# The Most Hated Man in Kentucky

# The Most Hated Man in Kentucky

## *The Lost Cause and the Legacy of Union General Stephen Burbridge*

Brad Asher

UNIVERSITY PRESS OF KENTUCKY

Scholarly publisher for the Commonwealth,
serving Bellarmine University, Berea College, Centre
College of Kentucky, Eastern Kentucky University,
The Filson Historical Society, Georgetown College,
Kentucky Historical Society, Kentucky State University,
Morehead State University, Murray State University,
Northern Kentucky University, Transylvania University,
University of Kentucky, University of Louisville,
and Western Kentucky University.


*Editorial and Sales Offices*: The University Press of Kentucky
663 South Limestone Street, Lexington, Kentucky 40508–4008
www.kentuckypress.com

Library of Congress Cataloging-in-Publication Data

Names: Asher, Brad, 1963- author.
Title: The most hated man in Kentucky : the Lost Cause and the legacy of Union General Stephen Burbridge / Brad Asher.
Description: Lexington, Kentucky : University Press of Kentucky, [2021] | Includes bibliographical references and index.
Identifiers: LCCN 2021006482 | ISBN 9780813181370 (hardcover) | ISBN 9780813181387 (pdf) | ISBN 9780813181394 (epub)
Subjects: LCSH: Burbridge, Stephen G. (Stephen Gano), 1831–1894. | United States. Army—Biography. | Generals—United States—Biography. | Kentucky—History—Civil War, 1861–1865—Biography. | United States—History—Civil War, 1861–1865—Biography.
Classification: LCC E467.1.B788 A74 2021 | DDC 973.7/3092 [B]—dc23

This book is printed on acid-free paper meeting
the requirements of the American National Standard
for Permanence in Paper for Printed Library Materials.

Manufactured in the United States of America

Member of the Association
of University Presses

*For Lila and Lucas*

# Contents

# Illustrations

# Introduction

For the last third of the nineteenth century, Union general Stephen Gano Burbridge enjoyed the unenviable distinction of being the most hated man in Kentucky. From mid-1864, just months into his reign as the military commander of the district of Kentucky, until his death in December 1894, the mere mention of Burbridge's name triggered a firestorm of curses from Kentucky's editorialists and politicians. By the end of Burbridge's tenure as head of the military district, Governor Thomas E. Bramlette, who had early on been a Burbridge ally, concluded that Burbridge was an "imbecile commander" whose actions represented nothing but the "blundering of a weak intellect and an overwhelming vanity."[1] Editorialists in the years after the war upped the ante from imbecile to tyrant. At various times in 1866, the *Louisville Daily Courier* branded Burbridge a "military dictator," a "blood-stained tyrant," a "demon in human shape," and the "plunderer and murderer of our innocent citizens."[2] The *Paris Democrat* pronounced itself "nauseated" when it spotted the "infamous murderer and notorious Hog-order Maj. Gen. Burbridge" on the streets. "The meanest convict in the penitentiary is more deserving of countenance than this notorious murderer."[3] A Frankfort correspondent wrote that he had never before regretted that a man was a Christian until one of Burbridge's wartime enemies refrained from murdering the general during an encounter in Washington, D.C. "I was savage enough to wish he had been a Bowie or a Burr, who looked upon it as a Christian duty to shoot a man who had done them wrong."[4] The *Maysville Bulletin* branded Burbridge a "paupered, lecherous, despised, and criminal outcast" whose soul would be eternally denied rest in the hereafter.[5] "He is a Robespierre without a motive, and a Caligula without courage," raged the *Louisville Courier-Journal* in 1882.[6] For fans of nineteenth-century editorial invective, there are few newspaper database searches as rewarding as "Burbridge."

How did Burbridge earn such opprobrium? He served eleven months as the military commander of Kentucky, from March 1864 until February 1865. During that time he used extreme measures, including retaliatory executions, to try and quell Kentucky's problem with guerrillas and Confederate partisans. He jailed, banished, and harassed those who expressed anti-Lincoln, anti-war, or pro-Confederate political sympathies. He suppressed the circulation of newspapers and other printed materials that advocated different wartime policies or that painted the Confederacy in a favorable light. He attempted to control trade and interfered in the markets for Kentucky's agricultural products, enriching some and impoverishing others. Most importantly—and most damning in the eyes of his enemies—he sped along the destruction of slavery in Kentucky by overseeing the recruitment and enlistment of slaves as soldiers. Along the way, he was branded as unfeeling, arrogant, corrupt, arbitrary, and tyrannical.

Like most black legends, the one that grew around Burbridge's reign had its genesis in actual events. Burbridge did enact harsh antiguerrilla policies; he did enforce the Lincoln administration's antislavery agenda; and he did clamp down on Kentuckians' political, economic, and civil liberties. But also like most black legends, Burbridge's actions were amplified and exaggerated to serve ideological ends.[7] In particular, postwar pro-Confederate apologists for the "Lost Cause" in Kentucky used Burbridge's sins to reinforce pro-southern sympathies among white Kentuckians. A frontal attack on the martyred Lincoln or even on Generals Sherman or Grant might have triggered a backlash among Kentucky's Unionists. Attacking Burbridge was a surefire way to keep picking the scab of Kentucky's wartime grievances, reminding the white population of the injustices wrought in the name of military necessity and of the misbegotten objective of emancipation.

Burbridge thus became an ideal scapegoat for Kentucky's Lost Cause partisans. Since Kentucky had never actually seceded and joined the Confederacy, it had been spared the wartime ravages inflicted on the South. Burbridge's supposed villainies, therefore, invoked a solidarity and a shared suffering between Kentucky and the defeated South—both had endured the Union's hateful wartime policies. This solidarity enabled many white Kentuckians to give full-throated support to a Lost Cause ideology that routinely extolled the honor of the southern soldiery, celebrated the glory of the southern cause, criticized the brutality of northern warmaking, and lamented the unforgivable error of emancipation. At the 1914 unveiling of a monument paid for by the United Daughters of the Confederacy, for example, and dedicated to two Confederate recruits who had been imprisoned and then shot in retaliation for guerrilla attacks per Burbridge's orders, the Reverend W. T. Ellis praised the young Kentuckians as "patriots" who "gave their lives in defense of a cause which all the world to-day concedes to have been a just cause. They were soldiers in an army whose splendid prowess and glorious deeds have been firmly anchored in the pages of our country's history." And they were ordered to their deaths by "a tyrant, a heartless despot, an unfeeling monster in human shape."[8]

Kentucky's Civil War experience can be divided into several separate conflicts. One might begin with the political battle over whether Kentucky should get involved in the war at all. Initially declaring neutrality, Kentucky found the fence it was sitting on threatened by the actions of the armies from both sides by late 1861. Its decision to stay in the Union, while supported by most, alienated a significant proportion of the population, many of whom would fight for or actively sympathize with the Confederacy. Then there was the regular war, which lasted in Kentucky from the beginning of the war to the Battle of Perryville in October 1862. This war consisted of the usual stuff of Civil War history, set-piece battles between opposing armies contesting for territorial control. It included several minor skirmishes, as well as the Confederate loss at Mill Springs in the eastern part of the state and the dramatic Union victories at Forts Donelson and Henry on the Cumberland River just over the state line in Tennessee. The Union victory at Perryville ended the final sustained effort by Confederate armies to invade and occupy Kentucky.[9]

Under and alongside this conflict there was the "irregular" war, marked by Confederate cavalry raids into Kentucky and by depredations against Unionist citizens by Confederate-sympathizing guerrillas. Famed Confederate cavalrymen like John Hunt Morgan and Nathan Bedford Forrest led raids into the state, but these celebrated forays were only occasional compared to the incessant attacks by guerrillas who roamed the state in small bands, attacked Union infrastructure and Unionist citizens, and then faded into the general population before the Union army could muster a response. This irregular warfare grew especially intense during the last two years of the war.[10]

In addition, there was the political war among Kentucky's Unionists, which became especially pronounced during Burbridge's reign, but took root with Lincoln's announcement of the Emancipation Proclamation in January 1863. Many of Kentucky's so-called Conservative Unionists had argued against secession on the premise that the Constitution and the Union offered the best hope of preserving slavery. With Lincoln's turn toward emancipation, they felt betrayed and increasingly hostile. Many would campaign for Lincoln's opponent, General George McClellan, in the 1864 presidential race. Their rallying cry became "The Constitution as it is; the Union as it was," suggesting that once the southern rebellion was quashed, things would return to the antebellum status quo, with the slaveholding states' property rights in human chattel fully recognized and legally protected. Their opponents, the so-called Unconditional Unionists, were willing to follow the Lincoln administration wherever it might lead, even to emancipation and amendment of the Constitution, in the name of unity and for the sake of ending the question of whether states could withdraw from the Union unilaterally.[11]

This intra-Unionist political battle was only a more visible expression of the more durable and violent conflict over slavery and the place of African Americans in Kentucky society. This was the conflict over emancipation not as a policy but as a ground-level reality. Of course, this conflict preceded the war itself and lasted beyond it, but during the years between 1861 and 1865 it reached an inflection point, especially when Kentucky's slaves began to gain their freedom by enlisting in the Union army. It was waged in hundreds of local-level confrontations—between freedom-seeking slaves and freedom-denying slaveholders, between slaveholders and army recruiting parties, between local vigilantes and slaves trying to make it to Union camps.[12]

Finally, there was the war after the war, the contest over how the Civil War would be remembered in Kentucky. Rather than a celebration of Union victory, as might be expected, this conflict would culminate by the end of the nineteenth century into a lamentation of southern defeat.

A coalition of returning Confederates, wartime Democrats, and increasingly disillusioned Conservative Unionists ensured that Kentucky's politics and culture were thoroughly identified with the South and the Lost Cause by 1900. Kentucky's southward turn coincided with a broader turn in national culture toward reconciliation between North and South, a turn that required the downplaying of slavery as a cause of the war and African American freedom as a principal goal of the victorious Union.[13]

Burbridge played a part in most of these conflicts. Although no records indicate his position on Kentucky's neutrality, he adhered to the Union cause early and eagerly. He recruited and commanded a regiment early in the war that patrolled the southern boundary between Union and Confederate Kentucky. While he did not participate in the battles of Shiloh or Perryville directly, his regiment was at both those battles, and Burbridge went on to command a brigade in Sherman's campaign against Vicksburg and later on in Louisiana. He played a part in the irregular war when he came back to Kentucky as military commander and confronted the guerrilla conflict that was convulsing the state, leading to his orders calling for harsh reprisals. He also commanded the troops who defeated John Hunt Morgan at Cynthiana in 1864, ending Morgan's final raid into Kentucky. His recruitment of slaves into the army and his clampdown on dissent as commander deepened the divide between Conservative and Unconditional Unionists, fueling another of Kentucky's civil wars. Those policies also shaped the ground-level conflict over slavery, motivating and encouraging greater freedom-seeking behaviors among the enslaved people of Kentucky. And the blackening of his reputation by Confederate apologists after the war made him a lightning rod in the conflict over Civil War memory in the state.

Despite his participation in various facets of the war, his months as district commander take on an outsized importance in his story. Thus this biography is peculiar in that it devotes well over half its pages to a short period in its subject's relatively long life. But those eleven months are crucial to understanding why so many people hated Burbridge for so long. It is ironic that Burbridge, who expressed his desire to be named commander of the state quite early in his military career, got what he wanted. "We ought to have one of our own state men in command here and if the citizens have confidence in me I would like to have the place," he wrote to his uncle in 1862.[14] Had he been frustrated in his ambition to "protect the citizens of the state," he would probably be remembered as a competent if unremarkable Union general from Kentucky. Instead, he earned the vilification of contemporaries, the loathing of his fellow Kentuckians, and the criticism of historians.

Historians have generally not been kind to Burbridge, reflecting for the most part Lost Cause-inflected views of the conflict in Kentucky. Basil Duke, a lieutenant in Morgan's command and an ex-Confederate returnee to Kentucky who did much to shape wartime memory in the state through his writings, labeled Burbridge an "insensate bloodhound" who shot all the prisoners he could lay his hands on. Nathaniel Shaler, a Union veteran who published a history of Kentucky in 1884, condemned Burbridge's "overbearing spirit" and the "brutal violence" of the retaliatory executions of guerrillas, which were "extremely distasteful to all fair-minded people." One of the lone voices of pushback came from Union veteran Thomas Speed, who, disheartened by his state's southward turn and its embrace of the Lost Cause, sought to remind white Kentuckians of their allegiance to the Union and of the gallantry of the state's federal soldiers. Speed noted that Burbridge took command "during a most difficult and distressing period" and bemoaned the "maledictions of the Confederate element" that rained down on Burbridge for his "rough handling" of guerrillas "and their aiders and abettors."[15]

After Burbridge's death and as the war slipped further away in time, the judgments became less condemnatory of Burbridge's character and more focused on his policies. E. Merton Coulter labeled Burbridge's wartime arrests of prominent Kentuckians "tactless and insane," part of a "long list of mistakes" in dealing with Kentucky. Edward Conrad Smith, in his 1927 *The Borderland in the Civil War,* called out "the arbitrary and unreasonable acts of the military commanders within the state," naming Burbridge as "the worst of these." Other notable historians changed the emphasis from the ruthlessness of Burbridge's policies to his supposed corruption, particularly his decision limiting the meat packers to whom Kentucky's hog farmers were allowed to sell their stock. Thomas Clark, for example, labeled the so-called Great Hog

Swindle a "dastardly trick" played upon Kentuckians, and called Burbridge "that masterful hog thief."[16]

By the 1970s, historians came to view Burbridge not necessarily as venal or cruel, but merely out of his depth during his time as commander. Lowell Harrison wrote in 1975 that Burbridge's role "would have been a trying position for anyone, but the thirty-two-year-old farmer from Logan County lacked the experience and tact needed for the job." Another author concluded that Burbridge was a "man who had some talent but was thrust into too great a command where his judgment could not meet the exigencies of the test." More recent assessments have softened even further. Writing in the *Encyclopedia of the American Civil War,* James Prichard concluded that Burbridge lacked "the judgment and skill necessary to command in a politically turbulent district," but also called Burbridge "a victim of partisan politics" who claimed, "rightly in most cases, that he merely followed the orders of his superiors."[17]

Little of this ongoing reassessment has filtered down to the popular level. The only book-length treatment of the general is titled *Butcher Burbridge* and refers to his "reign of terror" in the subtitle. In works where one might expect more temperate treatment, such as the institutional history of the Kentucky Military Institute, which Burbridge attended as a young man, one finds instead indictments of Burbridge's "dictatorial measures" and his "fervent desire for absolute power." Even the poets have had their turn; in a 2009 book of "sonnets on the life of Abraham Lincoln," Kentucky poet Richard Taylor describes Burbridge as "a touchy zealot . . . whose policies [lost] Kentucky for the Union for at least one generation," and as Lincoln's "martinet."[18]

Any current review of Burbridge's career and his tenure as commander of Kentucky has to take into account the last two generations of Civil War scholarship. This work has overturned the Lost Cause view of the war, reevaluating claims of southern military prowess, Confederate unity, and northern brutality. Most significantly, it has reversed the tendency to downplay slavery as a cause of the war and emancipation as an ultimate and important objective of the Union war effort. It has elevated the crucial role of black troops and the self-liberating actions of slaves in making the case for abolition, and it has revisited the reputation of the Radical Republicans, even as it noted the persistence and virulence of northern racism and antiblack attitudes.[19]

This new wave of Civil War scholarship has been somewhat slow to impact Kentucky. Recent work on the guerrilla war, on political disagreements among Unionists, on prewar and postwar regional alignments, and on postwar memory have, however, started to reshape the contours of the state's Civil War history. Like the broader historiographical trends, this work has moved slavery and emancipation to the center of the story (whatever the authors' disagreements might be on other issues). "The enlistment of large numbers of black soldiers from central Kentucky . . . drove a wedge through the white community and stimulated a violent white reaction that would reshape politics in the border states for decades," wrote historian Aaron Astor. Historian of religion Luke Harlow seconded Astor: "Where for whites in Kentucky, the Civil War was once intended to preserve the Union alone, it had now become a war about slavery. From their vantage point, that change was unacceptable." And Anne Marshall, historian of Kentucky's Civil War memory, wrote that "nothing . . . shifted the sentiments of white Kentuckians away from the Union cause more than Lincoln's evolving policies regarding slavery."[20]

This book hopes to contribute to the development of this line of Civil War historiography about Kentucky. It posits that the hatred white Kentuckians felt toward Burbridge had its foundation in his assault on slavery through the mechanism of black enlistment. The attack on slavery fueled criticism of wartime policy by Conservative Unionists and spurred guerrilla activity to new heights. This prompted Burbridge's harsh treatment of prisoners and his suppression of political dissent as a heavy-handed means to attain the antislavery objectives of the administration. Burbridge was not by nature antislavery in ideology, but as an Unconditional Unionist charged with implementing the war policies felt by his superiors to be necessary in putting down the southern rebellion, Burbridge went all-in on the recruitment of black soldiers. After the war, Lost Cause ideologues focused on the harm Burbridge inflicted on white people who resisted emancipation to discredit the outcome of the war and the postwar policies needed to sustain and strengthen that outcome. White Kentuckians' intense hatred of Burbridge was in no small part a measure of their ideological success.

While Burbridge certainly had his flaws, and while his actions as military commander of Kentucky were far from perfect, viewing Burbridge through the lens of emancipation yields a portrait that diverges sharply from the prevailing image of the most hated man in Kentucky. His policies, seen through modern Civil War historiography, become comprehensible, even justifiable. As the destruction of slavery became an objective of war policy, the notion that Burbridge could have somehow finessed the absolute opposition of most white Kentuckians to that policy into a reasoned and peaceful acceptance seems far-fetched. Burbridge's arrests and crackdown on dissent stemmed not from some desire for dictatorial power on his part but from the unshakeable opposition to emancipation on the part of white Kentuckians, including many in the Unionist political elite. His executions of suspected guerrillas fell within the range of tactics used by other Union commanders faced with irregular fighters in other areas and within the bounds of the laws of war as articulated by the Union high command. After the war, they were transfigured into "military murders" of legitimate Confederate soldiers deserving prisoner-of-war status by a sustained cultural effort—carried out through public occasions and political campaigning—to sanctify Kentucky's Confederate sympathies by demonizing Burbridge's supposed villainies. As a Kentuckian and as the local architect of the destruction of slavery, Burbridge—more than other commanders of the state—became the scapegoat for this pro-Confederate cultural project, the person to whom all the perceived sins of Union war policy and Republican postwar policy could be attached.

Burbridge left behind few personal papers, although he was not afraid to spar with his opponents in the popular press and a good amount of his official correspondence during the war has been published in the *Official Records of the War of the Rebellion* and other government publications. Still, as Louis de Falaise commented over forty years ago, "the soul of the man cannot be . . . easily grasped."[21] As a result, most of the emotions and motivations attributed to him by his detractors and by historians are merely projections and guesswork. There is precious little evidence regarding his own thoughts on racial equality, on emancipation, on the morality or ethics of his policies, and even less on his private life, his family, and his personal trials.

The man depicted in these public writings showed a common set of mid-nineteenth-century masculine characteristics: a driving ambition, a strong sense of duty, and a prickly sense of honor. (Burbridge challenged at least four separate men to duels after perceived insults to his honor.) Whether and by how much the public man differed from the private, however, is impossible to know. What also showed in his writings was a growing sense of frustration, especially after the war, at the way his ambitions were thwarted, his devotion to duty went unrecognized, and his honor was attacked. As Burbridge the man was increasingly submerged into Burbridge the black legend of the Lost Cause, he found himself exiled from his home state and ostracized by his former allies, living out the last decade of his life in relative quiet in New York and Washington, D.C. Reviled and ignored by turns, Burbridge remains, as James Prichard wrote, "one of the most controversial figures in Kentucky history."[22]

# 1

# Gentleman

Stephen Burbridge grew up among Kentucky gentlemen. His family background and the circumstances in which he came to adulthood partook of a certain set of characteristics that one might call "typically" Kentuckian. More precisely, this "typical" Kentuckian was white, male, and a member of the landed gentry. In later years, this image rooted in the antebellum Bluegrass elite would become the caricature of the "Kentucky colonel"—goateed, bourbon-sipping, and hospitable. But the caricature had roots in the historical experience of the early colonization and development of the Bluegrass region. Stephen Burbridge was born among Bluegrass elites, and doubtless was raised with the expectation that he would grow up to be the same.[1]

One of the characteristics shared by many of the Bluegrass gentry was a lineage that extended back to Virginia, and before that to England. Burbridge's grandfather, George Burbridge, emigrated to Kentucky from Spotsylvania County, Virginia, in 1791 or 1792. George's father, Thomas Burbridge, had emigrated from England and settled in Spotsylvania County before the American Revolution.[2] So Stephen Burbridge had the right pedigree.

Many of the Virginians who left for Kentucky did so because of the land warrants that Virginia used to pay its soldiers who fought in the Revolutionary War. George had served two three-month hitches in the Virginia militia, both times as a draftee. He saw little action during his first term of service in 1780. During his second stint, in 1781, he took part in the Battle of Green Spring, near Jamestown, and was part of a guard detail that escorted prisoners to Winchester. In return for his service, George could claim one hundred acres of Kentucky land.[3]

George was thus one of many thousands of veterans from Virginia who crossed the mountains into Kentucky in the 1790s. Virginia had been abuzz with Kentucky fever since the 1770s, but it was the decade of the 1790s that saw the most massive influx of settlers. The census of 1790 counted 73,077 people in Kentucky; a decade later the number had swelled to 220,995—the highest rate of growth Kentucky ever experienced. And while emigrants came from other neighboring states, Virginia contributed the most. By 1820, thanks in part to the land warrant program, the ethnic make-up of Kentucky's population looked more like Virginia's than any other state's. Attracted by reports of cheap, abundant, and fertile land—Kentucky land was reported to be one-half to one-third the price of land in the Shenandoah Valley, and twice as productive—George traveled to Kentucky with his wife, Mary, three young sons, and likely a cohort of four family slaves.[4]

Family reasons also may have persuaded George to move. His father had died in or around 1790, just before George decided to relocate to Kentucky. Along with his brothers and sisters, George received as inheritance his father's Virginia lands. Early in 1792, the various heirs deeded two hundred acres of the land to one James Lewis, and later that same year one of George's brothers and three of his brothers-in-law granted George power of attorney to sell additional lands in Virginia that had belonged to Thomas Burbridge. Judging from the grant of power of attorney, it appears that at least four of George's siblings had already left Virginia and settled in Kentucky. With the inheritance from his father providing additional resources and with family members already settled in Kentucky, George may have reasoned that there was little holding him in Virginia.[5]

Another common characteristic of the antebellum landed gentry in Kentucky was a military heritage. Just as it was common to find a Revolutionary War veteran in their lineage, it was also common to find a veteran of the War of 1812 a generation later. Stephen Burbridge's father, Robert Burbridge, and his uncle Thomas Burbridge served in different units of the Kentucky militia during the later conflict. Robert was an ensign in Captain Stephen Ritchie's company in the regiment commanded by Lieutenant Colonel John Francisco. Raised late in the war (February 1815), the regiment was ordered to Detroit to relieve soldiers about to be mustered out. Before they arrived, however, the war ended and the men returned to Kentucky. So while it was not glorious service, it was sufficient for Robert to join the list of those receiving a military pension.[6]

Another characteristic, obviously, was wealth. When Stephen was born—on August 19, 1831, in Scott County, near the town of Stamping Ground—it was into comfortable circumstances. For antebellum Bluegrass elites, wealth was measured primarily in land and in slaves. By the mid-1790s, shortly after he emigrated from Virginia, George Burbridge owned 205 acres of land and had doubled his slaveholdings to eight. In the years following, George invested more in slaves than he did in land, for while his acreage stayed steady, the number of his slaves increased to fifteen by the turn of the century. In 1820, his slaveholdings had grown to twenty-one, and the tax man assessed the total value of all his holdings—land, slaves, livestock, and taxable household items—at $7,600, making him one of the wealthiest men in Scott County.[7] George died in 1838 at the age of seventy-seven. At the time of the final settlement of his estate in August 1841, his six heirs—his two living sons, Sidney and Robert (Thomas had died in 1837), his two daughters Marion and Wilmina (through her husband), and the heirs of Thomas and James Burbridge—divided $23,282.[8] In 2020 dollars, that works out to almost $700,000, a sizable estate, but not enough to propel George into the topmost ranks of the Bluegrass elite.

Stephen's father, Robert, did better. According to the Scott County tax lists for 1830, Robert owned 276 acres of land and thirty-one slaves. By the time of George's death, the value of Robert's holdings had surpassed his father's. By 1845, owing partially to the inheritances from George and from his brother Thomas (who died a bachelor), Robert owned 760 acres in Scott County and an additional 350 acres in Livingston County in the western and less developed part of the state. According to a recent county history, Robert Burbridge's farm was one of the five most valuable operations in Scott County in 1850.[9]

The other component of wealth was human beings, and the Bluegrass gentry were the most stalwart defenders of the institution of slavery against early political challenges to it.[10] While they couched their ownership of slaves in kindly terms—referring to their paternal concern for "their people" and regarding the slaves as children who needed care and oversight—they also regarded their slaves as financial investments that needed to be managed wisely. Thus George Burbridge's slaves did not serve solely as his own agricultural labor force. Thanks to the development of the "hiring-out" system, there was an annual flow of slaves among different plantations and between rural plantations and urban manufacturers. Planter/slaveholders rented the labor of their slaves to their neighbors and to the manufacturers who processed their agricultural products. Rental contracts generally lasted one year and required the employer to provide suitable food, clothing, and care to the owner's slave. The hiring-out system allowed manufacturers the flexibility to expand and contract their workforce as demand for their products and the efficiency of their production methods changed, and it allowed planters to earn a return on their investment in slave property that could exceed the return from using slaves only on their own farm. The possibility of hiring out his slaves partially explains how George Burbridge could economically justify the steady increase in his slave holdings even as his landholdings remained static.[11]

George's participation in the hiring-out system is most visibly evidenced by a lawsuit filed by the administrators of his estate against John C. McGuffin for breach of covenant. McGuffin had agreed to pay $110 "in Kentucky currency and . . . furnish . . . good winter and summer clothing . . . in consideration of the hire of a negro boy hand," but he failed to make payment. The jury found for George Burbridge's estate in the amount of $123.[12]

Robert Burbridge owned significantly more slaves than his father ever had; the 1835 tax list counted forty-six slaves belonging to Robert, the bulk of those under sixteen years of age. Ten years later his slaveholdings totaled thirty, and ten years after that, in 1855, he owned fifty-five slaves. The fluctuation in number and the relative youth of the slaves in his possession suggests that Robert may have been an active participant in the interstate slave trade. By 1830, Kentucky's slave population had peaked as a proportion of the state's total population, and as the relative value of slave labor declined in the state, there was a lively trade between Kentucky and the slave-hungry states of the Cotton South. It is notable that the number of Robert's mature slaves (those over sixteen years of age) varied only slightly during this same twenty-year period, suggesting that his need for mature field hands to work his lands stayed steady even as his overall slaveholdings fluctuated significantly. Robert had married Eliza Ann Barnes in 1819, the daughter of Thomas Barnes, a well-to-do planter from Claiborne County, Mississippi. Given Robert's Mississippi connections through his wife, it may have been a profitable enterprise for him to regularly ship younger slaves "down the river."[13]

The Virginia heritage, the acceptance of slavery, and the marriage alliances with southern planters all point to another commonly shared characteristic of the antebellum Bluegrass gentry: a strong cultural orientation toward the South. In part, culture followed economics. Before railroads linked Kentucky to states north and west of the Ohio River, the bulk of its commerce flowed downstream to the southern states. Hemp, the principal cash crop grown on Bluegrass plantations, was primarily sold to southern cotton plantations for cordage, bagging, and material for slave apparel.[14]

Whether Kentucky was southern from the start or whether it "became" southern after the Civil War has recently become something of a scholarly debate. Anne Marshall asserts that "it is important to understand that Kentucky was, before, during, and after the Civil War, a southern state," but historian Christopher Phillips has recently argued that "the national confluence once represented as the West [including Kentucky] was remade as South and North" by the internal political conflicts of the Civil War. For purposes of understanding the cultural milieu that shaped Stephen Burbridge, such debates about the general character of Kentucky or of the border-state region are less important than the pronounced southern character of the Bluegrass elites among whom he grew up.[15]

That southern cultural orientation manifested itself in the aggressive conviviality that marked the social life of the Bluegrass elites. As described by historian Stephen Aron, Kentucky's landed gentry aspired to emulate their Virginian forebears. "Like Anglo-Virginians, Bluegrass planters lived for times spent convening and competing in the 'agreeable company' of other gentlemen." Through activities like fox hunting, squirrel hunting, dancing, and horse racing, the social lives of Kentucky gentlemen and ladies were marked by ostentatious displays of wealth, mannered decorum, and a fine-tuned attention to personal honor.[16]

Horses, in particular, assumed outsized importance for the Kentucky gentry. This, too, was part of their Virginian cultural inheritance. As T. H. Breen wrote about Virginia in the early 1700s, possession of a horse "became a social necessity. Without a horse, a planter felt despised, an object of ridicule."[17] In Kentucky, horses were more than just status symbols; they were also necessities for travel and for tilling the soil. Ninety-two percent of Kentucky taxpayers in 1800 owned a horse. Most of these, however, were draft animals. The practice of breeding, training, and racing thoroughbred horses, on the other hand, was a gentleman's enterprise. The Burbridges earned renown for their breeding and racing activities. George Burbridge garnered praise from a local historian for his work "to elevate the character of the race horse, and the turf in Kentucky." When it came to racing, George believed that a gentleman "should be content to run for the stakes . . . [he] should not turn gambler and use his horse as a gambling instrument." His brother Sidney trained the famed four-mile racer Grey Eagle, who sired a number of prominent winning race horses and, most notably, Robert E. Lee's horse Traveler. Grey Eagle was said to be such a beautiful horse that ladies swooned upon seeing him at the track. Robert was also a significant early breeder of race horses in Scott County and raced them in conjunction with his uncle Sidney.[18]

Stephen Burbridge's upbringing fit within this larger cultural complex of Bluegrass elites, and there is little to suggest that he challenged or questioned many of its presuppositions. Perhaps, given his Civil War history, one might wonder about his acceptance of the institution of slavery. But Stephen owned slaves before the war, showed no emancipationist inclinations during his early military career, and made a point of his own status as a slaveholder when implementing black enlistment, suggesting that it helped him to understand the feelings of his fellow Kentuckians.[19]

Stephen also retained his wealth. In addition to his seven slaves in 1860, the census valued his real estate holdings at $23,600 and his personal estate at $33,000. However, he had relocated to Logan County, along with his brother Thomas. Migration was, of course, common in the nineteenth century, but the move to Logan County was somewhat out of the ordinary for sons of the Bluegrass elite. Logan County lay to the south and west of the Bluegrass region and had once been touted as "a good poor man's country." Stephen and Thomas moved there sometime in the 1850s, perhaps to take advantage of lower land prices in the region and build something for themselves outside the crowded and competitive Bluegrass area. Interestingly, although both Thomas and Stephen had wives and children by 1860, they are listed as part of one household. So, while they probably held their lands under separate titles, they may have been developing their farms jointly.[20]

The path taken by the eldest Burbridge son, Oscar, followed more closely the expected contours of the Bluegrass gentry. He too left Scott County, but stayed in the Bluegrass, moving only to neighboring Bourbon County. His landed wealth in 1860, at $39,000, exceeded that of either of his brothers, and he owned twenty-six slaves. "One of the landed princes of Old Bourbon," as a newspaper referred to Oscar, he also earned a reputation as "one of the most judicious and successful breeders of stock in the county," although in Oscar's case it was not horses but his Durham cattle and Cotswold sheep that gained acclaim. This emphasis on blooded stock imported from England also fit right in with the prevailing interests of his Bluegrass neighbors.[21]

Even though he eventually settled into his status as a landed gentleman in Logan County, Stephen's earlier educational and occupational forays suggest that he might have harbored some other ambitions besides being a farmer. At around fifteen years of age, in 1845–1846, he enrolled in the Classical Course of the Preparatory Department of Georgetown College, near his home. His schooling required him to leave his father's house, and he lived with Dr. Stephen Gano, a trustee of the college. Gano, from whom Stephen got his middle name, was a Scott County physician, a close family friend related through marriage to Robert's sister, and the descendant of a rather illustrious family of preachers. Gano had also acted as the administrator of George Burbridge's estate. The Preparatory Department was meant to prepare students for admission into the college. Housed in a separate building, the department had a separate instructor and taught "all the branches of an academical education." Students had to be able to read, write, and "perform the first rules in Arithmetic" before being admitted. Stephen was remembered as a "good, clever boy" by a fellow student, and he finished the preparatory course and enrolled in the regular college program for the session beginning in August 1847. According to a note in his record, however, he took sick and never began the course.[22]

He did not try again to enroll in the college, and the 1850 federal census found him living back at home. Shortly afterward, however, he enrolled in the Kentucky Military Institute, which was located about six miles south of Frankfort. The institute opened in 1847, and Stephen probably enrolled early in the 1850s, although some sources say he graduated as late as 1858.[23] Like similar institutions in other states, the KMI was intended to help compensate for the lack of a national standing army. "Americans should not only be citizens but soldiers," read an 1855 article on the institute's commencement exercises. "When war comes upon us we look for volunteers. Let those volunteers, if possible, be well prepared."[24]

The institute's curriculum combined math, science, and the liberal arts (with a heavy dose of classical Roman literature). Students were organized into companies, and commissioned and noncommissioned officers were chosen from among the student body by the academic staff. There was at least one hour of infantry or artillery drill every day, and dress parade every evening. The school's code of conduct forbade drinking, fighting (or issuing a challenge), and all "vicious, immoral and irregular conduct." Students were expected to behave with the "decorum of gentlemen." Students paid $82 per semester and provided their own uniforms and clothing, but the institute provided their weapons.[25]

According to biographical sketches appearing in early twentieth-century compendia of prominent Americans, after graduation from the institute Stephen reportedly read law under Garrett Davis, a prominent Kentucky lawyer and politician in Bourbon County. He never practiced law, however, before the war. According to another brief biography, he also tried his hand at being a merchant before settling into his role as a Logan County farmer. None of these professions would have been "beneath" his status as a gentleman; indeed, many prominent Kentuckians combined lawyering or commercial ventures with their agricultural pursuits.[26]

Additionally, in his family life Stephen did not deviate from the expected path of Bluegrass gentlemen, in that he married a respectable woman from a well-to-do Scott County family. Elizabeth "Lizzie" Garth was born in 1837, the daughter of Albert and Margaret Lemon Garth. Albert died shortly after Lizzie was born, and Margaret soon remarried, wedding the Reverend James Frost in December 1839. Lizzie thereafter lived in her stepfather's household, and her mother gave the reverend three sons and two daughters—Lizzie's half-siblings—during the decade of the 1840s. Lizzie's status as the sole Garth in the Frost household may explain why she attended the Georgetown Female Seminary during her teenage years, from 1850 to 1853, perhaps hoping it would provide her a way out of the household. She never graduated, however; instead she found her way out of the Frost household by marrying (at not quite sixteen years of age) twenty-one-year-old Stephen on May 11, 1853. In the years before the war, Lizzie bore four children: the births of two sons, Albert (born February 1855) and Oscar (born February 1861), bookended the births of two girls, Margaret (born September 1857 and named after Lizzie's mother), and Lillie (born March 1859).[27]

Despite the Cinderella trappings of her family story, Lizzie was not destitute. Her mother, Margaret, was a significant property holder in her own right. She was assessed as a separate taxpayer in the years after her first husband died, obviously retaining her rights to the land she inherited as a widow. Her second husband makes no appearances in the Scott County tax lists. Margaret owned over one thousand acres in Scott County and an additional two hundred acres in Fayette County in 1845, along with thirty-one slaves. The total assessed value of her holdings equaled $89,390, financially outstripping the Burbridge clan. By 1855, the situation had reversed; Margaret Lemon had divested herself of all but 450 acres of Scott County land and held just seven slaves. That same year Robert Burbridge had expanded both his land holdings and his slave holdings. Whatever their relative positions in the wealth hierarchy, it is clear that Lizzie and Stephen shared the same class and cultural background.[28]

However, it is impossible to know how eagerly Stephen and Lizzie participated or how well they fared in the social world of the Bluegrass. Perhaps the move to Logan County was a bid to escape the competition for social standing within the community of the landed gentry. Burbridge did not enjoy a reputation as a gifted raconteur. In November 1864, deep into his tenure as commander of Kentucky, the staunchly pro-Burbridge *Lexington National Unionist* described him as "remarkably unsophisticated as a speaker. His sentences are short as a child's, and his words are uttered with no more force than those of a bashful school boy reciting his first speech."[29] It is conceivable that Burbridge knew the cultural rules of the game and, while not questioning them, simply did not play the game very well.

His cultural background may also help explain some of the vitriol expressed by Lost Cause Kentuckians toward Burbridge after the war. Burbridge was one of their own, but he had turned against his people. He had not done so by joining the Union army. A military career was not counter to the set of cultural expectations for a gentleman. Nor was being a Unionist. While the gentry may have had southern cultural sympathies, few were outright secessionists. Instead, Burbridge betrayed them by countenancing and implementing the destruction of the racial hierarchy that helped define their own social status. And then when they complained—or when their sons took up arms against this egregious insult—he retaliated against them through arrest, banishment, and even violence. In the eyes of those who hated him, his unforgivable transgression was that he became a traitor to his class and, especially, to his race.

## 2

# Soldier

When the Civil War began in April 1861, most white Kentuckians sat on their hands and hoped that the state's plea to remain neutral in the conflict would be respected. The majority of whites in the state blamed the outbreak of hostilities on fanatical abolitionists on the northern side and fire-eating secessionists on the southern side. Since both of these extreme positions were wrongheaded, Kentuckians reasoned, it was best to just stay out of it. Even the Central Committee of the Union party declared in 1861 that Kentucky "ought to hold herself independent of both sides." And the state's official position as adopted by state House members was that "the State and the citizens thereof shall take no part in the civil war now being waged." George Prentice, the influential editor of the *Louisville Journal,* wrote that anyone who advocated the abandonment of neutrality to follow "the line of apology for the Republicans becomes the ally of anti-slaveryism, and he who deviates from it into the line of apology for the seceders becomes . . . the ally of disunionism." This attitude filtered deep into the white populace. "Kentucky has never don [*sic*] nothing to for neither party that should cause here [her] to be the battle field," wrote one Kentucky student to his sister in 1861. Even after neutrality broke down, in September 1861, and Kentucky officially opted to stay in the Union, the state was "first [among southern states] in percentage of whites who fought for no one," according to historian William Freehling.[1]

In contrast, Burbridge almost immediately answered Lincoln's call for troops. He enrolled for service on August 27, 1861, in Louisville and was commissioned a colonel. Through the last half of 1861 he recruited and organized the 26th Kentucky Volunteer Infantry. The 26th was not immediately mustered into federal service, and so for the first few months of its existence it patrolled south-central Kentucky. Burbridge's unhesitating response to the call to suppress the rebellion became a standard line in his wartime resume. "He with promptitude raised a fine regiment, and . . . has formed his men into a fine soldiery," Senator Garrett Davis wrote to Lincoln in 1861, pushing Burbridge for an early promotion.[2] In November 1863, Colonel W. J. Sandram also wrote to Lincoln, urging him to promote Burbridge both for his actions on the battlefield and because "he was one of the first to raise a Regiment in Kentucky . . . at time when and in a section where it was dangerous to . . . recruit for the Government."[3] An anonymous letter to the *Cincinnati Enquirer* in 1862 extolled Burbridge for standing "prominent among the sons of Kentucky who, from the first, took a decided stand in favor of maintaining the Union."[4] After the war, General Sherman similarly praised Burbridge for being "one of the first Kentuckians to take up arms in defense of our common nationality."[5]

On September 18, the same day the Kentucky General Assembly formally ended the state's policy of neutrality and ordered Confederate troops (but not Union troops) to leave the state, Confederate general Simon Bolivar Buckner occupied Bowling Green. In October, Albert Sidney Johnston, commanding general of Confederate Department No. 2, moved his headquarters there and established a defensive line across southern Kentucky.[6] With the collapse of Kentucky's neutrality and the seizure of Bowling Green, a group of pro-Confederate Kentuckians hastened to form a provisional government of Confederate Kentucky. At a state sovereignty convention held in Russellville on November 18–20, 1861, the self-appointed delegates "severed connections with the United States and declared Kentucky a free and independent state." The provisional government then sent commissioners to Richmond to petition the Confederate government for admission. On December 9, despite the irregularities involved in the formation of its provisional government, Kentucky became part of the Confederate States of America. Bowling Green was named the capital; its territory extended only as far as the Confederate front line. By February 1862, the rump regime was forced to flee the state and spent most of the rest of the war as a nonfunctional government in exile.[7]

Burbridge's 26th Kentucky was stationed just north of this Confederate line, patrolling the Union's southern frontier. On October 29, 1861, near

Woodbury, along the Green River in Butler County, the 26th encountered a detachment of the 1st Mississippi Cavalry, composed mainly of "Mississippians, Alabamians, and Georgians," according to Burbridge's official report. The Mississippi unit had encamped on the south side of the river and contemplated an attack upon the Union troops at Camp Galloway, about thirty miles to the north, near Hartford. Burbridge marched south with about 125 infantrymen and 100 cavalry, who were reinforced by an additional 125 men of the 17th Kentucky Volunteers under Colonel John McHenry. McHenry took his force across the river at Morgantown, where he pushed Confederate pickets south. Burbridge, with the main body of troops, kept marching toward Woodbury, where he "found the enemy encamped upon a summit commanding the surrounding neighborhood." A detachment of his troops captured the ferry and Burbridge ordered his soldiers across the river. They soon took the high ground, overlooking the enemy camp. "A few shells were sent into their tents, and then charged . . . with bayonets, the enemy scattering in confusion and consternation," leaving some fifty dead behind them. "Our men, from the greatest to the least, fought bravely and nobly," Burbridge wrote. He was commended for his "marked success" by his commanding general, who said his thirty-mile march showed the "true soldier's spirit."[8]

Such confrontations were common occurrences along the thinly defended portions of the Confederates' long front line. As historians James Klotter and Lowell Harrison wrote, "the Green River country became a sort of no-man's-land, with a great deal of scouting activity and numerous skirmishes."[9] The early career of the 26th was no exception, and the regiment next saw action in December 1861 in a small skirmish at Whippoorwill Creek, a few miles south and west of Russellville. Company B of the 26th under Captain Gabriel Netter surprised a small detachment of CSA troops guarding a railroad bridge over the creek. Netter's men chased off the Confederate troops and burned the bridge, temporarily severing the supply line between Confederate Tennessee and Bowling Green.[10]

Burbridge eagerly touted these early successes, hoping for quick promotion up the ranks. He solicited several letters of recommendation for promotion to brigadier general in November and December of 1861, which were sent on to Lincoln. These letters extolled his bravery, his unhesitating response to the call for troops, and even ginned up the fracas at Woodbury as "one of the most brilliant fights that has yet graced the arms of our country."[11] His commanding officer, General Don Carlos Buell, was more sanguine, remarking in December 1861 that, although he was "greatly in need of staff officers and brigadiers," men he did not know were being pushed forward prematurely. "One of them is Colonel Burbridge," he reported. "I certainly hope they will have to wait until they are tried." The skirmish at Woodbury, in Buell's view, had not sufficiently tested the young officer.[12]

It did not help Burbridge's case that it was not at the middle of the Confederate line where the decisive battles occurred. Rather, it was at both the eastern and western ends where major Union advances took place. In the east, the Battle of Mill Springs in January 1862 resulted in a Confederate withdrawal across the Cumberland River. More crucially, in the west, Ulysses Grant took Forts Henry and Donelson in February, the latter loss resulting in the surrender of sixteen thousand Confederate troops. With the collapse of his flanks, Johnston abandoned Bowling Green in February 1862, retreating southward to make a stand against advancing Union troops in Corinth, Mississippi.[13]

With the Confederates expelled from Kentucky for the time being, Burbridge took the opportunity to request a leave of absence. In January 1862, he requested twenty days to see his family, from whom he had been separated for four months, and to attend to some urgent business. The 26th, meanwhile, was ordered to Nashville, where the troops were mustered into federal service. The mustering-in followed a lengthy period of delay and confusion. Lieutenant Colonel Cicero Maxwell, commanding the regiment in Burbridge's absence, complained that it had taken repeated appeals to General Buell to have a mustering officer appointed for the regiment. On top of that, so many of the men were sick and missing that the regiment did not have the numbers required to be mustered in. Many of the soldiers, Maxwell reported, had deserted or fled, claiming that the officers had no authority over them outside Kentucky, leaving those who remained demoralized. "It is disgraceful," Maxwell wrote, "now that our state is clear of armed rebellion, that our soldiers should sneak away from duty." Finally, in early March, a mustering officer was appointed and the men who were present were mustered into federal service and formally placed under the authority of the US Army.[14]

Burbridge arrived in Nashville a few weeks later and was belatedly mustered into federal service as well. However, he had fallen ill while on leave and, even though he returned to the regiment, he was unable to attend to his duties. His wife Lizzie's uncle remembered that he had urged Burbridge when he was home on leave to "take better care of him[self] and resign his army position because of his physical condition . . . he then being sorely afflicted with rheumatism."[15] As a result of his disability, Burbridge missed the Battle of Shiloh.

Instead, Maxwell remained in command when the 26th advanced to Pittsburg Landing, Tennessee, as part of Buell's Army of the Ohio. The plan was to join Buell's army to Grant's Army of the Tennessee and then proceed to Corinth, where the Confederates under Johnston waited. However, urged on by fellow Confederate General P.G.T. Beauregard, Johnston decided to take the offensive against Grant, hitting him before Buell's reinforcements arrived, and drive the Federals out of Tennessee. On April 6, he attacked the advance Union positions at Shiloh Church, Tennessee. On that first day of the battle, the Confederates drove back the Union right and left, but the center held long enough for Grant to reform his lines two miles back from their original position. It also bought enough time for Buell's army, including the 26th Kentucky, to be thrown into the battle on the second day.[16]

The 26th was part of the 14th Brigade, which was brought up on the left side of the Union line. After getting into position, the brigade made a "brilliant and daring charge" against the enemy, driving them back "nearly a mile with great slaughter," Maxwell wrote. The Confederates regrouped and pushed back, and in the dense thicket troops from different regiments all became intermingled. The Union advance held, however, and the 26th was ordered to fall back as another brigade came up. Later in the day they were ordered forward again to support one of the Union artillery batteries. Although the regiment of 270 men had only seen action for a part of the second day of battle, it sustained seventy casualties. When Burbridge rejoined the regiment on the battlefield three days later, he wrote "[I] find my regt [*sic*] very much cut to pieces. I have lost my Major [John L. Davidson], Lieut. [John Thomas] Higdon, and a good many men."[17]

After rejoining his regiment, Burbridge petitioned his superior officers to send the 26th back to Kentucky. In addition to the men lost in battle, it had many who were out of action due to sickness and thus was much diminished in size. Burbridge argued that a return to Kentucky would allow his remaining men to recuperate and enable him to recruit new blood to build up the regiment's numbers. He also commented on the parlous state of his own health, pointing out that the easier duty at home would enable him to fully regain his vigor. An army doctor certified that he suffered from dyspepsia and a sore throat that steadily worsened over the course of the next six weeks. If the regiment remained in the field, Burbridge wrote, he would be forced to resign, and on April 28 he did tender a letter of resignation in which he complained that the poor state of his health made it impossible for him to carry out his duties. Buell did not accept the resignation, but he did send Burbridge back to Kentucky to recruit. The 26th went a different direction, however. Under Maxwell, they were part of the siege of Corinth, campaigned over the summer with Buell in Alabama and Tennessee, and then were part of the Union's pursuit of Confederate general Braxton Bragg when he invaded Kentucky in autumn 1862.[18]

Back in Kentucky, Burbridge's promotional campaign paid off, despite Buell's earlier note of caution. He was offered and accepted a commission as brigadier general of volunteers in June 1862. As yet, however, he was a general without a command, so when the Confederates invaded Kentucky in August, Burbridge reported to General William "Bull" Nelson, who had been put in charge of Kentucky's defenses. Nelson could be a difficult man to serve, at times prone to fits of violent temper and outbursts of profanity, at others reported to be a sensitive and generous soul. As Bragg neared the city of Louisville, Nelson ordered Burbridge to deploy troops around the city in a defensive line. When Burbridge requested specific details about the deployment from Nelson, the irascible commander yelled, "Oh, you be damned. Get out of this and post the troops as you please." When Burbridge had organized the troops and posted them around the outskirts of the city, Nelson came out to inspect the placements. The general "found fault and cursed Burbridge, calling him a terrible name," according to an account published by Union general James Brisbin years later. In Brisbin's telling of the incident, Burbridge pulled a derringer out of his pocket and leveled it at Nelson's head, threatening to blow his head off if he did not withdraw the insult. Nelson apologized, scolding Burbridge for his quick recourse to firearms, and both men's anger subsided. But Nelson had it in for Burbridge, and when Burbridge refused to send some of his troops to Nelson because he believed the order had come from a junior officer, the general "cursed him, said he would put him in the Ohio River, and relieved him from command," ordering Burbridge to report to the general commanding at Cincinnati. Coincidentally, as he waited for the train to Cincinnati, Burbridge encountered two other Union generals who had been similarly treated by Nelson.[19]

Ultimately, no defense of Louisville was needed. By fast marching, Buell's Army of the Ohio overtook Bragg's invading army and arrived in Louisville first. Resupplying there, the army turned east and south and engaged the Confederates at the climactic Battle of Perryville on October 8. Perryville, which is just a few miles south of Harrodsburg in central Kentucky, ended the Confederate invasion and forced Bragg's retreat back into Tennessee. Once again, Burbridge missed a pivotal battle. At the time of Perryville, he had been given command of the 1st Brigade of the 1st Division, Army of Kentucky, under divisional commander General A. J. Smith. The Army of Kentucky, however, did not fight at Perryville. Burbridge's brigade, camped near Georgetown, scouted the surrounding countryside, protected the railroad, and drilled. On October 8, he reported to Smith that his men had gone as far north and east as Cynthiana, Owenton, and Williamstown and found "no large rebel force on the railroad at any point." A few days after Perryville, Burbridge wrote to Smith that his drilling of the men was paying off: "I now have hopes of making soldiers of them."[20]

Burbridge pestered Smith for more troops, for cavalry, for artillery. Demonstrating the numerous unanswered questions that surrounded army procedures at this early point in the war, he also wanted to know what to do with prisoners. And more significantly, he wanted to know what to do with the increasing numbers of refugees that were gathering around his camp seeking protection. "Numbers of Union refugees are coming into my camp running from the rebel conscription which is threatening them," he reported on October 8. Black refugees from slavery soon followed. "Shall I issue rations to negro men in my camp and furnish transportation for the women and children? What kind of vouchers shall I give to Union men in the Federal service who have slaves now in our camp? Must they have their services and value altogether?" he asked Smith. Although "contrabands" would continue to be a "problem" for Union officers for the rest of the war, Burbridge's problem in Kentucky was a little different. Slavery was legal in Kentucky, and men who went into the Union armies fully expected their slave property to be respected and protected. The actions of slaves themselves challenged this expectation, and Burbridge was not the first commander to ponder how to deal with this challenge. Surely the Union men would be compensated for their loss, receiving a voucher for the "value" of the slave. But were they also entitled to the slave's services? In other words, did the slave need to be sent back to the master's farm? If a Union officer issued a voucher, was that effectively buying the slave's freedom? "This is a delicate matter for me. Please advise me," Burbridge pleaded with Smith.[21]

By the end of October, Burbridge had instituted his own policy. He complained in a personal letter to his uncle that he had been promised by General Quincy Gilmore that orders would be issued "turning out all nigrous [*sic*] and preventing the soldiers from stealing [in other words, encouraging slaves to come into Union camps]," but Gilmore had not issued the order. So Burbridge took it upon himself. "I have ordered up nigrous to owners and issued orders giving three hours to have all [slaves] out of my camps and I have it obeyed. I had to arrest several officers at first but a little firmness is all that is needed." In these months before black enlistment in Kentucky and its promise of freedom, Burbridge held fast to the distinction between slaves owned by Unionists and slaves owned by Confederates. Slaves owned by Union men who fled to his camp were returned to their masters. "If you or any of our main friends have lost nigrous I can get them without any trouble," he told his uncle. With Kentucky's place in the Union barely secured, Burbridge shared the belief of many other officials that the expropriation of slave property would only drive Unionist Kentucky into the Confederate camp.[22] It would be almost two years before wartime policy—and Burbridge's mind—changed.

In the meantime, his actions caused him problems with some of the northern officers and troops now crowding into Kentucky as the war prepared to move south. Northern newspapers believed he was violating the Confiscation Acts by returning slave property. More abolition-minded officers, disregarding Kentucky's status as a Union state, looked the other way when their men allowed slaves into their camps. The influx of northern soldiers ratcheted up tensions within Kentucky, and Burbridge wrote that what Kentucky needed was a Kentuckian in charge.[23] Burbridge told his uncle that he aspired to be that Kentuckian, but he first had some hard fighting ahead of him.

In December, Burbridge was transferred from the Army of Kentucky to command of the 1st Brigade, 1st Division, Army of the Tennessee, remaining under General A. J. Smith. He was ordered to Memphis, where the Union army was preparing its campaign to take Vicksburg. At midnight on December 21, 1862, the troops boarded steamboats for the journey down the Mississippi.[24]

They arrived at Milliken's Bend, Louisiana, north of Vicksburg, on December 24, where Smith received orders to dispatch one brigade to cut the Vicksburg & Shreveport Railroad. On Christmas Day, Burbridge was sent with the 1st Division—six regiments of infantry, two companies of cavalry, and one artillery piece—to carry out this mission. Just a short distance from the landing, they destroyed the Lake Providence and Tallulah telegraph and captured several prisoners and horses, along with 196 head of beef cattle, which were sent to the rear. At this point, however, they found their progress impeded by the lack of "reliable maps, those furnished. . . being not only defective but inaccurate," and by enemy cavalry hounding their flank. By sundown, the troops had reached Dallas Station, Louisiana, where Burbridge concentrated his forces, sending out smaller detachments to accomplish the work of disrupting the railroad. They burned three bridges, five hundred yards of trestle work, and tore up the rails and ties for about a mile, returning to the boats about 10 p.m. on the 26th, having marched seventy-five miles in thirty-six hours, with a "cavalry dash of 30 miles beyond." Burbridge returned with a large number of confiscated mules and reported burning 1,000 bales of cotton, 2,000 bushels of corn, 250,000 yards of muslin fabric, medical instruments and sundry other items belonging to the Confederate government. "The result of this expedition is very creditable to the officer in charge," Smith wrote, and the commendatory sentiment was echoed by General Sherman.[25]

From Milliken's Bend, the boats proceeded downriver, joining the Union fleet on the Yazoo River on December 27. Smith debarked his men near Johnson's plantation, and they caught up with the rest of the army near Chickasaw Bayou, just north of Vicksburg. The plan was to punch through the Confederate defenses on the Walnut Hills rising to the east of the bayou, rendezvous with Grant's army, which was proceeding southward along the railroad from Oxford, Mississippi, and then make a direct attack on Vicksburg. Burbridge's brigade was ordered to the right of the Union line, close in on the bayou. Their orders were "to force a passage and proceed in an easterly direction to the crest of the hill toward Vicksburg."[26]

The plan failed. The bulk of the fighting fell to the 2nd and 3rd Brigades, although Burbridge's 1st Division engaged in "heavy skirmishing all along the line" on December 28 and 29. Attempts to skirt the Confederate defenses on December 28 did not succeed, and Sherman's effort at a frontal assault on December 29 resulted in heavy Union casualties. On the 30th, Sherman ordered a withdrawal to the boats, and he took his army back upriver to Milliken's Bend.[27]

General John McClernand, arriving from Memphis, took overall command of the army from the more junior Sherman at Milliken's Bend. Rechristened the Army of the Mississippi and divided into two corps—the XIII Corps commanded by McClernand and the XV Corps commanded by Sherman—the army turned its attention to Arkansas Post (also known as Fort Hindman), about 120 miles north and west of Milliken's Bend. Arkansas Post guarded the Arkansas River valley from Union incursions and permitted Confederate forays to disrupt Union shipping on the Mississippi, which lay fifty miles or so down the Arkansas from the fort. One of the prizes captured by the Confederate forces was the steamer *Blue Wing,* which was fired on by guerrillas and beached by its captain on December 29, 1862. Laden with ammunition, the *Blue Wing* was taken upriver by its captors. The capture of the *Blue Wing* was cited by the Union commanders as the immediate justification for the attack on the fort.[28]

On January 10, 1863, Burbridge and his troops debarked along with thirty thousand other Union soldiers at Notrebe's plantation, south and east of the fort. After a devastating Union gunboat barrage knocked out the fort's artillery, the troops moved into position, pushing hard up against the Confederate defenders, who were entrenched behind a line of rifle pits defending the fort. On January 11, the infantry attack began. Burbridge's 1st Brigade of about twenty-four hundred troops occupied the center of the Union line, directly facing the fort across four hundred yards of open field, over which his men would have to advance once the attack commenced. To his right, the soldiers of the XV Corps engaged a stubborn group of Texans and Arkansans firing from the rifle pits to the west of the fort. At the sound of musketry and cheering from Sherman's troops on his right, Burbridge's men advanced "under a most murderous fire of musketry, shell, round shot, and grape and canister." His front lines wavering under the fire, Burbridge ordered up his three rear regiments in relief. But "the three front regiments refused to be relieved, and supported by the three relieving regiments the whole went forward with great resolution and most unflinchingly, driving the enemy from the houses in front of their works."[29] Burbridge reported that he was within "hand-shaking distance" of the enemy.[30]

At about 4:30 that afternoon, as McClernand pondered mounting a full-out frontal assault to overwhelm the remaining defenders, white flags appeared along the Confederate lines. As Burbridge approached the front gates of the fort, however, the guards fixed their bayonets and announced that they had not surrendered. Burbridge told them they had fought gallantly but had been "whipped," and demanded their capitulation. They lowered their weapons and allowed him entrance. The commander of the fort, Thomas J. Churchill—ironically, a fellow Kentuckian who had relocated to Arkansas in 1848—personally surrendered the fort and its 4,791-man garrison to Burbridge. And it was Burbridge who raised the national flag over the captured fort.[31]

Burbridge's men—most of whom had never seen actual battle before Arkansas Post—had been under fire for three and a half hours. They had been in the thickest part of the battle and borne the brunt of the casualties. Of the 1,061 official Union casualties, Burbridge's 1st Brigade counted 349 losses. "It is but justice," General George Morgan, field commander of the XIII Corps, wrote, "to say that the honor of the day belongs to Brigadier General A. J. Smith's gallant division [of which Burbridge's brigade formed a part]." The plaudits flowed down through the chain of command. Smith accorded "great praise" to Burbridge, and Burbridge could not "say too much in praise of the officers and men under my command." His men returned the praise, urging Lincoln to award Burbridge "two stars" for his "gallant and heroic conduct." The "complete success" of the assault helped assuage the bitter memories of the failure two weeks earlier at Chickasaw Bayou.[32]

The focus of the Union high command remained Vicksburg, however, and the Army of the Mississippi was ordered back to Milliken's Bend on January 13. Grant took direct command of the expedition at that point, relegating McClernand's XIII Corps to duty along the west bank of the Mississippi and declaring that he had no confidence in McClernand's military ability to guide the expedition against Vicksburg. As part of the XIII Corps, Burbridge's brigade carried out mopping-up operations in Arkansas and Mississippi between Arkansas Post and Milliken's Bend. They mostly operated well north of Grant's main forces, who were trying various schemes, from digging canals to navigating the bayous, to breach Confederate defenses around Vicksburg.[33]

On February 13, 1863, Burbridge's men were ordered upriver to Greenville, Mississippi. They debarked on the 16th to find that the rebel forces they hoped to engage were moving toward Bolivar, twenty miles to the north. With rain making the roads impassable, Burbridge returned his men to the boats. They then moved to Cypress Bend, Arkansas, just across the river from Greenville, from which a Union troop transport had taken fire a few days earlier. Burbridge dispatched a detachment of cavalry that soon came under fire. Rushing up his infantry, he threw them into the fight, but nightfall, unfamiliarity with the roads, and swampy terrain halted his advance. He returned his men to the boats and moved again toward Greenville, to which the forces they had pursued earlier were now returning. At Fish Lake, a little north and west of town, his cavalry engaged a small force of the enemy and captured about fifty men. Most of these later escaped when the rebel forces brought up their artillery and shelled Burbridge's men. In the end, Burbridge returned to the boats on the 24th, having captured some stock and reporting that he saw plenty of cotton and corn in the vicinity.

Frustrated with the meager results of the expedition, Burbridge lamented the disadvantages faced by Union troops operating against mounted rebel detachments in the area, foreshadowing similar frustrations he would later experience in Kentucky. "It is impossible for infantry to be effective . . . in such a country. Their information is always better than our own; the citizens all sympathize with them. The only force which can capture any of those rebel forces that fire into our transports is cavalry or mounted infantry. . . . [I]t is not their intention to fight, they can only be captured by a chase."[34]

By April, all of Grant's canal-digging, channel-dredging, and bayou-exploring had resulted in nothing; he concluded that there was no way to assault Vicksburg from dry land to the north of the city. So he decided to try a dry-land approach from the south, where his army would be cut off from its supply lines and operating against an enemy of unknown strength. Grant ordered the army to progress south of Vicksburg along the west side of the Mississippi, and he ordered the fleet under Admiral David Porter to run the Union boats directly past the batteries that guarded the river at Vicksburg. It was a huge risk, but the fleet got through and thus could ferry the army across the river at Bruinsburg. The XIII Corps was anxious to go. General McClernand, the corps commander whom Grant had bumped from overall command and in whom he had expressed a lack of confidence, wrote that "my corps . . . was inspired by an eager desire to prove its usefulness, and impatiently awaited an opportunity to do so."[35]

Burbridge's brigade left Milliken's Bend on April 13, marched south to Somerset plantation in Louisiana, then boarded the boats to cross the Mississippi. They stayed aboard as the Union gunboats tried to reduce the Confederate batteries at Grand Gulf on April 29 and, when that failed, proceeded further downriver to disembark at Bruinsburg on April 30. They immediately formed up and marched through the night toward Port Gibson, where the only significant Confederate force was garrisoned. Grant's twenty-three thousand men overwhelmed the six thousand Confederate defenders on May 1. Burbridge's men, having marched all night, were put in the reserve during the battle at Port Gibson, shifting along the battle line to shore up weak points. Finally thrown into the battle in relief, Burbridge's men pushed farther to the front than any other unit, "driving the enemy from the hill," he reported.

As night fell, "our men sank exhausted upon the ground. They had marched all night and fought all day under a burning sun, and without having had a mouthful to eat since the previous evening."[36]

Burbridge's brigade entered Port Gibson the following day, and Burbridge raised the Stars and Stripes over the town. Over the next two weeks his soldiers marched generally north and east, then turned directly west toward Vicksburg. On May 16, Burbridge's brigade was in the advance when they engaged the enemy in the Battle of Champion Hill. Encountering Confederate pickets, his regiments formed skirmish lines and pushed the enemy back. The Confederates were generally retreating, but Burbridge feared they would "avail themselves of some prominent hills" in the distance, so he pushed the brigade ahead as rapidly as he could until they gained the crest of the hill. "[I] had abundant reason to congratulate myself on my speed, as the enemy had rallied and planted their battery on the second hill, not having had time to form on the first." Protected by the crest of the hill they had taken, Burbridge's men endured "a most terrific fire of shot, shell, grape and canister," while their commander called frantically for reinforcements. When additional troops arrived, backed up by artillery, the battle turned and the Confederates retreated "in great disorder." Smith ordered Burbridge to hold his position, and Burbridge lamented in his report that had he been properly supported "we could have captured the whole rebel force opposed to us."[37]

Moving forward toward Vicksburg the next day, his men again engaged the enemy in the Battle of Big Black River Bridge. Burbridge's soldiers had to charge across an open field under enemy fire, but they were rewarded with the waving of a white handkerchief over the Confederate entrenchments as his advance skirmishers approached. Burbridge took the surrender of the 60th Tennessee, even as the main body of Confederate forces retreated across the Big Black River toward Vicksburg, burning the bridge as they did so. By Monday, May 18, as part of the general Union advance, Burbridge encamped just two and a half miles from Vicksburg's outer defenses.[38]

Relentless, Grant ordered his troops forward the next day, hoping to take Vicksburg itself from the demoralized Confederates, who had lost five engagements over the previous seventeen days. But Vicksburg's landward side was protected by trenches, rifle pits, and artillery, and the hunkered-down Confederates now had the advantage. The defenders repulsed Grant's first effort on May 19, though for its part Burbridge's force pushed back the Confederates until it was just four hundred yards from the city's defenses. On the 20th, his men were ordered to charge the Confederate works. "The brigade, with tremendous cheering, rushed over the crest of the hill in front of them," then advanced up the next hill, company by company, until they had driven the Confederate sharpshooters behind the fortifications. Burbridge's men advanced until they lay close under the fortifications, shooting at any Confederate head that appeared over the top, and neutralizing the effectiveness of the enemy's artillery. Relieved that night about 10 p.m., Burbridge withdrew his men and they rested in the rear on the 21st. On the 22nd, as part of another direct Union assault to storm the city's defenses, Burbridge's brigade again charged the Confederate fortifications.[39]

By 10:30 a.m. on the 22nd, the right side of Burbridge's line had advanced to within "20 steps" of the fort. Confederate artillery had fallen silent for fear of injuring their own men, and Burbridge's troops had "their colors flying against the walls of the fort." He then received an order to withdraw half his regiments and bring them to aid the brigade to his right. He protested that to withdraw those troops would leave his front unsupported and vulnerable, but to no avail. "I returned to my command, and with a heavy and foreboding heart, gave the requisite orders." Sure enough, as the Union fire slackened, the Confederate defenders opened up with more vigor. After a hasty consultation with his fellow brigade commander, Burbridge brought his regiments back, receiving an order shortly thereafter from General Eugene Carr, who was in overall command of the attack, to use his discretion about removing his troops. "Such a message ten minutes before, or such consent when I pleaded for it, would have saved a hundred lives," Burbridge wrote. As night fell, Burbridge withdrew his men, who had held their ground during nearly ten hours of continuous fighting. Despite the fierce fighting, his brigade lost just fourteen killed and eighty-two wounded in the May 22 assault, which once again had failed to breach the city's defenses.[40]

After the failure of the direct assaults in May, Grant settled on a siege of the city. Soldiers dug parallel defenses and tunneled under Confederate fortifications, and Union engineers detonated mines to blow holes in Confederate defenses. All the while, Union artillery and naval gunboats kept Vicksburg under near-constant barrage. On June 18, Grant reported that "everything progresses well" and that "we scarcely ever lose a man." Deserters were coming out daily and all reported that rations in the city were growing short. After six weeks besieged, starved, and deprived of the hope that reinforcements would arrive to lift the siege, the Confederates surrendered Vicksburg on July 4, 1863.[41] Once again, Lincoln heard praise of Burbridge from various quarters. The officers of the 16th Indiana Mounted Infantry, which had served under Burbridge for the previous twelve months, praised his conduct as "kind and gentlemanly, wise and daring. . . . His name has become the battle cry of our Brigade."[42]

Grant told his superiors back in Washington that the army was so worn out from the siege and the battles that preceded it that they required "several weeks of repose before undertaking another campaign." Burbridge used these "weeks of repose" to return to Kentucky, but they were hardly restful, for just as Vicksburg was succumbing to the pressures of the Union siege, Confederate general and Kentuckian John Hunt Morgan was riding into Kentucky on his "Great Raid."[43]

By 1863, Morgan had nearly perfected the tactics of fast-moving, wide-ranging, guerrilla-style cavalry raids. The idea, wrote historian and Morgan biographer James Ramage, was to take the offensive: "hit and run, attack when you have superior numbers and power; withdraw to avoid decisive battle; . . . harass the enemy like a gnat, destroy his communications; force him to disperse his strength; . . . do anything necessary to win; and—most fundamental of all—always preserve yourself so you can continue destroying the enemy." Morgan was a hero to southern sympathizers in Kentucky and a role model for numerous aspiring guerrilla leaders. The "Great Raid" was his third incursion into Kentucky. The first came in the summer of 1862, intended to rally pro-southern citizens in Kentucky to join the cause. The "Christmas Raid" followed in December 1862, raising havoc over two weeks and four hundred miles in the Bluegrass. Now came the "Great Raid." Louisville was Morgan's initial target, but he changed his plan (and disobeyed orders) by crossing the Ohio River and marauding through Indiana and Ohio, sowing panic among the Union residents.[44]

To divert attention from Morgan, the Confederates ordered about two thousand infantry and cavalry under Colonel John Scott into Kentucky on July 25. Scott's lesser known raid moved quickly up from Williamsburg, on the Tennessee border, to Richmond, where on July 28 they routed Union troops under Colonel W. P. Sanders, who was forced to retreat in great disorder toward Lexington. Occupying Winchester on the morning of the 29th, Scott then sent out a detachment toward Paris with the goal of destroying a large trestle bridge of the Kentucky Central Railroad.[45] It was this detachment's movements that disturbed Burbridge's intended repose.

The army post at Paris was garrisoned by troops from Michigan, Indiana, and Ohio under the command of Lieutenant Colonel Thomas Young of the 118th Ohio. As news of Scott's raid spread, Burbridge offered his assistance to Young in preparing for a defense of Paris and the railroad bridge. Young's troops engaged the advance force of Scott's detachment on July 29, fully expecting an all-out attack the next day. None came. There was another skirmish on the 30th, but by 6 p.m. the Confederates were retreating "in great disorder" back toward Winchester. In his report, Young acknowledged the "valuable assistance" rendered by Burbridge. "He did not assume command, yet I was aided by his advice and plans for defense, and he took charge of the execution of the most important and dangerous part of it himself."[46]

Burbridge and Young were unaware at the time that Scott had called his men back after learning that trainloads of Union troops, fresh off the pursuit of Morgan, who had been captured on July 26 and imprisoned, were pouring into Lexington. Scott beat a hasty retreat, harassed repeatedly by Union troops, until he had crossed again into Tennessee. The capture of Morgan and the subsequent deployment of Union reinforcements had turned Scott's early success into "a partial disaster," in the words of Scott's commanding officer.[47]

On September 18, 1863, the army promoted Burbridge to divisional command, naming him leader of the 4th Division of the XIII Corps of the Department of the Gulf. His new assignment took him to Union-occupied Louisiana, where he would be chasing recalcitrant rebels who still thought the state might be reclaimed—much as he would be doing as commander of Kentucky a few months later. In September 1863, Burbridge was sent upriver from New Orleans to Donaldsonville, a town about halfway between New Orleans and Baton Rouge. The swamps around Donaldsonville, virtually impenetrable to Union infantry, served as an excellent base for guerrilla operations. Burbridge's orders were to "destroy, capture, or break up the enemy under [Confederate colonel John] Logan, as well as force the evacuation of all the space between the Mississippi River and Lakes Maurepas and Pontchartrain." Instead, his troops destroyed a single bridge over the Amite River, never encountered the enemy, and returned to base three days later.[48]

In early October, Burbridge and his men were ordered to the other side of the Mississippi, this time to support an effort to take and hold western Louisiana and establish a Union foothold in Texas. In conjunction with some 19,500 Federals under Major General William B. Franklin, the army pushed forward slowly north and west to Opelousas, skirmishing several times with a much smaller Confederate force. By the time they reached Opelousas, however, Franklin found the water level in the bayous so low that he had to abandon his plan to transport his army by boat. Rather than march west across Louisiana, Franklin decided to instead retreat southward by detachments toward New Iberia. On November 1, he ordered Burbridge to camp with one brigade from his division, about twelve hundred men, near Grand Coteau, about ten miles south of Opelousas, to serve as the main army's rear guard.[49]

On the morning of November 3, Burbridge sent word to his immediate commanding officer, General C. C. Washburn, that "the enemy had shown himself in some force," but by the time reinforcements were brought up the Confederates had disappeared. As Washburn withdrew from the front, he suddenly heard the sound of cannon. Dispatching two subordinates to bring up the reinforcements as quickly as possible, he returned to the front to find Burbridge's forces "assailed with terrible energy by an overwhelming force in front and on both flanks." The attack had shattered the Union line, and soldiers were "scattered over the field, and the utter destruction or capture of the whole force seemed imminent," Washburn wrote. Hard fighting on the right side of the line saved Burbridge from annihilation. It bought him enough time to save all but one of his artillery pieces, fall back, and reform them into a line and, with additional artillery brought up from the rear, unleash a "raking cross-fire" upon the attackers, which forced their retreat. Despite the near catastrophe, in which nearly half of Burbridge's men were either killed, wounded, or captured, Washburn praised the Kentuckian's behavior as "gallant and judicious" throughout the engagement.[50]

With the rebel forces driven off, Burbridge's men fell back with most of the rest of the Union forces to New Iberia. Having abandoned the idea of getting to Texas via an overland route, General Franklin watched many of his men be siphoned off to Texas via sea. To try and control western Louisiana, he posted troops in a line roughly following the southward course of the Bayou Teche, with detachments left behind in Opelousas, New Iberia, and Vermilion. For the remainder of his time in Louisiana, Burbridge sparred with Confederate guerrillas, sent out scouting expeditions, gathered intelligence, and confiscated abandoned cotton and sugar.[51]

On December 6, 1863, Burbridge was relieved of command at his own request. Several motives doubtless prompted this request. He was away from the main action of the war, and so unlikely to get noticed for further promotion. He was engaged essentially in garrison duty, repulsing small groups of Confederate irregulars and trying to safeguard Unionists and Union assets, a job he would much rather be doing in Kentucky than in Louisiana. Since 1862, his political patrons back home had been pushing for him to be named commander of the state, and the time may have seemed right for his return. Finally, there was his health to consider; the bayous and swamps of western Louisiana no doubt appealed to him less than the hills and meadows of his native state. Burbridge was going home.

# 3

# Commander

After his battles in Louisiana, Burbridge came back to Kentucky. The previous military commander in the state, General Jeremiah T. Boyle, had been relieved on January 2, 1864. Boyle had been born in 1818 in Mercer (now Boyle) County, Kentucky, the son of a prominent pioneer lawmaker and jurist (in whose honor Boyle County was named in 1842), and was appointed commander in June 1862. His appointment was made partly in recognition of his admirable service at the Battle of Shiloh and partly because it was felt that, as a native Kentuckian, his knowledge of the state would help preserve good relations between Kentucky and the federal administration. It was not to be.[1]

Shortly after his appointment, Boyle issued an order aimed at suppressing guerrilla activity in the state, providing for the arrest of suspected guerrillas, loyalty oaths from Confederate sympathizers, and assessments upon the disloyal population in the vicinity of a guerrilla attack that damaged Unionists' property. He followed this a few weeks later with an order to provost marshals throughout the state to "fit up quarters for the imprisonment of . . . disloyal females." These two orders resulted in the arrest of so many suspected rebels and Confederate sympathizers that by the end of July the prisons were full to bursting and the authorities began to require prisoners to post bond and swear an oath of loyalty in order to be released so as to make room for new prisoners. Vehement protests from Kentuckians to the federal authorities finally prompted Secretary of War Edwin Stanton to tell Boyle to show more restraint and to consult with the governor before making arrests.[2]

The discontent bred by the arrests of southern sympathizers was compounded by the military's interference in state elections, injunctions against commerce and trade, and meddling with the institution of slavery. Boyle issued General Order No. 5 in July 1862. It forbade any person

General Stephen Gano Burbridge. Burbridge was named military commander of the District of Kentucky in February 1864. (National Archives.)

"hostile in opinion to the government and desiring its overthrow" from running in the upcoming elections for county office. Statewide elections in August 1863 were held under a decree of martial law in the state that more or less guaranteed the election of solidly Unionist candidates.[3] After the 1862 Confederate invasion of Kentucky, Boyle introduced a permit system for "purchasing and shipping goods and merchandise for retail trading." A loyalty oath was required to obtain a permit, and the seizure of goods was authorized—permit or no—if shipped by someone who gave aid or comfort to the invading Confederate soldiers. He also shut down several religious newspapers for their less-than-enthusiastic reaction to his policies.[4] Finally, Boyle messed with the peculiar institution, impressing six thousand slaves in August 1863 to work on extending a railroad line in central Kentucky and threatening to emancipate all the slaves of those owners who did not answer the military's call for laborers.[5]

Nonetheless, some Unionists felt he had not been hard enough on Confederate sympathizers. "Under the policy of General Boyle, the union men of this state have but little to hope for," wrote a federal appointee in Bowling Green to Burbridge, on the eve of Burbridge's appointment as commander. "There are but few men more popular with rebels than Genl Boyle."[6]

For all these reasons—that he had been too harsh or that he had not been harsh enough—few Kentuckians shed tears when Boyle was relieved and ordered to report with all the able-bodied troops in his division to Knoxville. Boyle responded by resigning his commission on January 10, complaining to Lincoln that "my superior officers have shown distrust of me." He went on to make a fortune in the railway business.[7]

It is interesting—and somewhat ironic—to note the parallels between Boyle and Burbridge. Both were appointed commander of the district because of their battlefield accomplishments and because they were native Kentuckians. As they had hoped with Boyle, federal officials hoped that the native Burbridge might mollify the restive elements in the state. And as with Boyle, these hopes were dashed when the exigencies of the wartime situation—or the overweening desire to humiliate Kentucky, as some in the state perceived it—led Burbridge to enact policies to punish Confederate sympathizers, influence state politics, interfere with commerce, and, most especially, meddle with slavery. Unlike Boyle, however, Burbridge was never forgiven by the state's residents for his wartime actions. While historian E. Merton Coulter wrote that the arrests under Boyle would "make his name odious to many of his fellow citizens," he went to on to become president of the Louisville City Railway Company and the Evansville & Nashville Railway Company and died in Kentucky.[8] The odium attached to Burbridge's name, by contrast, enjoyed a long and healthy career.

General Jacob Ammen was initially named as Boyle's replacement as commander of Kentucky. Ammen was a native Virginian who had grown up in Ohio and worked as a mathematics professor at Georgetown College in Kentucky for a few years before the war. In January 1864, however, he was on court-martial duty in Cincinnati and could not immediately assume command in Kentucky. So, on February 15 General Grant appointed Burbridge as a temporary fill-in until Ammen became free. Burbridge's supporters in the state, meanwhile, had gone to Governor Thomas Bramlette in January, after Boyle had been relieved, and urged him to get behind Burbridge's appointment as commander in the state. "He [Bramlette] expressed himself as being very much in favor of your holding command in Kentucky," Logan County's state representative wrote to Burbridge.[9] On March 8, Bramlette wired both Grant and General John Schofield, commanding the Department of the Ohio, pushing Burbridge to be named commander of the district. Ammen "does not desire the command, and I deem it important to our condition that General Burbridge be retained in command in Kentucky," Bramlette told Grant. On March 14, Grant wrote to Schofield that "General Burbridge seems to be doing so well in Kentucky that I think he had better be retained permanently in command of the district." On March 25, Schofield officially named Burbridge commander.[10]

At the time of Burbridge's appointment, Confederate forces in the West still remained concentrated in Tennessee, and intelligence regularly circulated that they were planning large incursions into Kentucky. The principal risk to the war effort from Confederate military action in Kentucky was from cavalry raids to disrupt Union supply lines. Burbridge was particularly instructed to guard the Louisville & Nashville Railroad line, a crucial link to the federal troops in Tennessee. Schofield ordered Burbridge to organize his command into two divisions. One division was to guard the L&N and the region to the west. The other division was to guard the region east of the railroad, keeping tabs on the restive Bluegrass region, the heart of pro-Confederate sentiment in the state, and the mountain gaps through which Confederate raiders might enter the state from western Virginia or eastern Tennessee.[11]

Repeated rumors of Confederate invasions came to Burbridge's ears. Within days of his appointment as commander, Burbridge's attention was drawn toward Pound Gap, a passage through the mountains on Kentucky's eastern border with Virginia. "There is but little doubt that a large rebel force is about to invade the State by way of Pound Gap," he instructed Edward Hobson, his divisional commander. In early April he relayed military and civilian reports of threatening Confederate troop movements to commanding general Sherman. Sherman counseled Burbridge to keep the threat in perspective. "There is no real army to threaten Kentucky but [Confederate general Joseph] Johnston's, and he can't advance," Sherman wrote. "The mountains of eastern Kentucky are a barrier against anything but a maraud." And a maraud could be easily contained by the available forces in Kentucky.[12]

The marauder *par excellence* in Kentucky was John Hunt Morgan, and by May 1864 rumors were rife that the flamboyant Kentuckian was planning another raid into the Commonwealth. In 1863, Morgan's "Great Raid" through Kentucky into Ohio and Indiana had culminated in his capture and imprisonment, but Morgan and six of his officers tunneled out of the Ohio State Penitentiary and escaped on November 27, 1863. Making his way through Kentucky and across the Confederate lines, Morgan was hailed as a returning hero. By 1864, however, Morgan was hell-bent on redeeming his reputation as a leader and cavalry raider. Union leaders from General in Chief Henry Halleck in Washington to Sherman on the march in Tennessee to Burbridge circulated reports that Morgan was preparing to attack Kentucky again. Sherman was sanguine: "There remains plenty of troops in Kentucky to watch Pound Gap," he told Halleck. Theodore Allen, a cavalry captain with the 7th Ohio Cavalry encamped at Nicholasville, Kentucky, noted in his diary on May 26, "Come on John and Basil [Duke, Morgan's second-in-command], we would like to renew our slight acquaintance. We like you. Your [*sic*] hard to catch but when caught are easily whipped."[13]

General John Hunt Morgan. The "Thunderbolt of the Confederacy" led cavalry raids into Kentucky four times over the course of the Civil War. His final raid ended in a defeat at the hands of Burbridge at Cynthiana, Kentucky. (Library of Congress.)

In response to the threat, Burbridge organized an expedition of five thousand men. Anxious about leaving key points of the state essentially undefended, he asked Governor Bramlette for four regiments of state troops to stand in for the Federals. Burbridge worried about the readiness of his forces and complained to Schofield that most of the experienced veterans had been removed from the state and sent to the front lines. Responding from the field in Georgia, Schofield was unsympathetic: "Give my compliments to the Governor and tell him I expect him and you to take care of Kentucky while I help to dispose of Johnston. I want all the veterans here."[14]

Burbridge's plan was to hit Morgan before he got to Kentucky. The plan made strategic sense. As historian Brian McKnight noted, "Morgan's force was at its most dangerous when in the field." Therefore, if Burbridge could take the fight to Morgan while the Confederate leader was still preparing for the raid, he would not end up like other Union commanders who had confronted Morgan, constantly on the chase after an elusive and cunning enemy. Halleck's message to Sherman essentially endorsed this proactive approach: Burbridge "should organize and meet Morgan before he reaches Richmond [Kentucky]."[15]

By late May, Burbridge was in the field with some twenty-one hundred men near Prestonsburg, at the mouth of Beaver Creek, intending to pass through Pound Gap and attack the Confederates at Abingdon, Virginia. His movement was delayed, however, waiting for supplies, and he did not actually move out until June 5. After one day on the march, he learned that Morgan had beaten him to the punch, crossing through Pound Gap with between two thousand and three thousand men. "General Burbridge's enterprise was bold and patriotic in its intention," the *Louisville Journal* noted, "but the wily and ever active guerrilla chief foiled it." Burbridge fell back to the mouth of Beaver Creek and sent General Edward Hobson downriver and on toward Covington with orders to gather a force to protect Lexington, while he determined—just like Union commanders before him—to pursue Morgan.[16]

Morgan took the town of Mount Sterling on June 8, taking 380 Union prisoners and robbing the local bank. In the predawn of June 9, Burbridge fell upon the dismounted troops that Morgan had left in possession of Mount Sterling. He destroyed Morgan's largest brigade, killing fifty-one men, wounding eighty-three, and taking one hundred prisoners, while only losing twenty-five men. He delayed at Mount Sterling, however, to allow his men to rest, giving Morgan the opportunity to enter Lexington and then move up to Georgetown on June 10, taking horses and destroying railroad bridges all along the way. In the towns where Morgan stopped, the *Journal* reported, "the rebels and rebel-sympathizing population, including pretended deserters and refugees, who have taken the oath of allegiance and the oath of amnesty, exulted and shouted and clapped their hands, giving the invaders all the comfort and encouragement and aid in their power."[17]

Now well-mounted, Morgan's men turned northeast and took the town of Cynthiana after a fierce battle with its small detachment of Union defenders. Morgan's men eventually resorted to setting the town on fire.[18] Meanwhile, Hobson and his staff had been stranded in Covington by Morgan's cutting of the railroad line. Hearing that Morgan was moving toward Cynthiana, Hobson gathered what troops were available in the vicinity and, with a force of about six hundred men, moved southwestward as far as they could on the Kentucky Central Railroad. Arriving at Keller's Bridge, about a mile north of Cynthiana, they met the advancing Confederates. According to Hobson, his men twice drove Morgan's troops from the field, but were eventually driven back to a small hill that they "stubbornly defended for five hours." Just as Morgan's men began to run critically low on ammunition, they gained reinforcements—including some sympathizers from the local militia, according to Hobson—and were able to completely surround Hobson's force, now reduced to three hundred men and officers. Soon after, Hobson waved the white flag and surrendered his command to Morgan.[19]

Hobson and his officers refused to be paroled and were escorted under a flag of truce to Falmouth, Kentucky, to communicate with Union authorities about arranging an exchange for officers of equal rank. Hobson believed that his negotiations over the terms of his surrender crucially delayed Morgan, allowing Burbridge, who had remounted and reinforced at Lexington, to catch up with the Confederate force. But equally important was Morgan's decision to stay and fight when his command had run dangerously low on ammunition, much to the consternation of his senior officers.[20]

Burbridge hit Morgan at Cynthiana at daybreak on June 12. Using his cavalry effectively and taking advantage of Morgan's lack of ammunition and surplus of confidence, Burbridge succeeded in completely routing the Confederate forces in a battle of about two hours. Morgan's men fled in confusion, some drowning while attempting to cross the South Fork of the Licking River, as their commander headed northeast toward Claysville. Burbridge ordered his cavalry commanders to pursue the fleeing Confederates, rounding up any stragglers, but Morgan made it back to Virginia. "The commanding general desires me to say that he considers the raid over," Burbridge's assistant adjutant general wrote to Governor Bramlette. "Morgan's command is wholly broken up. His men have thrown away their arms, are out of ammunition, and are being captured in small squads by our cavalry."[21]

In truth, the Morgan's raiders that Burbridge defeated were not the same Morgan's raiders of past incursions into Kentucky. While his brigade commanders were largely competent leaders, Morgan was missing Basil Duke, his right-hand man, who was still behind bars. And the men that made up the force consisted only partially of men who had previously ridden with the Confederate leader. The others were a mixed bag collected from all over the Confederacy, some of whom had dreamed of riding with the great man, some who merely who wanted to avoid conscription or infantry service, and some who inhabited the "criminal fringe" of the crumbling Confederate war effort.[22]

Nonetheless, the defeat of Morgan earned Burbridge high praise and commendation from his superiors. President Lincoln and Secretary of War Stanton both sent telegrams expressing their congratulations and gratitude for Burbridge's success. On July 4, Burbridge was breveted to major general (from his rank of brigadier general) for his "meritorious and distinguished service." The *Lexington National Unionist* boasted that, at age thirty-three, Burbridge had become one of the "younger double stars [major generals] in the Federal firmament."[23] Hobson was not so fortunate. Accused of violating orders by accepting a parole (which Hobson fervently denied), Hobson was arrested by order of the War Department. Burbridge campaigned for his release, which was eventually obtained, but Hobson was relieved of his divisional command and ordered to report to the new divisional commander, Nathaniel McLean.[24]

Despite his victory over Morgan, Burbridge continued to be haunted by the "Thunderbolt of the Confederacy." By mid-July, Burbridge was again warning that an invasion of the state was imminent. The colonel commanding the forces watching Cumberland Gap passed along reports that Morgan had amassed eleven thousand troops at Tazewell, Virginia.

A month later, Kentucky's adjutant general warned Burbridge that Morgan planned to invade the state "with a large force" on or around the 26th of August, intending to take "Camp Nelson, Lexington, Frankfort, and Nashville railroad, and all boats on the Ohio." By August 21, Burbridge was telling Halleck that "Kentucky is to be invaded by a large force under Morgan and [CSA General Joseph] Wheeler."[25] None of these purported movements by Morgan turned out to be true. As Grant told Halleck, "John Morgan . . . has no command." These repeated rumors, however, point to the hold that Morgan had on the imaginations of Union commanders and to the fact that a large part of Burbridge's role as commander was to distinguish good intelligence from bad and deploy his troops to counter the real threats faced by the state.[26]

As it turned out, Grant was correct. Morgan had been relieved of command pending investigation into the depredations that occurred during his last Kentucky raid. But Morgan, characteristically, ignored the suspension in the hopes of striking a rousing blow against Union forces to offset the growing opposition toward him among the Confederate high command. He was not aiming at Kentucky, however, but at Tennessee. From his headquarters at Abingdon, Virginia, Morgan had been ranging into eastern Tennessee on foraging expeditions when he learned that Governor Andrew Johnson had sent General Alvan Gillem to expel him from the area to protect the Unionist citizens. Morgan hoped to redeem his fortunes by defeating Gillem. Instead, helped along by Morgan's usual excess confidence and by Unionist sympathizers in the area who betrayed Morgan's whereabouts, Gillem's men were able to surprise and surround the house where Morgan was staying in Greeneville, Tennessee, on the morning of September 4. Seeking a way out and having vowed never to be captured again, Morgan disobeyed an order to halt and was shot and killed by Private Andrew Campbell.[27]

Even with Morgan out of the picture, rumors about pending invasions of Kentucky by other Confederate forces continued to circulate in the summer of 1864. On August 19, both Sherman and Halleck warned Burbridge that Wheeler had passed to Sherman's rear in eastern Tennessee and that he might contemplate a raid into Kentucky.[28] If the 1904 memoirs of Confederate officer Adam Johnson can be believed, however, a secret and much grander plan was afoot that August. Johnson began his military career as a scout for Nathan Bedford Forrest,

Colonel Adam Johnson. Even though Johnson claimed to be operating as a legitimate Confederate military unit, he and his men were routinely viewed as irregular forces by federal authorities. (Library of Congress, Prints and Photographs Division.)

then recruited a band of Confederate irregulars in western Kentucky. He eventually received the official "partisan ranger" designation from the Richmond government and operated against Union troops and Unionist civilians in the area around Henderson, Kentucky. He served under Morgan during the "Great Raid" but escaped capture and made it to Virginia. In the summer of 1864, he was ordered back to Kentucky ostensibly on a second recruiting mission. However, he also had secret orders to make contact with the shadowy Sons of Liberty organization, a supposed network of civilian sympathizers with the Confederacy. If Johnson enlisted or conscripted enough men, and if the Sons of Liberty arose, and if Forrest led a cavalry force into the state, then the Confederate army under Joseph Johnston would try to outflank Sherman's army and invade Kentucky. If successful, Johnson wrote, they would "drive any Federal force out of Kentucky" that could be brought against them, "capture Louisville and Cincinnati, . . . compel Grant to withdraw his forces from Virginia and perhaps induce the Federal government to cease the war and acknowledge the Confederacy."[29]

Most of this plan was wishful thinking by the Confederates, although Burbridge and the governors of Ohio and Indiana treated the threat from the Sons of Liberty quite seriously (see chapter 4). Johnston and Forrest were held down by Sherman, and the Sons of Liberty proved to be more bluster and promise than actual uprising. Johnson, however, enjoyed significant recruiting success. He arrived back in Kentucky in mid-July 1864 and believed he could raise three thousand cavalry to operate against Sherman's rail and river transportation links by early September. "This is the golden moment for securing an army from Kentucky," Johnson wrote to the secretary of war in Richmond. Even without the grand plan coming together, had Johnson been able to raise a regiment in western Kentucky, he could have posed a grave threat to Sherman's supply lines, especially the L&N railroad.[30]

Johnson was thwarted by Burbridge's ordering General Edward Hobson to the western part of the state on August 10. "It is of great importance that you move quickly," he told Hobson. He also ordered additional forces from Paducah and Hopkinsville to meet up with Hobson, giving him a force of about three thousand to confront Johnson's eight hundred to one thousand troops. Hobson's "rapid and unexpected movement," Johnson wrote in his memoir, "compelled me to move on toward the Cumberland river," frustrating his goal of capturing Evansville, Indiana. On August 20, learning that about three hundred to four hundred Union soldiers were encamped at a place known as "Grubb's Crossroads" near Princeton, Johnson decided to attack. Although he captured about fifty prisoners at first, his own men opened fire on the Federals and mistakenly shot Johnson in his right eye. The ball came out his left temple, disabling his left eye as well. In the ensuing confusion, the prisoners escaped, the Union men regrouped, the now-blind Johnson was captured, and his men fled. "Adam Johnson's men are scattered," wrote a group of Hopkinsville citizens to Burbridge, "but there are still hundreds of them all around us." They begged Burbridge to leave troops in the area to protect citizens from reprisals.[31]

Morgan's June raid had disrupted Burbridge's original plan to attack Confederate troops in southwestern Virginia, and Burbridge continued to believe that the best strategy was to take the fight to the forces that threatened the state. In particular, he lobbied his superiors to approve an attack on the Confederate saltworks at the appropriately named Saltville, Virginia. As part of targeting the saltworks—which were important to the Confederacy for the preservation of meat for troops and civilians—he meant to clear southwestern Virginia of Confederate troops. He remained convinced that an attack into southwestern Virginia would help secure Kentucky and ultimate Union victory.[32]

His commanders were not so sure. Schofield questioned the advisability of the attack, hinting that "more important movements will probably require all the troops we can raise." Sherman was likewise unconvinced. "I doubt the necessity of your sending far into Virginia to destroy the salt-works, or any other material interest," Sherman wrote. "We must destroy their armies." Nonetheless, after meeting with Burbridge in Louisville, Schofield approved the expedition, largely because Halleck had already okayed it, provided that Burbridge moved quickly.[33]

With fifty-two hundred men, including members of the 5th U.S. Colored Cavalry, Burbridge set out on September 20. The image is striking: Burbridge, a Kentucky slaveowner, leading armed black men, many of whom had been enslaved in Kentucky just months earlier, into battle against white soldiers, at least some of whom were Kentuckians themselves. As will be discussed in further detail in the next chapter, Burbridge embraced the use of black soldiers both out of necessity and out of his commitment to the Union cause, though he was hardly a diehard emancipationist. Earlier in the war, in fact, he had argued that his status as a slaveowner would reassure other Kentucky slaveholders with Unionist sympathies.

The men of the 5th U.S. Colored Cavalry had endured abuse and insults from the time of their enlistment. At Camp Nelson, where black troops in Kentucky were sent for training, one white officer remarked that it was rare for his men to go through the day without a violent attack. On the march with Burbridge, they were subject to "insult, taunts, and ridicule from their fellow white soldiers." The inhabitants of the mountains of eastern Kentucky and southwestern Virginia through which they marched were probably slack-jawed as they saw the columns of mounted and equipped black soldiers pass. Although the mountaineers had little direct experience with slavery, they harbored fierce ideas of white supremacy and racial animosity. As one historian of the region speculated, seeing the troops "probably gave rise to many wild thoughts of racial vengeance that might be perpetrated on the Virginians by the former slaves."[34]

Burbridge's plan was to cooperate with General Alvan Gillem, who would bring forces from eastern Tennessee into the fight. Gillem was met by a Confederate force at Bulls Gap, however, and never met up with Burbridge. Meanwhile, Confederate general John Echols was cobbling together a defensive force for the saltworks, calling on troops from several different commands to help him repel Burbridge's men. Burbridge met armed resistance up to and through Laurel Gap, only four miles from Saltville, but he got through the mountains late on October 1. He camped there and prepared to attack the saltworks the following morning. That decision cost him the definitive victory he sought, for it allowed seventeen hundred battle-hardened Confederate veterans to reinforce the four hundred defenders at Saltville.[35]

By early morning on October 2, Burbridge's men were pushing back Confederate pickets about three miles from the works. They continued to make slow and steady progress through the day. The defending force had swelled to about twenty-four hundred with the arrival of reinforcements, facing off against about forty-two hundred Federals. The Union forces pushed in the Confederate left and center and held the right until a shortage of ammunition compelled Burbridge to call off the fight at about 5 p.m. Receiving word from Sherman that his troops were needed for the upcoming campaign against General John Bell Hood's army, Burbridge withdrew during the night and headed back to Kentucky.[36]

What happened next has been shrouded in controversy ever since. What is indisputable is that on the morning of October 3, after the battle was over, Confederate soldiers were found on the battlefield killing wounded black soldiers. Burbridge had left his wounded on the field under the care of regimental surgeons, and a group of Confederate soldiers moved among them, singling out black soldiers for execution. Controversy has arisen over whether any officers were involved, who they might have been, and to what extent Confederate general officers tried to stop the killing. At least one historian has suggested that the Saltville Massacre exceeded the brutality of the more famous Fort Pillow Massacre of black troops. Unlike Fort Pillow, the battle at Saltville had been over for hours when the killings took place. The Confederate troops had rested for the night and found the federal forces withdrawn; they then proceeded to vent their anger over the Union's use of black troops. Estimates of the number killed have ranged from lower than a dozen to over one hundred, with more recent and more careful estimates falling around forty-five to fifty murdered.[37]

More knowable and perhaps more significant than the precise number of soldiers killed or which, if any, Confederate senior officers were directly involved is the clear and unmistakable rage that black soldiers triggered in white southerners. The killings at Saltville, along with the growing list of sites where atrocities were committed against black soldiers, gives bloody testimony to the fury kindled in Confederate soldiers at seeing and confronting armed and uniformed African Americans. Much of white Kentuckians' antipathy toward Burbridge, the man responsible for enlisting and arming those soldiers in Kentucky, grew out of this elemental rage toward their former slaves who were now uniformed in blue.[38]

The killings continued after the wounded had been transferred under the care of paroled Union surgeons from field hospitals to Emory and Henry College, near Abingdon. On October 7 and 8, a group wearing Confederate uniforms, led by Champ Ferguson, a Confederate guerrilla from Kentucky, came into the hospital and dispatched two more wounded black soldiers, as well as a white officer against whom Ferguson carried some sort of vendetta.[39]

Burbridge did not mention the massacre in his official report, instead doing his best to put a positive overall interpretation on the battle at Saltville. His report to Schofield overstated the size of the rebel force against him and maintained that his failure to overrun the saltworks was due to a lack of ammunition and Sherman's order to come back. Still, he concluded, "The result of the expedition may be thus stated: We whipped the rebels in every engagement, fighting from the Virginia line up to the salt-works."[40] The fact was, however, that the Confederacy remained in control of the saltworks, with only some of the outer works damaged. In addition, Burbridge had been out of contact for several days, so

Sherman's message to turn back, which had been sent on September 23, reached him only ten days later, while other pleas for Kentucky troops to hurry to Tennessee went unanswered.[41] Brigadier General J. D. Webster, in command at Nashville, wrote on October 6 that he had repeatedly forwarded the recall order to Burbridge, "but he can hardly get back to do any good in the matter occasioning his recall."[42] On October 11, Schofield wrote resignedly to Sherman that Burbridge had returned to Kentucky, "having failed in his expedition. His troops will require rest for some time before they will be fit to take the field again."[43] Having failed to take the military objective on an expedition that had met only the marginal approval of his superiors, Burbridge had also prevented the main Union army in Tennessee from using the troops stationed in Kentucky.

Rumored and actual incursions by Confederate troops and attacks by rebel guerrillas left Burbridge continually begging for more troops with which to defend Kentucky. Sometimes he was successful, as in July when he asked the governor of Indiana and the military commander of Ohio for additional troops, and persuaded Halleck to order two regiments back to Louisville from Nashville. On July 16, Burbridge pressed the urgency of his need for more troops by telling his military counterpart in Ohio that he believed that between five thousand and seven thousand enemy troops had already invaded the state by way of Pound Gap.[44] More often, though, he was told to make do with the troops he had. When his request for troops to repulse the threatened invasion by Wheeler was relayed to Grant, Grant responded that "there is no place from which troops can be withdrawn to send General Burbridge. I do not think Wheeler can get to Kentucky to do much harm, nor do I think he can be spared from [Confederate general John Bell] Hood's army." If Wheeler did turn north into Kentucky, Grant wrote, Burbridge would have to deal with him using the troops available to him in Kentucky.[45]

Sherman, from the front in Tennessee, echoed this sentiment. "General Burbridge . . . must take care of Wheeler and Morgan with the force he has."[46] To Burbridge himself, Sherman wrote, "Of course I cannot turn back for a cavalry raid. . . . Get your people well in hand, and in no event allow alarm to spread in Kentucky. The enemy cannot spare a large force now to invade Kentucky. It is a raid designed to make clamor and nothing more."[47]

This pattern of request-and-deny recurred in Burbridge's correspondence with higher-ups in the army. Of course, the feeling of being undermanned and insecure was not unique to Kentucky, and Grant, Halleck, and Sherman were frequently deflecting requests for more troops to secure areas in the rear of their armies. The overriding desire of the generals at the front was to be able to cut loose and stop worrying about the areas already subdued. Shortly after Burbridge's appointment as commander of the district, Sherman optimistically declared that "we are now independent of Kentucky," forecasting that the combination of the federal troops already in the state and the state forces would be able to control military affairs there. Instead, until the end of the war, Sherman received reports of rumored invasions and requests for additional troops to be deployed in Kentucky.[48]

After his failure to take Saltville, Burbridge was buffeted with orders to send all the troops that could be spared to Nashville to General George H. Thomas, who had been charged with the task of holding Tennessee while Sherman began his march through Georgia. On October 14, he told Schofield that in obedience to orders he was sending three regiments to Nashville, which he complained left his forces in Kentucky "entirely inadequate."[49] On the very next day, Burbridge passed on information that Confederate general John C. Breckinridge "will soon invade Kentucky with a formidable force of cavalry and infantry. I will do my utmost, but have so few troops left that I fear the result of an invasion." Schofield, again, was notably unsympathetic: "You were left to consult your own judgment as to what troops you could spare from Kentucky, and should not weaken your command too much."[50]

Meanwhile, the western part of the state was besieged by Confederate cavalry raids, both real and threatened. In October, Solomon Meredith, the commander in western Kentucky (and thus outside the military district of Kentucky and Burbridge's formal authority) pleaded with Burbridge to send him reinforcements to repel a raid by Confederate general Nathan Bedford Forrest, thought (as usual) to presage a larger invasion of the western part of the state. Burbridge had none to

Table 1. US Forces in Kentucky, 1864–1865

| *Date* | *Number of officers and men reported present* |
|---|---|
| April 1864 | 11,728 |
| May 1864 | 8,576 |
| June 1864 | 9,606 |
| July 1864 | 10,512 |
| August 1864 | 15,742 |
| September 1864 | 16,453 |
| October 1864 | 13,724 |
| December 1864 | 9,382 |
| January 1865 | 9,708 |
| February 1865 | 7,997 |

*Sources: O.R.*, vol. 32, pt. 3, 570; vol. 38, pt. 4, 376; vol. 38, pt. 4, 654; vol. 38, pt. 5, 319; vol. 38, pt. 5, 745; vol. 39, pt. 2, 561; vol. 39, pt. 3, 569; vol. 45, pt. 2, 461; vol. 49, pt. 1, 622; vol. 49, pt. 1, 801–2. No returns for November could be located.

spare. As it turned out, Forrest's true target was the federal supply depot at Johnsonville, Tennessee, but the panic he created in Kentucky kept US troops from knowing his true intentions. At the same time, Confederate general Hylan B. Lyon entered the state east of the Cumberland River (and thus within Burbridge's district), briefly occupied the town of Eddyville (Lyon's hometown), and then moved east toward Princeton. Lyon's raid, meant to divert attention from Forrest's designs on Johnsonville and to scoop up any Kentucky recruits, likewise taxed the available forces in Kentucky. When Burbridge's divisional commander requested more troops to repulse Lyon's raid, Burbridge could only advise him to concentrate his available forces and go on the offensive. "No other troops can be spared from other parts of the district."[51]

How many men did Burbridge have? According to the monthly returns submitted to the War Department, there was in fact a sharp decline in the number of officers and men reported present for duty in the District of Kentucky after October 1864. Table 1 shows the number of men and officers reported as present for duty in the official records during the months Burbridge was commander of Kentucky. Between April and October, the average number of men present for duty was

12,337, a number inflated by a significant increase in troop strength in the wake of Morgan's June raid. However, as Burbridge noted, the absolute number of troops in the state overstated the military readiness of his command. "Many of the troops which I have had in the department have been dismounted cavalry, sent here to be reorganized and equipped." As soon as that was accomplished, Burbridge complained, they "were ordered to the front." Other regiments in Kentucky were there to be mustered out since their terms had expired. "While it appeared that I had a very large force, I was left with a very insufficient force for the responsible duties imposed upon me."[52]

Additionally, after October and the failure of the Saltville expedition, as well as the continued push of Sherman's army deeper into the South, the number of troops in Kentucky fell dramatically. Between December 1864 and February 1865, the average number of officers and men reporting present for duty averaged just over nine thousand, a 25 percent decline in troop strength.

In spite of those reduced numbers, in November Burbridge was given a final crack at taking Saltville and chasing the Confederate forces out of southwestern Virginia. Since the demise of the first expedition, Union troops under General Gillem in eastern Tennessee had been regularly harassed by Confederate forces. On November 13, Gillem was routed by three thousand Confederates under General John C. Breckinridge. Gillem retreated to Knoxville with Breckinridge following, but the arrival of fifteen hundred Federals from Chattanooga under General Jacob Ammen forced Breckinridge to withdraw. In response to Gillem's defeat, Major General George Stoneman, who had been left in command of the Department of the Ohio while Schofield was operating in the field with Sherman, ordered Burbridge to push all his available mounted force through Cumberland Gap and then open communications with Stoneman in Knoxville.[53] Burbridge believed he could bring at least two thousand soldiers to the front, possibly as many as four thousand, but when he arrived in Crab Orchard, Kentucky, about one hundred miles from Cumberland Gap, on November 21, he found only a smattering of forces. "I wish the troops collected and sent forward," he chided Nathaniel McLean, his divisional commander. "Clear out Lexington, Nicholasville, and Camp Nelson of all officers and men. . . . Let all move, night and day, and have them armed and equipped and supplied with ammunition."[54]

By November 24, Burbridge was at Cumberland Gap, with his forces still arriving from various spots around Kentucky. Three days later, he informed his adjutant that he planned to move on the 29th for Bulls Gap in Tennessee to attack Breckinridge. "There is no danger to Kentucky from any quarter," he wrote.[55] Breckinridge now had Stoneman in his front with nine thousand to ten thousand men and Burbridge coming up behind him with four thousand more. The Confederate leader pulled back into the Virginia mountains, although rumors began to spread that he was planning a countermove by invading Kentucky. "I do not credit it," Burbridge wrote to his subordinates back in Kentucky, but he urged them to "be vigilant. I will watch the lower gap, and [you] look out for Stony and Pound Gaps. . . . Hold the State until I return."[56]

By December 12, Stoneman had concentrated his forces under Burbridge and Gillem, and pushed further into Virginia. At first he put Burbridge's forces at the head of his column, ordering them to intercept General John C. Vaughn's command at Bristol. Only encountering pickets there, Stoneman pushed Burbridge deeper into Virginia to Abingdon, with orders to destroy the railroad connection between Saltville and Wytheville to prevent Vaughn's forces from reinforcing Breckinridge's. Stoneman then held him back and sent Gillem's forces to the fore. Gillem's men met Vaughn's forces at Marion, routed them, pursued them back to Wytheville, and scattered them into the mountains. Gillem then destroyed the supplies left in the town and an important railroad bridge some miles beyond, and Stoneman sent a force to destroy the lead mines near Wytheville. "The only thing now left for us to do was to destroy the far-famed salt works," Stoneman wrote.[57]

Breckinridge had cobbled together a defensive force for the saltworks, but he left the fortifications behind in order to follow Stoneman. This was exactly what Stoneman had hoped he would do. The two forces met near Marion on December 17 and the fighting continued into the next day. Burbridge's forces were the first to meet Breckinridge, and Burbridge's performance did not seem to impress Stoneman. Stoneman reported that he received "repeated applications from him [Burbridge] for reinforcements[.] I pushed forward past the column to the front, and assumed the immediate control of his command." In the morning, Stoneman sent Gillem around to the left of Breckinridge's forces, getting between him and Saltville. As night set in on the second day of the fighting, "Breckinridge . . . finding himself nearly surrounded and cut off from Saltville, withdrew by the road leading over the mountains into North Carolina and escaped," Stoneman wrote.[58] The Confederate defeat at Marion was the pivotal event in this second Saltville campaign, and the actual attack on the saltworks the next day proved somewhat anticlimactic.

At this point, the works were thinly defended by about seven hundred Virginia militia. Burbridge was ordered to take a direct route into the town, while Gillem was to circle to the south and bring artillery into play. Again, Stoneman's report betrayed his disdain for Burbridge's overcautious approach. Once Gillem's guns had opened up, Stoneman ordered the Kentuckian to "attack at once, and with the utmost vigor. I received in reply the assurance that he would attack in half an hour. Night, however, overtook us, and nothing of material advantage had as yet been accomplished." After dispatching a regiment of Tennessee cavalry to the task he had initially set Burbridge, with the result that "by 11 o'clock in the night all the works were evacuated . . . and the town of Saltville was in flames," Stoneman received a message from Burbridge at 4 a.m. the next morning announcing that his "advance guard had reached the town of Saltville and . . . that the enemy had first burned and then evacuated the place the night before." The following day and night (December 21) were devoted to the destruction of the saltworks.[59]

While not directly contradicting his commanding officer, Burbridge's reports on the expedition into Virginia did not cast himself in the same light as Stoneman's. No mention was made of the delays and over-caution that sparked Stoneman's comments. Instead, Burbridge depicted the entire expedition as an unqualified success in which everyone executed their assigned roles well.[60] For their part, the official Confederate reports on the attack downplayed the damage to the saltworks and the lead mine, and held that Burbridge's "statement of the stores, cars, and engines taken is greatly exaggerated."[61] Nonetheless, by the time the Federals withdrew, the Confederate forces in southwestern Virginia had been scattered or pushed into North Carolina, and the destruction of the railroads, resources, and forage in the area left little, in the words of one historian, "worthy of the attention of an army."[62]

The second attack on Saltville was the last time Burbridge would lead troops in the field. By the time he got back to his Kentucky headquarters, powerful voices were clamoring for his removal as commander, and he would be replaced in February 1865. Two months after that, of course, the war would be over. Judging from his performance during his tenure as district commander, it seems clear that Burbridge had lost some of the aggressiveness he had shown during his time as a brigade commander in Mississippi and Louisiana. He performed well against Morgan at Cynthiana, of course, but the failure at Saltville in October and Stoneman's critiques of Burbridge during the December expedition indicate that, like many Union commanders, he had become overcautious in the field, prone to delays, tended to exaggerate the size and strength of Confederate forces, and confident only when he was absolutely certain that his troops outnumbered the opposing force.

It is also evident that Burbridge viewed commanding troops in the field as a critical part of his role as district commander. When Paducah was reportedly threatened by an attack from Nathan Bedford Forrest in October, there is a hint of bravado in his message to Halleck that he had sent troops to reinforce the Paducah garrison and that he was on his way to Paducah in person.[63] Similarly, when Stoneman was organizing the second Saltville expedition and ordered Burbridge to concentrate his troops at Cumberland Gap, Burbridge responded, "If my troops are wanted at the front, I am ready to command them."[64] Some of this doubtless stemmed from the cultural pressures of nineteenth-century masculinity and the expectations attached to being an officer and a gentleman. Despite having campaigned for the job as commander of Kentucky, Burbridge knew that administrative work and directing other men to lead troops was no avenue to promotion. His ambition to rise, his sense of honor, and his pursuit of military glory all motivated his desire to be the man riding at the front of a line of troops as they headed into battle.

That said, Burbridge's desire to lead troops into the field makes a certain strategic sense. Burbridge's repeated warnings of impending invasions of the state show that he viewed Confederate raiding from outside the state as a primary threat to Kentucky's security. In the 1862 letter to his uncle that first expressed his ambition to command in the state, his stated goal was to protect Kentucky's citizens. He clearly believed that one way to do that was to eliminate the external threats by taking the offensive against the Confederate forces that threatened the state. As he told a group of supporters in February 1865, "I . . . thought it better to carry the war into the enemy's country, than to submit to their incursions upon ours."[65]

Burbridge's expeditions—against Morgan and twice against Saltville—always targeted the mountainous Kentucky-Virginia borderland. That too made some sense militarily; the Confederate troops in the area could mount—indeed, had mounted—raids into Kentucky. And the Wytheville lead mines and the works at Saltville did constitute valuable Confederate infrastructure, although their value to the war effort by December 1864 had ebbed. But southwestern Virginia was also the only geographic arena where he *could* lead troops into the field in his role as commander of Kentucky. To venture south into Tennessee—also the source of attacks upon Kentucky—or west into Missouri—the source of an influx of guerrillas—would be to transgress beyond his boundaries of command. Expeditions into Virginia aimed at extirpating threats to Kentucky allowed him to lead men into battle and mostly preserve his independence as a military leader.

Finally, it is clear that Burbridge's focus on external threats was a misplaced priority. For the citizens of the state, the predominant risk came not from Confederate invasions or cavalry raids, but from incessant guerrilla attacks. Burbridge's official correspondence is riddled with reports of guerrilla activity, and he responded to it by deploying his forces in different ways, but he never once assumed command of anti-guerrilla forces in the field, even though some of the attacks were carried out by bands that could bring together hundreds of men. Meanwhile, his two trips to Saltville took him out of the state and out of communication for weeks at a time. They also took men from the state who might have been better deployed against the guerrillas than against the Confederate forces in Virginia. "Salt and negroes seem to be the only objects created by Divinity which claim the attention of the District commander," wrote one disgruntled Louisvillian to General Edward Hobson.[66]

One might also question the distinction between guerrilla activity and Confederate cavalry raids. As Sherman pointed out to Burbridge early in his tenure as district commander, no Confederate army threatened Kentucky; the most they could mount was "a maraud." In hindsight, it is not clear why a "maraud" by Morgan or Wheeler or Breckinridge should command so much of Burbridge's attention and resources when a similar raid by an in-state guerrilla leader commanded so little. The distinction was surely lost on the Unionist citizens of a locale who had their horses stolen, food taken, and men shot.

# 4

# Liberator

Given the overwhelming importance that emancipation has assumed in modern scholarship on the Civil War, it is strange that Burbridge's role in ending slavery in Kentucky has gone largely unremarked in favor of the gorier aspects of his tenure as district commander. Yet it was during Burbridge's reign that black enlistment in Kentucky finally became a reality. And it was black enlistment in the army—with its promise of freedom for the soldiers and, eventually, for the soldiers' families—that dealt the killing blow to slavery in Kentucky. Burbridge's significance in this regard was recognized by Kentucky's black veterans themselves immediately after the war. At a ceremony at Camp Nelson (the primary black recruiting and training base in the state) on April 24, 1865, veterans from the 5th and 6th U.S. Colored Cavalry presented Burbridge with a "thousand-dollar sword, belt, and spurs." The address, by General James Brisbin, called Burbridge "the pioneer of freedom in Kentucky."[1]

Paying due attention to Burbridge's role in no way diminishes the role played by the African American people themselves in ending slavery. From the very first presence of Union troops in the state, slaves began to leave their masters' farms and plantations and come into Union camps. When slaves impressed for labor by the military were paid wages, others back on the farms began to refuse to work without being paid. As slaveholders joined the army or fled South, discipline broke down and black laborers moved freely about the state. Many other African Americans left Kentucky to enlist in other states. When refugees from further South came into Kentucky claiming freedom under the Emancipation Proclamation, numerous Kentucky slaves joined in the stream, even though technically the Proclamation did not apply to Kentucky. As historian Victor Howard noted many decades ago, "the initiative taken by the masses of blacks lay at the heart of slavery's decline in Kentucky."[2]

However, while all these multifaceted acts of self-liberation seriously undermined Kentucky slavery, and while slaves could free themselves from the physical and psychological shackles of bondage, those who remained in the state were legally still slaves, facing retribution, sale, and possible reenslavement by state and local authorities.[3] Before passage of the Thirteenth Amendment and the legal abolition of slavery, it was enlistment in the army that made them, in the words of the Emancipation Proclamation, "thenceforward and forever free."

Both Kentucky and Burbridge followed tortuous routes to black enlistment and, by implication, to the destruction of slavery. Burbridge was not, as at least one historian labeled him, an abolitionist.[4] He was a slaveowner before the war, and he claimed more than once during his time as district commander that his ownership of slaves gave him unique insight into how to handle relations with other Kentucky slaveholders.[5] But if he was not a committed emancipationist from the start of things, neither was he irrevocably committed to the preservation of slavery or lukewarm in his enforcement of federal policy once black enlistment began in Kentucky, as Ira Berlin suggested.[6]

He viewed himself primarily as a soldier engaged in the task of preserving the Union and suppressing the southern rebellion; in other words, he followed orders and enforced the policies handed down by his superior officers in the military and the War Department. "Much has been said against the organization of colored troops in Kentucky," Burbridge remarked in a speech to Unionists at the time of his removal. "This matter was entrusted to me by orders from the War Department, and I have organized eighteen thousand troops under those orders."[7] When black enlistment and service in the military came to be a necessary war measure, Burbridge did his duty.

Two episodes from different periods in the war illustrate Burbridge's changing sense of duty as the aims of the war changed. In the fall of 1862, during his time as a line officer, Burbridge was publicly called out by a colonel from a Wisconsin regiment that was under Burbridge's command for arresting and returning a fugitive slave who had sought refuge inside the army lines. The colonel accused Burbridge of violating the army's prohibition on Union soldiers being used for the purpose of returning fugitive slaves to their owners. A Wisconsin newspaper broadcast similar accusations, attacking Burbridge for repeatedly giving "orders to return fugitive slaves and to guard rebel property. . . . We supposed the disgraceful duty referred to had ceased to be required in our army, but it seems the practice is still continued in Kentucky." Burbridge protested that he had only excluded slaves from coming within the lines, which was the stated policy of the generals in charge of the army in Kentucky. He also added that the slaves "belonged to firm and staunch Union men" and so, according to the Second Confiscation Act of July 1862, were still legally in bondage. In Burbridge's mind, he was just following orders, although he clearly did not share the antislavery leanings of many of the Midwestern soldiers who came to Kentucky for the first time in 1862.[8]

The second episode occurred in June 1864, after black enlistment had begun in Kentucky. As per his constant requests to Washington, Burbridge wanted more troops in Kentucky. He wrote to Secretary of War Edwin Stanton: "I can have five regiments of colored troops ready for service in a very short time. . . . I need colored troops for garrison duty. May I use them?" Stanton wrote back that Burbridge's report was "very gratifying" and told him he could use colored troops for infantry or artillery duty, in garrison or in the field.[9] For Burbridge, the use of black troops was based on necessity more than principle. But military necessity overrode any predilection on his part to try and preserve slavery in the state; he knew that enlisting and employing black troops meant the destruction of slavery, yet he was willing to accept that consequence in service of what he saw as the larger cause of protecting the state militarily.

In that sense, he moved farther down the road toward an acceptance of black freedom than many other Unionist officials in Kentucky, both civilian and military. Kentucky's halting and resistant steps toward black enlistment and the widespread rejection of emancipation as a war aim bedeviled the implementation of Republican war policy from the initial issuance of the Emancipation Proclamation. "Unwise, unconstitutional and void," charged the Kentucky legislature in a resolution passed condemning the proclamation in March 1863. An Ohio soldier in the state during that 1863 legislative session wrote in his diary that "the Pres.

Proclamation of freedom seems to have engrossed their attention principally. They are loud in their denunciations." During speeches in the state Senate, he wrote, the proclamation "was roughly handled and such epithets bestowed upon it as 'unconstitutional, infamous, barbarian.'" He declared that "this Legislature is not wanting for secession votaries. In fact, Kentucky loyalty is very questionable as far as my experience goes."[10]

Benjamin Buckner, a young Kentucky attorney who had joined the Union army at the outset of the war, called the proclamation "an abominable infamous document" in a private letter. "[I]f announced 12 months ago, [it] would have driven us all . . . into the ranks of the Southern Army." A few weeks later, he wrote to his fiancée that "all men of decency ought to quit the army," and made good on that pledge by resigning from the service two months later.[11]

Numerous other federal officers from Kentucky followed suit. "My enlistment was for the purpose of suppressing a rebellion only," Major Henry Kalfus of the 15th Kentucky Infantry stated. "Since President Lincoln has seen fit to issue an Emancipation Proclamation, I decline to participate further in a war aimed at freeing the negro." Lieutenant Colonel Charles Hanson, the commander of Buckner's unit, the 20th Kentucky Volunteers, and a slaveholder, told his commanding officer that he would "not fight to free his own negroes." John McHenry, who had fought with Burbridge at Woodbury early in the war, did not adapt to the new regime as readily as Burbridge. He issued orders that prohibited slaves from coming into his camp and allowed owners—loyal or not—to claim those who remained. As a result, he was dismissed from the army.[12]

Each step along the road toward ending slavery precipitated defections from the Union army by Kentuckians and spluttering protests from Kentucky politicians and editorialists. Even the enrollment of a few free blacks in June 1863 brought such a storm of protest that General Boyle (still the district commander) and department commander General Ambrose Burnside both wrote to Washington and asked the War Department to stop the process. Enrolling the free blacks of Kentucky, who numbered just over four thousand, at the expense of alienating a much greater number of potential white volunteers made no sense, the officers argued. The army, Burnside pointed out to Lincoln, was already making excellent use of blacks in Kentucky as impressed laborers. Lincoln sent Burnside's message on to Stanton with the comment:

"I really think the within is worth considering." The end result was that black recruiting was put off in Kentucky for the rest of 1863.[13]

Kentucky's civil authorities also took their stand against black soldiers. In the gubernatorial campaign of 1863, both the Peace Democrat Charles Wickliffe and the Union Democrat and former Union army officer Thomas Bramlette promised to resist black enrollment. Bramlette, the eventual victor, proclaimed he would do away with "emancipation, confiscation, and negro regiments." In his inaugural address, he criticized the idea of recruiting black soldiers as a "humiliation to the just pride of loyal men" and called black regiments "uncalled for and needless experiment[s]." The official platform of the Union Democrats stated bluntly: "This is the white man's government; he is abundantly able to defend it." After the election, Bramlette's lieutenant governor stated that he was against black soldiers because "it is against the laws of civilized warfare, to incite the slave against the master. . . . I am opposed, and must continue to be opposed, to the use of negroes in this contest, as at war with civilization and humanity."[14]

Kentucky's sensitivity on the question of black enlistment thus made it the only Union state exempt from black recruiting as of December 1863. With black Kentuckians leaving the state in significant numbers to enlist in Indiana, Ohio, and especially Tennessee, federal authorities began to press for an end to Kentucky's exemption. Some whites in Kentucky were sympathetic to the idea simply because they wanted Kentucky's blacks to count as Kentucky recruits against the state's draft quota. US Adjutant General Lorenzo Thomas approached Governor Bramlette in January 1864 to discuss black enrollment in the state. The idea was firmly rejected by the state's leaders, and Thomas was convinced that forcing black enrollment on Kentucky would endanger its loyalty to the Union.[15]

Nonetheless, the privileged position of Kentucky's slaveowners was on increasingly wobbly ground. Even before Thomas's meeting with Bramlette, federal recruiting officers were rumored to be at work in the state among the black population. One farmer complained in November 1863 that nine of his slaves had been "induced by a Federal officer" to leave his service and join "the Government's negro regiments." In January 1864, Bramlette's annual message to the General Assembly proclaimed that the "authorities at Washington do not contemplate recruiting 'colored men' in

Kentucky," but the governor was firing off threatening letters to federal recruiting officers just days later, warning them that "summary justice will be inflicted" upon any officer who attempted to recruit black soldiers in Kentucky.[16] Meanwhile, Colonel Richard Cunningham was raising hackles in western Kentucky by opening a recruiting station at Paducah and making nighttime visits with squads of soldiers to neighboring farms to enlist slaves, promising enlistees a $300 bounty and their freedom if they joined up, although his actions were apparently not authorized by Washington.[17]

On February 8, 1864, Dr. S. P. Cope of Paducah wrote a letter to Bramlette, endorsed by two federal officers, complaining of Cunningham's methods. "While I was seated at breakfast this morning four negro soldiers armed with musket and bayonets came to my house and demanded my only negro servant," Cope wrote. He had been loyal since the beginning of the rebellion, he told Bramlette, but now found himself, along with other Kentucky Unionists, being made "to pay the penalty of rebellion by having my property violated, the feelings of my wife outraged, and my children alarmed by the forcible, insolent, and offensive intrusion of armed negroes upon my premises." He appealed to Bramlette for protection of his rights. "As a citizen of a free country, and as the birthright of a loyal Kentuckian, I claim that my right of property shall be sacred and inviolate."[18]

Bramlette tried to meet his constituents' demands. On February 1, 1864, he sent a long letter to Lincoln, protesting the recruitment of blacks in Paducah. His argument relied on both principled and practical premises. The principle was states' rights. Kentucky was a loyal state in control of its own militia and able to meet the central government's demand for troops with white soldiers. Therefore, the federal government had no legal right to recruit blacks or whites in Kentucky, as the state was still a sovereign member of the Union. As a practical matter, Bramlette stated, the use of blacks as soldiers was simply unacceptable to most white Kentuckians. Moreover, under Kentucky law, black recruitment subjected recruiting officers to jail time of up to twenty years for interfering with slaveholders' property rights. Bramlette requested an immediate halt to the recruitment of Kentucky blacks and its "wanton disregard of the rights of our people." Lincoln forwarded the letter to Stanton, who refuted Bramlette's points by asserting federal supremacy for the purpose of suppressing a rebellion. Stanton insisted that the federal government had the legal right to recruit any ablebodied male in any state, and that such action neither abridged the state's sovereign rights nor showed any disrespect toward the state's people. He hoped Bramlette would, upon further reflection, agree with the policy.[19]

In late February 1864, Congress amended the Enrollment Act and ended Kentucky's exemption from slave enlistment. The amendment allowed for the conscription of slaves, and the provost marshals in the state were ordered to add the names of black men to the pool of potential draftees.[20] Almost immediately there was a storm of protest, as the conservative Unionism of the bulk of white Kentuckians foundered on the shoals of emancipation. Many began to voice an increasingly strong opposition to the Lincoln administration's war policies and especially the president's continued insistence that slavery had to end.[21] This was the crisis situation into which Burbridge stepped when he took over as district commander.

In March 1864, a wave of Conservative Unionist opposition to black enrollment, spearheaded by Colonel Frank Wolford of the 1st Kentucky Cavalry, broke over the Commonwealth. Wolford was a genuine Union war hero. Early in the war he had recruited the 1st Cavalry, and he had been in almost constant action since, participating in over three hundred skirmishes and taking seven wounds in battle. He was very seriously wounded at the Battle of Lebanon, Tennessee, in May 1862, taking a ball in the left side just above the hip, which would plague him for the rest of his military career. "The blood was dripping from his wound into the road," one of his men remembered, "as he offered to take care of himself" so his men could continue the pursuit of the retreating enemy. He was the nemesis of John Hunt Morgan, whom he pursued during Morgan's first three raids into Kentucky. During the Great Raid, Wolford and his men doggedly chased Morgan through Kentucky and into Ohio, even as Wolford's unhealed wound from the prior year soaked his saddle with blood. When Morgan's luck finally played out in Ohio, the Confederate cavalryman sought out Wolford to offer his surrender, even giving the Union colonel silver spurs that had been gifted to Morgan by the southern-sympathizing citizens of Lexington.[22]

However, Wolford could not countenance the idea of emancipation or of black troops. As early as 1863, shortly after the Emancipation Proclamation had been released, Wolford reportedly told his higher-ups in the Army of the Cumberland that "my boys came out to fight the rebels, not to steal niggers." When black enrollment began in Kentucky, Wolford spoke out against the policy in dramatic fashion. In speeches given in Lexington and Danville in March 1864, he denounced Lincoln as a tyrant and pronounced the decision to enroll blacks as "unconstitutional, unjust, another of a startling set of usurpations." He called the enrollment of blacks a "violation of their [Kentuckians'] guaranteed rights," and pronounced it the "duty of the people of Kentucky" to resist the order. "The people of Kentucky did not want to keep step to the 'music of the Union' alongside of Negro soldiers," Wolford said. "It was an insult and a degradation for which their free and manly spirits were not prepared." Since it impinged on the rights of the state, as well, the governor had an equal obligation to "resist with all the constitutional power of the Commonwealth." The first enrolling officer who appeared to carry out the policy should be thrown in prison, and Wolford declared his troops ready and available to assist the state authorities. The silence of Bramlette, who shared the platform with Wolford in Lexington, was viewed widely as assent to the colonel's fiery propositions.[23]

Most of the state's editorialists and opinion leaders backed Wolford's sentiments. "Wolford became the hero of the day," wrote historian E. Merton Coulter, "and was everywhere applauded." In a letter to Congressman Brutus Clay, a relative informed him that "the gallant Wolford is now the most popular man in our part of the State & the President universally condemned for his tyrannical course."[24] Unionist voices supporting the enrollment, on the other hand, were weak. "Unfortunately there is no really loyal newspaper in the state," wrote Major W. H. Sidell, the acting assistant provost marshal general in Kentucky, to his superior in Washington, "so that no means exist to set forth loyal views."[25] Unconditional Unionists like William Goodloe and Robert Breckinridge tried to blunt the impact of Wolford's speeches with orations of their own, defending the enrollment provision as a legitimate exercise of federal authority. The military authorities even ordered Wolford's arrest, but he was soon released upon his promise to report to General Grant in Nashville.[26]

Colonel Frank Wolford. A Union war hero from Kentucky, Wolford could not countenance the enlistment of black troops and spoke out forcefully against Lincoln's emancipation policy. (Library of Congress, Prints and Photographs Division.)

Sidell worried that although Wolford and his ilk "may not sympathize with the rebellion, the State is filled with such as do," and that speeches like Wolford's would fan the flames of discontent not only regarding black enrollment but in other areas of military policy as well, like recruitment and the draft. "To-day the colonel of a veteran Kentucky regiment, returned from furlough and on its way to the front, informed me that the bad spirit had even appeared in his regiment," Sidell wrote.[27] One Union solider in the 3rd Kentucky Cavalry, hearing of Wolford's speech while in the field in Tennessee, wrote sarcastically to his sister that "it is a wonderful thing this Kentucky loyalty."[28]

Sidell's fears of noncooperation were not unjustified. In Taylor County, the provost marshal told General Edward Hobson that "there will not be a man in our country" who would enroll black recruits and predicted it would take "400 men" to accomplish the task. Hobson also heard reports of civil disturbances in other Kentucky towns when black enrollment was attempted.[29] As news of Wolford's speech and Bramlette's seeming embrace of the colonel's views spread across the state, a Unionist sympathizer from Hawesville in Hancock County wrote to Lincoln ally James Speed that when the provost marshal in Hawesville received the order to enroll eligible African Americans, he had announced his hope that "Kentucky would call out the militia to oppose it and hoped Gov Bramlett [*sic*] would do it." Further, the informant told Speed, the man said that "when ever Abe Lincoln interfered with the Negro he would shed the last drop of his blood in the cause of the South."[30] Sidell predicted in his report on the progress of the enrollment that "little more will appear than reports of refusals of enrolling officers to act."[31]

Bramlette now faced a critical choice: would he actually advocate open resistance to black enrollment and back it up with force if necessary? On March 13 he sent off a letter to Lincoln stating that as governor he was obligated to execute the laws of Kentucky against those who would interfere with the property rights of citizens. He also invited the Unconditional Unionist leader Robert Breckinridge to come to Frankfort to confer with him on the issue. On March 14, he wrote to Burbridge expressing similar sentiments as he had in his letter to Lincoln. "I am determined to execute our laws—and if any man violates them he must abide the penalty. The forcible abduction of slaves—the enlistment without consent of owners[,] enticing them to run away[,] etc. are all crimes against the known laws of the land, and instead of commanding the commission of crime it is the duty of officers to arrest the violators and hand them over to the Civil Magistrate for trial." His plan, he told Burbridge, was to send Breckinridge to Washington to persuade the administration to back off, as it had been cajoled into doing previously. "I wish to avoid if possible any semblance of collision and will therefore use every means to remove the occasion of such evil—before accepting the last resort of arresting persons who claim to act under federal authority."[32]

At either Bramlette's or Breckinridge's invitation, Burbridge was at the meeting the two men had arranged on March 15. They met at the Capitol Hotel in Frankfort, along with Louisville physician Theodore S. Bell and *Frankfort Commonwealth* editor Albert Hodges, who had used the *Commonwealth*'s pages to vigorously denounce the idea of black troops.[33] Like Bramlette, Burbridge also faced a critical choice. He had not even been officially named district commander at the time of the Wolford controversy. Now the governor, one of his main supporters in his bid to be named to the position permanently, was threatening to nullify a federal law by force. Would Burbridge side with Wolford and Bramlette, using his military powers to "protect the people of the state," as he had promised to do back in 1862? Would he, like Boyle and Burnside had done before him, counsel patience and prudence on the part of military authorities when it came to recruiting African Americans, and recommend that Kentucky continue to receive special treatment?

The meeting was a marathon, beginning about 8 p.m. and lasting until after 3 a.m. Bramlette showed the men a draft of a proclamation he intended to release the next day. In one version, published later, Bramlette advised slaveowners that "when your slave is taken, or enticed, or persuaded to leave you, or is harbored by officers and soldiers to prevent you getting him, the courts are open to you, for a civil remedy against all who command, counsel, advise, aid, promote, or adopt the act." He also said criminal proceedings could be instituted against those who interfered with the rights of property, promising the "whole power of the Commonwealth" to support such proceedings. He denounced those legislators in Congress who were foisting black enlistment on Kentucky as "cold blooded," "disloyal," and "ignominious" men who have "perverted their sacred trusts to the base uses of partisan ends and fanatical purposes." In the words of one witness to the meeting, by advocating resistance to the enrollment of Kentucky slaves, the original draft would have been "a firebrand if published." In a speech a week later, Breckinridge alleged that Bramlette's original proclamation was even more inflammatory, calling for an uprising at the same time as the Confederacy planned to invade the state as part of a general conspiracy to "bloodily baptize Kentucky into the Southern Confederacy."[34]

Whatever the precise wording of the initial document, Burbridge, Bell, and Breckinridge spent the next several hours talking Bramlette down from his proposed course of resistance. Bramlette reportedly fought every excision, but the revised proclamation was about one-third the length of the original draft and was published the next day in Hodges's *Commonwealth.* In the published version, Bramlette urged the peaceful submission of Kentuckians to the enrollment of slaves. He emphasized that the federal authorities at this stage were only enrolling slaves, not enlisting them. The mere entry of names on a list did not "affect any right of the citizen" and should not spur Kentuckians to violence, Bramlette stated. "Your indignation should not move you to commit acts of violence nor unlawful resistance." Instead, he urged Kentuckians to "submit to the law and trust to legal remedies," suggesting that the most effective form of resistance would be via the ballot box. "Trust the American people to do us the justice the present Congress may not do."[35]

While many proslavery Unionists were dismayed by the moderate tone Bramlette struck, for Burbridge the meeting had been a success. The general telegraphed Lincoln the same day the proclamation was published. "We came to Frankfort . . . in fear of trouble," he wrote. "We have spent the night with the Governor. Heard his proclamation. . . . It has the national ring. Kentucky will do her duty to the Nation. There need be no fears about the enrollment in this State. The law will be obeyed."[36] Ten days after Bramlette's proclamation, Breckinridge wrote to Burbridge that "every thing like opposition to the enrollment of negroes, and every thing like trouble to the government, in this region—gave way before the proclamation of the Governor." While many Unionists in the state credited Breckinridge with getting Bramlette to back down, Breckinridge himself credited the presence of Burbridge and Bell as making the difference in the discussion. "While I feel grateful to the Governor for taking the course he did at the last moment, I should be utterly faithless not to assert my conviction that if you and Dr. Bell had not been there, every thing this day would have been widely different from what it is all around us."[37]

As always, it is nearly impossible to get inside Burbridge's head during this troubled time; he left no memoir, diary, or letter about his views on black enrollment. From the documents that are available, however, Burbridge's role in this affair showed his soldierly commitment to his military duty above all. Major Sidell, in appraising Burbridge's role for his superiors in Washington, wrote that he was "firm in his determination to use all the force at his control in carrying out the law," and praised the general's decision to send a company of troops to each district under his command to assist the district provost marshals in the enrollment.[38] It was not, however, a principled adherence to the cause of black freedom that undergirded Burbridge's determination. Burbridge liked to say that the eighteen thousand African Americans he enlisted from Kentucky "saved just that number of white men from the draft," hardly the sentiments of a racial egalitarian.[39] More broadly, though, it was his perception that enrollment of slaves was legal and a justified measure to suppress the rebellion, and that the resistance exhorted by proslavery Unionists like Governor Bramlette and Colonel Wolford was illegal, unjustified, and would only serve to prolong the rebellion. While these are not the heroic actions of a man utterly committed to racial equality, they stand well above the craven actions of his predecessor General Boyle, who urged the federal government to abandon the recruitment of free blacks because white Kentuckians found it repugnant, and the political maneuvering of Governor Bramlette, who wanted desperately to square the circle of his devotion to slavery and his devotion to the Union.

After the meeting in Frankfort, Bramlette changed his mind about sending Breckinridge to Washington, deciding instead to seek an interview with the president personally. On March 22, he traveled with editor Hodges and former US senator Archibald Dixon to Washington, D.C. During his meeting with Lincoln, Bramlette reiterated his acceptance of black enrollment and received a promise from the president in return that no blacks would be enlisted from any county that met its draft quota with all white soldiers. Moreover, Lincoln told Bramlette that any blacks who were mustered into the army would be sent out of state for training. In a memorandum to Secretary of War Stanton, Lincoln deemed the Kentucky requests "just and reasonable," and after his return to Frankfort Bramlette pronounced himself well satisfied with the results of the trip.[40]

For his part, in early April Burbridge was given "general superintendence" by the War Department over the raising of troops in Kentucky, whether through voluntary enlistment or through drafting. What this meant was that should Kentucky fail to meet its quota of troops through white volunteers, it would fall to Burbridge to authorize the enlistment of black troops. This was a step beyond mere enrollment, for it meant that former slaves would actually be serving in the army.[41] By late March it was clear that Kentucky would fall well short of filling its quota of troops with whites alone. A draft call was then made for some nine thousand men, which yielded less than half that amount. Although the Unconditional Unionists denied the connection, the controversy over the enrollment of slaves and the growing distaste among proslavery Unionists for the emancipationist policies of the Lincoln administration clearly had dampened already waning enthusiasm for the war among white Kentuckians. "[N]early every county would have filled its quota," wrote Kentucky adjutant general John Boyle, "if the unfortunate attempt to recruit negroes had not been begun."[42]

On April 18, Burbridge issued General Order No. 34, which instructed provost marshals in each district and county to "receive and regularly enlist as soldiers . . . all able-bodied negro slaves and free colored persons of lawful age who may apply to them to be enlisted, and in cases of slaves whose owners may request the enlistment." The order also vested sole recruiting authority in the provost marshals, threatening the arrest of any unauthorized recruiter, and ordered provost marshals to prepare documentation for any owners that presented their slaves to enable them to file compensation claims with the federal government. Slaveowners might present their slaves for enlistment for a number of reasons: loyalty to the Union, preservation of discipline on the plantation by getting rid of "troublesome" slaves, or, most likely, to preserve a record of their cooperation in meeting the state's troop quotas. Eventual compensation for voluntary cooperation was a possibility in April 1864, and some slaveowners may have thought it better to take a chance on compensation rather than have their slaves run off to enlist on their own. Ultimately, of course, the Thirteenth Amendment prevailed and no compensation was paid for slave property.[43]

In line with the agreement between Lincoln and Bramlette, the order also specified that black recruits, once mustered into the army, would be sent out of state for training, equipping, and assignment to companies and regiments. "It is thought [the order] will be satisfactory to the Government and the people of this State and if it is, indeed a very God-send has occurred," confided Burbridge's adjutant to his diary.[44]

Burbridge's order was a radical departure for Kentucky. For the first time, slaves in Kentucky would be enlisted into the federal army and, by Section 24 of the February 1864 amendment to the Federal Conscription Act, such slaves would be legally free once mustered. No longer would Kentucky's African Americans have to leave the state in order to gain their freedom. Questions persist among historians, however, about the clause that mentioned slave enlistments made at the slaveowner's request. Did it restrict slave recruitment *only* to those slaves whose owners requested it? Was Burbridge's intention, as Ira Berlin charged, to "obtain black recruits without threatening slavery?"[45] Again, Burbridge was no abolitionist, so it was likely that he leaned toward conservatism when ordering the enlistment of slaves; still, it seems improbable that he only intended to enlist slaves whose owners requested it. Certainly he had no sympathy for disloyal owners, and so it would seem that slaves who deserted the farms of southern sympathizers would have been enlisted, the lack of their owners' request notwithstanding. General Order No. 34's provision regarding enlistments made at the owners' request probably aimed at protecting the interests of loyal slaveholders. In sum, General Order No. 34 was a conservative document that held within it the seeds of revolution.

Those seeds soon sprouted, largely because Kentucky's slaves did not pause to parse the fine points of the order. Rather, they saw their chance and they took it. The central Kentucky counties that had the most slaves felt the greatest impact. In May, seventy-two blacks from Mercer County made their way to the Lexington provost marshal's office to volunteer; in Boyle County, the provost marshal opened his

View of Camp Nelson. The camp was the primary recruitment and training center for African American troops in Kentucky. (University of Kentucky Library, Special Collections.)

office on a Saturday to receive recruits and nearly one hundred enlisted; and when he kept it open on Sunday, nearly two hundred recruits showed up. In Jessamine County, the entire quota was filled with black volunteers; the same was true in Marion County. Four hundred potential recruits had gathered at Camp Nelson by late May, simply awaiting an enlistment officer.[46] One correspondent wrote to James Speed in May 1864 that "we have been unfortunate in the way of our men servants. One of our black men ran off . . . weeks ago with a party of eight others from the neighborhood and one left yesterday."[47]

The African Americans who flocked to the recruiting centers faced substantial risks in doing so. White Kentuckians frequently attacked blacks trying to enlist, and owners at times inflicted harsh retribution on slaves who came back if they were turned away. According to historian Victor Howard, eight slaves were killed in Nelson County between May and July for trying to volunteer for the service, slaveholders in Marion County cut the left ears off two slaves captured while trying to get to an enlistment center, and masters whipped fifteen black men in Lebanon because the men wanted to enlist. Even without the physical threat, slaves who wanted to enlist without permission from their masters still had to endure the uncertainties of escape, with the potential of being captured and returned to slavery. A slave named Paul Kennedy was recaptured on his first attempt to escape from his master near Elizabethtown, but he was successful on his second try after walking the fifty miles or so to Louisville. Peter Bruner traveled with a small group of other aspiring black volunteers, but a group of whites broke up the band and recaptured them all. When such reports reached Burbridge, he issued General Order No. 45 on June 2. The order did not offer the far-reaching protections that were needed for blacks who wanted to volunteer, but it at least addressed part of the problem. Burbridge declared that those who punished rejected enlistees were "discouraging enlistments," and thus subject to trial by a military court. He also ordered provost marshals to issue passes to any blacks rejected for service, granting them immunity from any punishment upon their return.[48]

Eventually, reports of the outrages on black recruits filtered back to Washington, and in July the War Department ordered Judge Advocate General Joseph Holt to travel to Kentucky to investigate. On July 31 Holt filed his report. In the beginning, slaves attempting to enter military service "were waylaid, beaten, maimed, and often murdered," he wrote. "When we consider the perils and menaces which these downtrodden men have to brave in making their way to the recruiting stations we cannot but regard the example of their courage, and loyalty, and zeal as among the most noblest and cheering signs of the times." More recently, however, opposition to black recruitment in Kentucky had faded because of an "improved public sentiment" and "the vigor and success with which the Government has continued to press its policy." According to Holt, about one hundred blacks per day came to the recruiting centers.[49]

Under this onslaught of recruits, any restrictions or limitations on black enlistment soon fell away. When Adjutant General Lorenzo Thomas returned to the state in June, he issued General Order No. 20 urging "unconditional Union men" to "cheerfully bring forward their slaves to assist in crushing the rebellion." But if they did not, Thomas's order went on, it did not really matter, "as all who present themselves for enlistment will be received and enlisted." Moreover, General Order No. 20 established "camps of reception" in each congressional district where the new recruits would be "organized into companies and regiments, armed, fully equipped, and prepared for service."[50] Bramlette's carefully negotiated agreement with Lincoln regarding black recruitment in the state was falling apart. At the end of May, Bramlette wrote to Burbridge that if black enlistment was not stopped, "bloodshed will be the consequence, and *Fort Pillow will be re enacted.*" In June the governor complained to both Burbridge and Stanton about the many "abuses" that were occurring in the recruitment of black soldiers. His understanding with Lincoln was that recruitment of slaves would cease when the state's quota of troops was met, that the new recruits "were to be removed for organization without the state" in order "to remove all occasion for excitement or offense," and that the "offensive" recruiting methods of Colonel Cunningham in Paducah would be halted. He was particularly aggrieved that Cunningham had not been reined in, and asked Stanton to tell him clearly whether the colonel's actions were authorized by the War Department.[51]

Burbridge felt that Bramlette was simply being obstructionist. He responded to the governor on June 16 citing the federal statutes that authorized enlistment and conscription in the state and asserting that they provided "ample authority for all that is being done in Ky. within my knowledge in relation to the enlistment of slaves in the Army." He told Bramlette that he had no copy of the agreement that the governor struck with Lincoln and therefore he could not possibly know whether its terms were being violated. And he fell back on his notions of duty as a federal officer: "My orders charge me with the execution of the laws above referred to, and I hope in so doing, to have the cordial cooperation of your Excellency."[52] Bramlette was powerless to stop the steady erosion of slavery in the state.

The reports coming out of Kentucky regarding the large number of black troops continued through the summer. In late June, Burbridge reported having five regiments of black troops ready for service. By the end of the month, Thomas reported to Stanton that there was a full one thousand-man regiment in Louisville, with three hundred others available for a second regiment, and some fifteen hundred men at Camp Nelson. Just a few days later, he raised his estimate to three thousand men at Camp Nelson. On July 10, Colonel Thomas Sedgwick, commander of Kentucky's black troops at Camp Nelson, reported to Burbridge that he had just finished "a grand review and drill of seventeen companies organized and clothed." In his report at the end of July, Holt stated that ten thousand black troops had been enlisted in the state and prospects were good for ten thousand more.

Recruiting slowed, however, during the fall and winter. In October, Thomas reported that fifteen thousand black troops had been recruited in the state, but in his final summary report after the war was over, he gave the total of black troops raised in Kentucky as just over thirteen thousand.[53] (Thomas's number is significantly lower than historians' usual estimate of nearly twenty-four thousand black Kentuckians who served in the Union army because Thomas's figure includes only those who were recruited in the state, and not those who fled the state to enlist elsewhere before black enlistment began in Kentucky.[54])

One reason the recruitment of black soldiers slowed later in the year was the risk that volunteering entailed for a soldier's family, often left behind to suffer the master's wrath. As a result of this fear, many soldiers brought their families with them when they went to a recruitment center. As early as mid-July, Thomas was complaining of the number of "old men, women, and children" at the recruiting centers in Louisville and at Camp Nelson. His solution was to send them back to their owners, out of respect for the state's law allowing slavery and in line with his charge to recruit only ablebodied men. The families were needed on the farms, he added, to gather the crops, which would surely be needed by the army. The local colonel in Louisville, however, refused to send them back, believing that such actions would constitute rendition of fugitives, which was prohibited. Such conflicts of legal interpretation meant that, often, the makeshift camps of soldiers' families continued to grow.[55]

The Reverend Thomas James, a former slave and abolitionist in the American Missionary Association, was charged with the oversight of the refugee camp that sprang up on the outskirts of Louisville. "Nearly all the persons in the camp were women and children," he wrote in his autobiography, "for the colored men were sworn into the United States service as soldiers as fast as they came in." James courted controversy by

Reverend Thomas James. Sent to oversee the African American refugee encampment at Louisville, James found his life threatened by some of Louisville's white leaders. (Local History and Genealogy Division, Rochester Public Library, Rochester, New York.)

visiting Louisville's slave pens and liberating the African Americans who were confined there; at another point, he brought a squad of soldiers to a room in the National Hotel where nine men were being held by a slave trader. He mustered the nine into service and "made them freemen," he wrote. James's actions riled the municipal authorities, who complained to Burbridge. They hinted darkly that unless James left the city within forty-eight hours, he would be killed. According to James, Burbridge told them that if James were killed, he would "hold responsible for the act every man who fills an office under . . . city government" and threatened to "hang them higher than Haman was hung. . . . Your only salvation lies in protecting the colored man's life." The city fathers backed down, but James spent the rest of his time in Louisville with a military guard outside his quarters.[56]

The largest of the refugee camps was at Camp Nelson, and camp commander Speed S. Fry repeatedly expelled the residents, forcing them to choose among the tender mercies of their owners, vagrancy, or returning to the camp. Many soon returned.[57] With no official government policy in place, Burbridge wrote to Stanton in November about the "large number of colored women and children . . . accumulated at Camp Nelson. . . . There will be much suffering among them this winter, unless shelters are built and rations issued to them." He urged Stanton to issue the necessary orders "for the sake of humanity" to protect the soldiers' families.[58]

On November 23, Fry ordered over four hundred women and children out of the camp into the freezing Kentucky countryside. Recruit Joseph Miller recounted the experience of his family in an affidavit from November 26. "A mounted guard came to my tent and ordered my wife and children out of Camp. . . . I was certain that it would kill my sick child to take him out in the cold. I told the man in charge . . . that my wife and children had no place to go. . . . He told my wife and children that if they did not get up into the wagon . . . he would shoot the last one of them." Miller's family had fled their master with few clothes and thus had little protection against the cold. He found them later that evening about seven miles from the camp "shivering with cold and famished with hunger. . . . My boy was dead. . . . I know he was killed by exposure to the inclement weather." In all, one quarter of the refugees driven from Camp Nelson died of exposure. When Captain T. E. Hall

Refugee camp at Camp Nelson. Facing retribution from slaveowners, many families followed black recruits to recruiting centers. (University of Kentucky Library, Special Collections.)

saw the results of Fry's order, he immediately telegraphed Burbridge, who rescinded it and ordered that "all colored women and children seeking refuge in Camp Nelson should be received and cared for."[59]

Missionary John G. Fee, who had begun working among the black soldiers and their families at the camp soon after black enlistment began, had outlined a plan by which the army in conjunction with missionary societies would construct a camp for the families, but the War Department ignored him. The suffering occasioned by Fry's expulsion order, however, got noticed by the northern press and ignited an outcry that finally got the War Department's attention. On January 10, 1865, Fee's plan was referred from Washington to Burbridge for approval, which he granted "with all his heart." As details mounted about the treatment of black soldiers' families in Kentucky and about the numerous deaths caused by the expulsion order, pressure grew for further protections. This pressure led the government in March 1865 to grant freedom to the families of soldiers who enlisted in the military. The order sparked a late-war surge of African American enlistment, although Burbridge had already been replaced as district commander by then.[60]

As with black enlistment in general and the abuse suffered by black enlistees, Burbridge's measures to protect the families of black soldiers did not go as far as some would have liked; they certainly did not end the suffering from disease, overcrowding, and poor sanitation that continued to afflict the refugee camps. His compassion and sympathy for the soldiers' families, however, do stand in contrast to the callousness of generals like Fry and the legal nitpicking of even strong advocates of black recruiting like Lorenzo Thomas. By ordering the families to be received at Camp Nelson, Burbridge struck yet another blow at slavery, facilitating recruitment by providing resources for recruits' families.

Thomas irked Burbridge in other ways, too, particularly when he tried to assume control of the recruiting process after he returned to the state in June 1864. Thomas's General Order No. 20, for example, charged Brigadier General Augustus Chetlain with the "supervision of the organization of colored troops in Kentucky."[61] Chetlain had worked with Thomas recruiting black troops in western Tennessee, and Thomas lauded him as a "most valuable officer" with "intelligence and zeal [and] with a rare qualification for the organization of troops."[62] Burbridge felt, however, that the adjutant general was invading his turf. Early in July, he wrote to Thomas that the War Department had given him authority over recruiting, including the "enlistment and organization of colored troops," and that he had already taken steps toward doing so that would arouse "the least possible feeling upon the subject by the people." Given Kentucky's hostility to the idea of black troops, Burbridge stated, "I regarded it as eminently necessary to proceed with some caution in the matter." His plan, he said, was to appoint Kentucky officers for all the regiments raised in the state and to use the black regiments as much as possible for garrison duty, freeing up "my white troops for other and more active duties." However, now he found General Chetlain working at cross-purposes to his, removing control of the black troops in the state from his supervision. He pointed out to Thomas the numerous difficulties that might occur due to the overlapping authority claimed by both

Chetlain and himself, and he urged Thomas to consider that because he was a Kentuckian and a large slaveholder, "the people of Kentucky will feel less hostility to the organization of colored troops in the state if conducted under my supervision than if controlled by any authority outside the state."[63]

Thomas conceded quickly. On July 6, he relieved Chetlain of his duties regarding the organization of black troops in Kentucky, even though he felt, he said later, that Burbridge would have too many things on his plate as district commander to give due attention to black recruiting.[64] Still, it is telling that Thomas never publicly questioned Burbridge's commitment to the idea of black troops or felt that Burbridge was anything less than forceful when it came to implementing the government's policy. On July 3, at the same time as Burbridge was telling him to back off, Thomas told Stanton that Burbridge was "a good commander" who rendered him "every assistance, and . . . [was] fully impressed with the idea of arming the negroes." In his postwar report, he described Burbridge as having taken "special interest" in the recruitment of slaves, "advocating it on all proper occasions."[65]

It is also telling who Burbridge appointed when, as Thomas had predicted, he had to delegate recruiting authority to others. His first choice, Lieutenant Colonel John H. Hammond, was the assistant adjutant general in charge of the camp for draftees in Louisville. But Burbridge would later complain that while Hammond was "energetic and capable," he lacked "moral integrity,"[66] and the general replaced him with Colonel James Brisbin. Brisbin had strong antislavery credentials from before the war, establishing a reputation in his native Pennsylvania as a speaker for antislavery causes. In addition to supervising the recruitment and organization of black troops in Kentucky, he commanded the 5th U.S. Colored Cavalry, which accompanied Burbridge on his first expedition into southwestern Virginia in October 1864. After the war, he helped establish the Freedmen's Bureau in Kentucky and organized more black regiments.[67] The appointment of Brisbin, rather than an officer less committed to the idea of raising black troops, again illustrates Burbridge's determination to carry out the government's policies.

As he described it to Thomas in July, Burbridge's original plan was to use black troops as garrison soldiers, freeing up white troops for "more active" duties. Burbridge's course here hints both at a racist distrust of the capabilities of black troops—he wanted "to avoid sending away slaves who are not fit to bear arms," he told Stanton[68]—and a sensitivity to the racial feelings of white Kentuckians, whom he believed would not relish the sight of armed black soldiers among them. Even garrison duty, however, undermined Bramlette's preference to have all the black troops raised in Kentucky sent out of the state.

Burbridge's planned use of black troops, however, played out much as his plans regarding their initial enlistment had played out: circumstances soon overrode his cautious approach. As previously mentioned, he felt constantly undermanned in the fight against internal threats from guerrillas and external threats from Confederate raiders. The black troops in the state, therefore, could not be kept solely at garrison duty. Already by the end of July 1864, he was seeking authority to mount two regiments of black cavalrymen on horses seized from disloyal Kentuckians. Judge Advocate General Joseph Holt, who was in Kentucky investigating conditions in the state, urged Stanton to approve the request. "These regiments, composed of men almost raised, as it were, on horseback, of uncompromising loyalty, and having an intimate knowledge of the topography of the country, would prove a powerful instrumentality in ridding the State of those guerrilla bands of robbers and murderers," Holt wrote. "Besides, their presence in the different counties engaged in this popular service would exert the happiest influence in favor of the Government policy of employing colored troops."[69] And when Burbridge advanced for the first attack on Saltville in late September, Brisbin's 5th U.S. Colored Cavalry rode with him. "General Burbridge speaks in the highest terms of the gallantry of the Fifth Colored Cavalry—they doing better service than any other regiment," Thomas reported to Stanton after the expedition returned. The 5th had taken the enemy's rifle pits after two failed attempts by white regiments and suffered the bulk of the losses in the battle: four officers and 116 men killed and wounded. According to Brisbin, the taunts and ridicule to which the 5th had been subjected on the march out disappeared on the march back.[70]

Soon after his return from Saltville, Burbridge found himself relying to an even greater degree on black troops. Most of the white veterans in the state were ordered to Nashville to join General George Thomas in confronting Hood's army. This was followed by an order to send five thousand black troops east to the Potomac, which, one officer wrote to departmental commander General John Schofield, "will pretty well strip the state."[71] Burbridge was left with seven thousand black troops and between two thousand and three thousand white troops by the end of October. "It is very important that I should have more white troops," Burbridge pleaded with Schofield, describing the guerrillas in the state as gaining in boldness and his own forces as "entirely inadequate."[72] When the commanding general at Paducah pleaded repeatedly for reinforcements in the face of a feared Confederate attack in late October, Burbridge relied on African American cavalry troops to go to his aid.[73]

Burbridge even used black troops for the activity most hated by white Kentuckians: deployment of recruiting squads into the countryside. Nothing generated more complaints than the reported forcible recruitment of blacks from Kentucky plantations. Kentucky's Senator Garrett Davis complained to his fellow legislators in Washington that the "entire Negro military population" of Bourbon County had been "swept from their owners," decimating the agricultural labor force and threatening the state's harvest. Representative Brutus Clay echoed the charges on the House floor, and Bramlette lambasted the military's use of force to gather in troops in his annual address to the state legislature. Many of these complaints reflected the dismay of proslavery Kentuckians over the administration's antislavery policies in Kentucky. Its peculiar institution was under assault by the very institution that was supposed to be protecting the state: the US Army. "I take every way I can to get the slaves," Brisbin wrote to Senator Benjamin Wade. "If left alone [I] will kill slavery in Kentucky."[74]

The tactics of Brisbin's recruiters, however, often crossed the line into coercion. There was forcible recruitment of black soldiers, impressment of blacks who had drifted off the farms to the cities, and threats and violence used to "persuade" African Americans to enlist. Humphrey and Charles Green, enlistees in the 120th U.S. Colored Infantry, for example, reported that both initially refused when asked if they would like to enlist, whereupon the lieutenant colonel in charge of the regiment threatened to throw them in jail. Under the threat, both joined up. It got worse. In February 1865, reports reached Lincoln's ears that African Americans were being tortured—"riding them on rails, and the like"—to extort their consent to enlistment.[75] Kentucky's slaves were thus caught in a double bind: many of those who desired to enlist faced violence or other retribution from their masters, while those who did not wish to enlist faced violence or other retribution from the Union army. When the provost marshal in Kentucky—under pressure from his superior in Washington—appealed to Burbridge for help in stopping acts of violence or coercion against black recruits, Burbridge responded quickly, informing him that all officers who had been accused of such practices had been "called to account." Burbridge's reaction did not stop all the abuses—his hold on the position of district commander was growing increasingly tenuous by early 1865—but it again showed his willingness to protect the integrity of the recruiting process and the black recruits themselves.[76]

The army relieved Burbridge as district commander in February 1865, naming General John M. Palmer as his successor. Palmer was an abolitionist from Illinois, and a month into his appointment he told a cheering crowd of African Americans at Louisville's Center Street Church that slavery had essentially ended in Kentucky. According to federal estimates, approximately sixty-five thousand blacks remained enslaved in Kentucky as of March 1865; 71 percent of slaves had been legally freed.[77] Although Palmer did not acknowledge Burbridge in his speech, most of the work of destroying slavery had happened on Burbridge's watch. He had resisted the state government's efforts to torpedo black enrollment and enlistment; he had overseen the recruitment, organization, and deployment of black troops; and he had offered military protection to slaves who tried to enlist, to their families, and to the provost marshals who had to endure the local community's wrath for their part in the recruitment of black troops. He did all this without believing in the essential justice of emancipation or in racial equality, however. He was inclined to move cautiously and to mollify the proslavery Unionists in the state. But circumstances, driven largely by African Americans' willingness to take risks for freedom and by Burbridge's own need for troops, overcame his caution, and the white supremacist ideology of Kentucky's Conservative Unionists foreclosed all attempts at mollification short of the preservation of slavery. It is to Burbridge's credit that he did not back down from the implications of black enlistment when his caution and temporizing proved unavailing; rather, he pushed forward out of a sense of duty and loyalty, and a belief in the necessity to take all measures required to defeat the southern rebellion.

Since he was not an outspoken advocate for black freedom, however, his outsized role in ending slavery in Kentucky has not been widely recognized by historians. His contemporaries were a different story. The assault on slavery signified by black enlistment fomented a wave of discontent with Unionist war aims and a backlash among white Kentuckians against the Lincoln administration and against Burbridge's reign as district commander. As proslavery unionism began to look a lot like disloyalty or—even further—like Confederate sympathizing to Burbridge, his attempts to enforce administration policy in Kentucky came to look more and more like federal tyranny in the eyes of his opponents.

# 5

# Tyrant

Historians have for too long conflated Kentuckians' wartime protests against Burbridge with their postwar hatred of him. During the war, it was Burbridge's crackdown on dissent and his interference with the economic interests of the state that earned him the wrath of the Commonwealth's politicians and editorialists, whereas much of the postwar loathing of Burbridge focused on his harsh treatment of suspected guerrillas and Confederate prisoners of war, albeit without neglecting Burbridge's suppression of the opposition. Burbridge's antagonists during the war—who were, it is worth remembering, almost universally pro-Union—did not complain much about his executions of suspected guerrillas, but they came to detest Burbridge because of his enforcement of the policies of the Lincoln administration, most especially the enlistment and use of black troops.

It is important to distinguish between the epithets attached to Burbridge—between the "tyrant" who squelched opposition to Republican wartime policy and the "butcher" who sent suspected guerrillas to their deaths. It is important because much of Burbridge's "tyranny" was aimed at those who turned against the Unionist cause as a result of the emancipation policies emphasized by the administration after 1863. Thus, attitudes toward slavery and the use of African Americans as soldiers are critical in understanding the nature of the dissent that roiled Kentucky late in the war. Remembering this moves the historical understanding of Kentuckians' wartime conflict with Burbridge away from a case merely of federal heavy-handedness or overzealousness, as it has typically been understood. E. Merton Coulter, for example, wrote that "the military authorities throughout the war failed to evaluate and understand Kentucky." And James Klotter and Lowell Harrison characterized Burbridge and his predecessor Boyle as "abrasive and perhaps overzealous in their efforts to maintain military control of the state." This interpretation has led to the impression that a more diplomatic, subtle, or flexible commander would not have alienated the state's white citizenry the way Burbridge did. As Coulter put it, "the Federal commanders sent to Kentucky were particularly unfortunate in their understanding of the best way to perform their work." Historian William Gienapp echoed him six decades later. "The situation [in Kentucky] required tact and forbearance, but the commanding general, Stephen G. Burbridge, . . . was devoid of both."[1]

However, if the hostility between Burbridge and the influential political actors in the state was the result of a white supremacist backlash against the end of slavery, then it becomes less clear that a smoother man at the top could have resolved the conflict. If antipathy toward the enlistment and use of black troops and the assault on slave property that it represented drove the speeches, the political meetings, and the stream of petitions to Washington, then finessing the political impasse in Kentucky would have meant suspending the recruitment of black troops and removing emancipation from the list of Republican war aims—which was in fact exactly what proslavery Kentucky Unionists called for. In a speech in September 1864 endorsing McClellan for president, for example, Governor Bramlette chastised the Republicans in Congress for adopting "radical and unconstitutional legislation" and urged Lincoln not to make the overthrow of slavery an objective of the war. "The truly loyal men are not willing that the status of the negro shall be made a condition of the restoration of the Government." In a speech in May 1864, Lieutenant Governor Richard T. Jacob denounced "the radicals [who] now turn on the loyal men of Kentucky and say our slave property must also be wiped out and destroyed. . . . They . . . say they will draft our slave property. They do it, simply because they wish to destroy slavery."[2]

Of course, the conflict between Burbridge and proslavery Unionists in the state did not play out explicitly as a debate about emancipation. It was more a matter of "whose side are you *really* on?" Did speaking against the use of black troops constitute an unlawful discouraging of enlistments? Did branding Republican war policy "radical and unconstitutional" signal an illegal sympathy for the southern rebellion by sapping Unionist morale? Did campaigning for McClellan—who promised immediate peace negotiations with no preconditions regarding the status of slavery—cross the line into illegitimate political activity? Or were all such activities merely exercises of free speech and freedom of conscience? Finally, did the fact that Kentucky was besieged by pro-Confederate guerrillas and subject to Confederate cavalry raids matter in the answers to these questions? Did hostility to Lincoln, to emancipation, and to the military administration of the state make it easier for guerrillas to operate by creating sympathy for their cause and hostility toward their targets? The analytical separation of "political" dissent from the primary cause of such dissent, which was the turn toward emancipation as a war aim, has made it easy to turn Burbridge into a free-speech-quashing, election-interfering dictator. But if emancipation fueled much of the dissent, and emancipation was not going to be abandoned in order to buy political agreement, then the suppression of that dissent takes on a more understandable logic, a logic independent of the abrasiveness or tactfulness of the individual commander. As one recent historian noted, Kentuckians' "political opinions were not simply swayed by the hard hand of General Stephen Gano Burbridge. . . . [T]he linkage between emancipation and the preservation of the Union had poisoned the cause for Kentucky whites."[3]

Burbridge's hand was actually quite light in the first months of his tenure as district commander. Most of his official correspondence focused on Confederate troop movements, rumors of invasions, and deployment of his own men to counteract the guerrillas operating in the state. Sherman, in fact, encouraged him to be more aggressive with the press, complaining in April 1864 that Kentucky's newspapers were "falling into the bad habit of publishing rumors and nonsense. Check this as much as possible," Sherman advised. Burbridge took no overt actions to suppress the expression of dissent, however, until mid-May, three months after his appointment as district commander and as black enrollment transitioned to black enlistment.[4]

Sensing a rising tide of anti-administration sentiment among Kentuckians, Burbridge began to take action against the shapers of public opinion—especially the press—as Sherman had earlier encouraged. In

May, he banned the book *Life, Services, and Campaigns of Stonewall Jackson* from his district. "The object of such books is not to afford the people correct information regarding the history of the rebellion and its leaders, but are put forth by the traitors themselves . . . for the purpose of stirring up discontent and sedition."[5] In mid-June Burbridge also banned the *Cincinnati Enquirer*—a "newspaper in the interest of the rebellion"—from being circulated in Kentucky. The *Enquirer* was a Democratic organ that routinely denounced the Lincoln administration, especially the policy of black enlistment. Commenting on the beginning of black enrollment, for example, the paper blamed all the sins of the Lincoln administration—from the trampling of the Constitution to the suspension of the writ of habeas corpus to the imprisonment of those expressing disloyal sentiments—on one overriding cause: "miscegenation."[6]

Burbridge also began in May to target southern sympathizers more directly. General Order No. 41 stated that "none but citizens of unquestionable loyalty to the United States Government . . . be given employment or contracts in the military service in this district." Such a directive was needed, he wrote, because "rebels and rebel sympathizers" had "almost" a monopoly on military contracts and employment in the state.[7] Two days later came General Order No. 42, reminding Kentuckians of Lincoln's proclamation of September 1862, which announced that "all persons discouraging volunteer enlistments, resisting militia drafts, or guilty of any disloyal practice" were "subject to martial law and liable to trial and punishment by courts-martial or military commission." General Order No. 42 came in the wake of reports of attempts to "prevent the enlistment of persons desiring to enter the United States service" in Kentucky.[8] While the order did not specify that African Americans were the persons being discouraged, General Order No. 45, issued eighteen days later, clarified the issue. Maltreatment of slaves who tried to enlist constituted "discouraging enlistments," Burbridge declared, and offenders would be treated per the terms laid out in his earlier General Order No. 42.[9]

The actions taken in May presaged much harsher actions in the summer of 1864. The harsher policies followed a series of events in June and early July. First, Morgan's raid had been repulsed in early June and his command scattered; this triggered an upsurge of guerrilla attacks in the state, as some of Morgan's men who remained in the state began to freelance on "detached duty." Second, African American recruitment had begun in earnest and black troops had begun to be deployed in the state. This came after a debacle in the recruitment of white troops. The War Department told Bramlette to raise ten thousand troops to serve six months, and Bramlette put Frank Wolford in charge of raising the troops and named him commander, much to the chagrin of some Unconditional Unionists, who thought it lunacy to give Bramlette and Wolford their own personal army. However, the War Department rejected these troops when it learned that their term of enlistment was only three months, not the six months it had requested. The state adjutant general explained that it had been impossible to get men to commit for six months because the army had begun its "unfortunate attempt" to recruit black soldiers.[10] Finally, in early July, reacting to the frequency of guerrilla raids and the opposition to the enlistment of black troops, Lincoln renewed his order suspending the writ of habeas corpus and urged enforcement of a previous declaration of martial law in Kentucky. Informing Burbridge of the president's action, Stanton told him, "It is expected that you will spare no effort to protect loyal citizens, and carry into effect the enlistment of troops, white or black, and suppress treasonable and disloyal practices within your command."[11]

Martial law gave Burbridge a great deal of power over Kentucky's civilians. Since the beginning of the war, the Lincoln administration had operated under the legal presumption that the executive could declare martial law where needed in the case of insurrection or rebellion and that civilians who committed an "offense against the military"—such as aiding the rebellion or resisting a draft—were subject to military jurisdiction. In laying out the reasons why renewed application of martial law was needed in Kentucky, Lincoln's order stated that many Kentuckians had joined the rebellion and had made incursions into the state several times, "not without aid and comfort furnished by disaffected and disloyal citizens," and made "flagrant civil war," which had overwhelmed the civil authorities and threatened the lives and property of citizens.[12]

In fact, Burbridge had been receiving encouragement from his superiors to take harsher measures even before the reemphasis on martial law. After the battle of Cynthiana, reports reached Washington that Confederate sympathizers in the town had aided Morgan and then buried the Confederate dead with honors. General in Chief Henry Halleck told Burbridge to arrest all "such persons, male and female, and send them under a proper guard to Washington."[13] At about the same time, General Sherman was concocting a plan for the mass exile of "malcontents." "We will never have peace as long as we tolerate in our midst the class of men that we all know to be conspiring against the peace of the State, and yet who if tried by jury could not be convicted," he wrote to Stanton. In a letter to Burbridge that got wide circulation in Kentucky, Sherman elaborated on the plan. He counseled Burbridge to arrest not only guerrillas but "all males and females who have harbored or encouraged guerrillas and robbers." When "enough" had been accumulated, "say 300 or 400, I will cause them to be sent down the Mississippi through their guerrilla gauntlet, and by a sailing ship send them to a land where they may take their negroes and make a colony with laws and a future of their own." He warned Burbridge to be careful that "no personalities are mixed up in this" or that mere love of home, country, or section be a pretext for arrest. Only those with "that devilish spirit" that used war as an excuse for "murder, arson, theft . . . , perjury, and all the crimes of human nature" were subject to exile.[14]

It is difficult to take Sherman's idea of mass exile of Confederate sympathizers to a faraway land very seriously—and the idea that they could take their slaves with them probably would have killed any chance of presidential approval—but Burbridge took Sherman's advice to heart about acting against guerrilla supporters and Confederate sympathizers. In ordering a post commander to aggressively pursue the guerrillas in the area, Burbridge's adjutant also reminded the post commander that the guerrillas frequently received help from citizens. "Arrest any citizen, male or female, against whom you can obtain positive written evidence of their complicity with rebels and send them under guard to these headquarters . . . for trial by military commission." Later in July, Burbridge ordered all those who had been banished from Missouri for "the expression of rebel sentiments and other acts tending to weaken the authority of the United States government" to leave Kentucky as well.[15] And then on August 1 he queried Sherman about his plan to exile Confederate sympathizers. "What must I do with men arrested—aiders and guerrillas? I have many. Must they go to South America or the Tortugas? . . . It is no use to try them. We must imprison them or send them off." Sherman responded promptly, telling Burbridge that it would take

General William Tecumseh Sherman. Burbridge's commanding general urged Burbridge to get tough with guerrillas in Kentucky and their sympathizers. (Library of Congress, Prints and Photographs Division.)

the permission of the secretary of war to ship them to the Tortugas, but that he would surely give it. "I approve your course and want you to make it thorough, and clean out Kentucky of all suspicious men."[16]

Moves against alleged guerrillas and their sympathizers, however, did not land Burbridge in hot water with state officials—even his harshest measures went largely unremarked upon at the time. In fact, they seemed to build on Bramlette's own earlier directives for dealing with guerrillas and their citizen abettors. In a proclamation issued January 4, 1864, Bramlette had decried "the frequent outrages perpetrated . . . by lawless bands of marauders" and traced their origin to "the active aid of rebel sympathizers in our midst, or their neglect to furnish the Military Commander the information in their possession, which would lead to the defeat and capture of such marauders." Like Burbridge, Bramlette viewed not providing all possible aid to the authorities as the equivalent of "a culpable and active assistance." He then directed the "various military commanders in the State of Kentucky" to "immediately arrest at least five of the most prominent and active rebel sympathizers in the vicinity of such outrage for every loyal man taken by guerrillas." These citizens were to be held as hostages for the return of Unionists who had been kidnapped by guerrillas. Bramlette called for relatives of the guerrillas to be "the chief sufferers." "This may seem harsh," the *Louisville Daily Journal* opined, "but the rebel outrages must be stopped at all hazards." According to the newspaper, the experiment had first been tried at Maysville after a guerrilla raid carried off some citizens behind rebel lines. Bramlette requested that the military authorities seize hostages for their safe return "and the result justified his expectations, for the prisoners were promptly released."[17] In his proclamation, Bramlette did not spell out the consequences that the hostages would suffer if Unionist citizens were killed, but his endorsement of retribution upon the disloyal in the neighborhood of a guerrilla attack augured Burbridge's retaliatory policies against community members who sympathized with the guerrillas or their cause.

It was Burbridge's actions in three other areas that really triggered the hostility of the state's civilian administration and of many white residents toward him. First, he began to arrest prominent and powerful citizens for speaking out against wartime policy, alleging that some of them were involved in a conspiracy to launch an insurrection in the North. Second, he interfered in the electoral process by barring particular candidates who did not seem sufficiently loyal and by using troops to ensure that disloyal men could not vote. Third, he interfered briefly with the economic life of the state via the infamous "Hog Order" of 1864, which gave the military first claim on farmers' pork. It was these actions, more than the arrests of Confederate sympathizers or the executions of accused guerrillas, that earned Burbridge his ill repute among Kentucky's Conservative Unionists.

To be clear, arrests of suspected Confederate sympathizers long preceded Burbridge's tenure as district commander. The General Assembly passed laws early in the war targeting those who enlisted in the southern armies and who encouraged others to enlist. Several ministers and a former governor were arrested and sent to prison under these laws. In June and July 1862, Burbridge's predecessor General Boyle had moved against Confederate guerrillas and their sympathizers—including women—and filled the jails to overflowing. But Burbridge went further; his arrests reached deep into the proslavery Unionist elite who controlled the state. Some of these men were army veterans who had fought against the Confederacy during the early years of the war. At one point even Boyle himself came under suspicion. Boyle (who was not arrested) wrote indignantly to Lincoln to protest. It is "well known to you that I differ from you in regard to your policy of enlisting negro slaves, especially in Kentucky. I believe the policy unwise, unconstitutional, and unjust and cruel to the negro." So, while Boyle's actions as commander had angered many white Kentuckians and few lamented his dismissal, the arrests of 1862 did not trigger the antipathy that Burbridge's actions did, especially since Burbridge's actions ultimately aimed at clamping down less on overt Confederate sympathy and more on resistance to black enlistment.[18]

One of Burbridge's first targets was Frank Wolford. The colonel's prominence among Kentuckians had made the authorities halting and hesitant about punishing him for speaking out against black enlistment. After his initial denunciation of the enrollment of black troops in March, the provost marshal general ordered Wolford's arrest, although he was soon released on his pledge to report to Nashville for trial. In Nashville, he was ordered instead to Knoxville, but he was never tried. Instead, he was dishonorably discharged for speaking disrespectfully of the president and for disloyalty, which simply freed him to return to Kentucky and continue making speeches denouncing the policy of black enlistment.[19] In a long justification of his actions published in the *Louisville Journal* in September, Wolford blamed his discharge on the influence of "some wicked men in Kentucky" who persuaded Lincoln, on the grounds of a "mere rumor," that Wolford had violated the Fifth Article of War and was guilty of disloyalty and of conduct unbecoming an officer and a gentleman.[20] Doubtless one of those "wicked men" was Burbridge.

Following his discharge, Wolford tried to rejoin his old regiment as a private, but due to his injuries he could not pass the physical. Wolford probably knew that the severity of his wounds barred him from another cavalry campaign, but he also knew that the failed attempt to enlist cleared the way for him to enter politics. "Being thus cut off from doing anything for my country in the army," Wolford wrote, "I accepted the nomination of the Conservative Union Convention as candidate . . . for the office of elector at the next Presidential election." The Conservative Unionists—an alliance of War Democrats and Peace Democrats that backed McClellan in the election—formed when Unconditional Unionists in the state announced their intention to support Lincoln's renomination. In his new political role, Wolford began canvassing the state. On April 2, in a speech at Lexington's Melodeon Hall, Wolford charged that the war had been "perverted from its original purpose to one of fanaticism," and announced his support for McClellan as a candidate who was "opposed to stealing negroes." At the Union Democratic Convention in Louisville on May 25, Wolford branded Lincoln a "despot," and on May 28 the Fourth Congressional District provost marshal telegraphed Burbridge from Lebanon that "Col. Wolford denounced the enlistment laws, the enlistment of negroes & provost marshal in a speech just now. Shall I arrest him[?]"[21] Burbridge, however, took no immediate action until word of the nature of Wolford's speeches reached Washington. On June 11, Halleck wrote to Burbridge that if he had evidence that Wolford's speeches were of "an insurrectionary and treasonable character" then he should arrest him and send him to Washington. On June 14, Burbridge replied that he would attend to the matter "immediately" and Wolford was arrested for the second time.[22]

Wolford was charged with two offenses by the judge advocate's office. The first was "aiding the enemies of the country by the public expression of disloyal sentiments." The second was "discouraging, denouncing, and opposing the enlistment of colored troops." Governor Bramlette was outraged, denouncing the arrest of "this battle-scarred patriot-hero" who had just recruited a regiment of white soldiers to meet the War Department's call for ten thousand volunteers. Bramlette released correspondence between himself and Lieutenant Governor Jacob that branded Wolford a victim of "political arrest" for which the citizens of Kentucky might justly retaliate by seizing hostages among those urging such arrests. "Kentuckians must be permitted to hold and express their own political sentiments, without being restrained by arrests," Bramlette wrote.[23]

Wolford was sent to Washington, D.C., but was paroled by President Lincoln to await trial on the condition that he refrain from public speaking. In July he returned to Louisville, where he received a revised parole offer from Lincoln. The president offered to discharge Wolford if the ex-colonel signed a pledge "to neither do nor say any thing which will directly or indirectly tend to hinder, delay, or embarrass the employment and use of colored persons as soldiers, seamen, or otherwise."[24]

Wolford penned a long reply to Lincoln, the gist of which was that he could not accept parole on such terms. "I will fester in a prison or die on a gibbet, before I agree to any terms that do not abandon all charges against me," Wolford wrote. He argued that he had broken no law nor contravened any military order. He told Lincoln he had no sympathy for the rebellion and that all his energies since the outbreak of the war had been devoted to "the triumph of the national arms, the preservation of the Union, the maintenance of the Constitution, and the restoration of the supremacy of law over all the states." The charge against him of discouraging enlistments was absurd, Wolford wrote, because the May 28 speech for which he was arrested was a speech aimed at encouraging enlistments. "I may say without presumption that I have done more to enlist white men in the army of the Union than any other man in the State of Kentucky." He admitted his opposition to Lincoln's "abolition" policy but denied that his actions had in any way discouraged the enlistment of black troops. "I have done nothing to hinder the enlistment even of negroes, because I do not associate with them and have no influence over them." He challenged Lincoln to find one African American who had been hindered or discouraged from enlisting as a result of his speeches. Find one, he told Lincoln, and Wolford said he would produce "one hundred white men who have been kept out of the army by your proclamations."[25]

Wolford's response eloquently vented the Conservative Unionist argument against Lincoln's measures. It asserted the underlying loyalty to the Union of those who, like Wolford, opposed emancipation. It asserted as a fundamental civil right the privilege of disagreeing publicly with the government, including "the criticism of your [Lincoln's] whole course, conduct, and policy, the policy of enlisting slaves not excepted." It charged Lincoln with violating—and thus endangering—the Constitution, which he had pledged to uphold and which, as of 1864, still allowed slavery. Lincoln had thus changed the war into "a war of conquest, plunder, and subjugation." It challenged the notion that the use of black soldiers and the Emancipation Proclamation were truly military necessities. "Do you really mean to say that the white citizen soldiers could not whip the rebels, that . . . you had to force the negroes to fight in order to save the country?" If not for the Emancipation Proclamation, the slaves would be in the fields producing corn that could be used by the army, Wolford argued, and their places in the army would be filled by five hundred thousand white men who would have volunteered except for emancipation. It charged that the crackdown on dissent was illegal and unconstitutional and was an underhanded political ploy to ensure that Lincoln and the Republicans remained in power. It is worthy of note that Wolford's long response to Lincoln makes no mention of the recently introduced policy by Burbridge of executing suspected Confederate guerrillas, although it does fault military authorities in Kentucky for their interference in elections. Again, it was not the "butcher" that troubled Burbridge's wartime critics; it was the "tyrant."

At its root, however, the Conservative Unionist complaint against Lincoln was about emancipation. It was emancipation that had changed the war into a war of "plunder," emancipation that had dissuaded white men from enlisting, emancipation that violated the Constitution, emancipation that McClellan's election promised to reverse. Indeed, Lincoln's revised parole offer to Wolford—which threw out the charge of disloyalty—and Wolford's response illustrate that racial issues were at the center of Wolford's ongoing legal travails. Wolford's high-profile speeches merely illustrated the more general point that dissent in Kentucky spiked and remained high after the issuance of the Emancipation Proclamation and especially after the enlistment of black troops began. Burbridge's harsh crackdown on that dissent resulted from white Kentuckians' fundamental disagreement with the Lincoln administration's decision to utilize black soldiers and thereby crush the institution of slavery. It is somewhat naive to believe, as some historians have asserted, that tact and forbearance on the part of the commander of the state would have led to some unspecified better outcome. The only acceptable outcome, from the administration's point of view, was an acceptance of emancipation by white Kentuckians. With or without Burbridge's repressive policies, that was unlikely.

Wolford was not the only prominent Kentuckian to come under military suspicion. In mid-July, rumors of yet another impending invasion of Kentucky reached Burbridge, but this invasion rumor contained a twist. "The day is fixed for a general insurrection in the State of rebel sympathizers to assist the raiding forces and act in concert with them," Burbridge informed General John Schofield, the departmental commander. A few days later, he fixed a positive date for the planned uprising: August 3, although he suspected it might be delayed if the Confederate invasion did not come off as planned. "The conspiracy referred to is much more formidable in Ohio, Indiana, and Illinois, than in Kentucky," he told Schofield. The conspirators called their shadowy organization the Sons of Liberty, echoing the revolutionary organization of the country's forefathers. It was this organization with which Adam Johnson had been instructed to make connection during his summer 1864 mission to recruit Kentucky fighters for the Confederacy who would rise up to support the rumored invasion.[26]

Judge Advocate General Joseph Holt, himself a Kentuckian, had been dispatched by the secretary of war to investigate conditions in Kentucky and Missouri, and he reported at the end of July on "the existence of a treasonable association in Kentucky," and in Illinois, Indiana, Ohio, and possibly Missouri. "It is secret in its meetings, has its ritual and passwords, and aims, through a co-operation with the enemy, in striking at General Sherman's communications, or otherwise to overthrow the Government as now administered." Holt reported on what he called the group's Declaration of Principles, which included a belief that "all men have equal rights insofar as they are equal in their capacity to enjoy and exercise those rights." People lower on the "ascending scale of humanity" needed to be "subject to a just and humane servitude and tutelage to the superior race" until they could be brought up to appreciate those rights and the benefits of civilization. In this proslavery understanding, emancipation ran counter to natural law and jeopardized the benefits that accrued to blacks under the slavery regime.[27]

Holt wrote to Stanton in late July that Burbridge planned to move in a few days against the conspirators, who included "a large number of influential men in Kentucky, embracing several occupying the highest positions under the State Government." Holt also predicted that Burbridge's actions would "have the support of Governor Bramlette, intensely conservative as he is, and all truly loyal men of the State," and the arrests would make "treason . . . socially infamous" in Kentucky. These last two predictions both proved dramatically wrong.[28]

During the first week of August, Burbridge arrested at least seventy-one alleged members of the Sons of Liberty from eight counties. Among those taken were Appeals Court Judge Joshua Bullitt, former Union officer Henry Kalfus, Democratic party leaders John W. Leathers and Joseph R. Buchanan, and several other state and county officials. Others, alerted to the military roundup, fled the state to avoid arrest. On August 6, Burbridge telegraphed to Stanton news of the arrests and urged that similar action be taken by General Samuel P. Heintzelman, who was in command of Indiana and Illinois, if the conspiracy was to be thoroughly uprooted. Stanton quickly relayed his approval of Burbridge's actions "against disloyal persons in your command."[29] Some of the alleged conspirators were sent to Tennessee and slated for eventual removal through the lines to the South, although few were actually banished. Others were imprisoned in Louisville and then eventually released after giving the oath of allegiance. None of the Kentuckians arrested were ever tried for their part in the conspiracy.

The true extent and nature of, and the actual threat posed by, the Sons of Liberty conspiracy continues to be debated by historians,[30] but it was Burbridge's reach into the upper echelons of Kentucky's Conservative

Unionist political elites that sparked outrage. James B. Guthrie, head of the Louisville & Nashville Railroad, wrote to Sherman to complain of the arrests. "I regret exceedingly the arrest of many gentlemen and persons in Kentucky," Sherman replied, "and still more that they should give causes of arrests. . . . It does appear to me when our national integrity is threatened and the very fundamental principles of all government endangered that minor issues should not be made by Judge Bullitt and others. We cannot all substitute our individual opinions, however honest, as the test of authority." Sherman told Guthrie it was time for individuals to defer to government authority on matters of "right and policy," trusting that errors would be revealed and corrected in due time. "I notice in Kentucky a disposition to cry against the tyranny and oppression of our Government." Sherman argued that if there was any oppression, it was the inevitable result of war—and then asked which side had started the war. His answer: The secessionist South. Now there was only one question that mattered to the citizens in the northern states, including Kentucky: "Shall we have a government that must be obeyed, and will you fight for it?" If the answer be "negative or doubtful, they are enemies or mere denizens of the land, stript [*sic*] of the right of suffrage, debarred from speaking or writing, yea even from marrying, for I would stop the breed." At the conclusion of his lengthy response, Sherman told Guthrie that he would "sustain General Burbridge if satisfied he is not influenced by mere personal motives, and nothing has occurred to evince anything of the kind."[31]

The timing of the arrests—and the timing of the releases of some of the central figures in the alleged conspiracy—betrayed the political motivations of Burbridge's actions. He meant to exert control over who would serve as local officials and, hopefully, over who Kentucky would choose in the presidential contest in November. The bulk of the arrests, beginning in late July and continuing into the first week of August, coincided with an August 1 election for several state and local offices. As the *Cincinnati Enquirer* commented upon receiving news of the arrests, "This is a part of the programme to control the election." Joshua Bullitt's mother, trying to make sense of her son's arrest, wrote in a letter that she figured "that the Ky ultras resolved that no democrat should hold office."[32]

Burbridge and his subordinates intervened more directly in the August election as well. Just a few days before the polling was to take place, for example, Burbridge issued an order to the county sheriffs in the Second District of the Kentucky Court of Appeals that Alvin Duvall's name was to be stricken from the poll books as a candidate for appellate judge. Duvall "is a man of considerable legal ability, and a courteous and pleasant gentleman in the private circle," wrote the *Lexington National Unionist,* which supported Burbridge's action, "but he has been a sympathizer with the South and the rebel cause ever since the commencement of the national trouble, and although he may never have done any overt act in favor of the rebellion, the influence of his name and his official position have given weight and respectability to the rebel cause in the estimation of others." Duvall, tipped off that he was to be arrested by the military authorities, fled the state. Similarly, General Hugh Ewing, who commanded Kentucky's Second Military District under Burbridge, ordered Charles Nourse of Elizabethtown not to run for the office of county clerk after receiving letters from Union men in the area that Nourse was "secessionist" and "a most uncompromising rebel." Likewise, Ewing barred S. W. Stone from standing for sheriff of Hardin County.[33]

Why bother with these local-level offices? For Conservative Unionists, it looked like straight-out partisanship. The military was favoring one party over another, rewarding Unconditional Unionists with political office. Lewis and Richard Collins's 1874 history argued, for example, that with the removal of Duvall's name from the judicial ballot, "the track seemed . . . adroitly and arbitrarily cleared for the success of . . . the Unconditional Union nominee." Indeed, Nourse, gently challenging Ewing's decision to bar him from running for clerk, wrote that he supposed since the office was without much influence, it would be free from military interference. However, he told Ewing, "I don't wish to incur displeasure. . . . I don't wish to be a martyr. I have a family to support and my ambition is to take care of my wife and five children."[34] From Nourse's point of view, Ewing's decision blocked him from making a living and threw the salary and fees that accrued to the clerk's office to a political ally of the Unconditional Unionists.

There was more to the arrests, however, than mere partisanship. Local officials were critical to the governance of the state. Despite the great powers of the military under the martial law regime, the army needed the active cooperation of local officials to detect and punish disloyalty, to furnish the lists upon which military enrollment and enlistment were based, and generally to keep an eye on the local population when federal troops were scattered too thinly to do so. After all, it was not just federal law and policy that sought to ensure support for the war effort; Kentucky's Unionist legislature also passed laws aimed at quelling and punishing dissent. In February 1864, for example, the legislature passed a law providing for civil remedies for civilians who suffered damage or injuries at the hands of guerrillas or any armed band "acting in the interest of, or professing to act in the interest of, the so-called Confederate States of America." The law specifically extended civil liability beyond the armed combatants who committed the injury to include those who "shall aid [or] . . . encourage such acts" and those who harbored or concealed the wrongdoers. It also defined harboring and abetting to include the failure by "any disloyal person" to notify the civil or military authorities of the presence of guerrilla bands within their county of residence. Under Kentucky's county-centric system of local government, enforcement of this law would fall to local sheriffs, judges, and court officials.[35]

That same February, the legislature also passed "an act to punish disloyal and treasonable practices." This act imposed criminal penalties on those who aided, abetted, harbored, or concealed guerrillas or Confederate soldiers "making or levying war upon the government of the United States, or State of Kentucky, or upon any citizen or resident of the State of Kentucky," essentially adding a criminal component to the civil liabilities imposed by the earlier law. Such crimes were declared "high misdemeanor[s]," punishable by fines of not less than $100 and not more than $10,000, and by jail time of not less than six months or more than one year. The law also called for fines and jail time for those who did not report the presence of guerrillas to civil or military authorities. More interestingly, it also mandated punishment of those who, "by speaking or writing against the Government of the United States," endeavored "to excite the people of this State . . . to insurrection or rebellion," or who tried through threats and terror to hinder or prevent the state's citizens from supporting the "legal and constitutional authority of the Federal Government or of this State," or those who opposed the suppression of the rebellion. The law also included a proviso that it should not be construed as a restriction on the "constitutional right of speaking and writing in reference to the manner of administering the government" or on the "exposing and correcting" of government maladministration or official misconduct.[36]

The act thus left a lot of room for interpretation. Was criticism of the enlistment and enrollment of black soldiers protected speech? Or did it "excite the people" to insurrection against the policies of the administration? Was denouncing Lincoln as a tyrant—or Burbridge, for that matter—a mere "exposing and correcting" of government maladministration, or did such denunciations seek to hinder the citizens from supporting the government? Part of the answer, of course, depended on whether one thought the government was acting within the bounds of its legal and constitutional authority. Critics like Wolford clearly thought the government had exceeded such authority. Jacob, another prominent critic, railed that when the administration goes "beyond the Constitution, I am for resisting them by every constitutional means. When they are sinking our institutions into the night of oblivion and destruction, I am for fighting this base and damnable Administration." On the other hand, Unconditional Unionists—especially military men—believed its actions were legal and constitutional. In the context of the actual working of the law, who would make those interpretations? It would be county judges, sheriffs, and court officials—the elected positions where Ewing and Burbridge intervened most directly in August 1864. They wanted Unconditional Unionists in those positions not solely for partisan reasons—although such reasons doubtless influenced their thinking—but because they needed and wanted a cooperative local administration to help keep the lid on a situation that they worried was getting out of control.[37]

Not surprisingly, however, Kentucky's political elites did not take kindly to military interference in the electoral process. In response to Alvin Duvall's name being stricken from the ballot, Governor Bramlette sent an inquiry to the local officials in Duvall's district, asking for information on whether they received an order from the military excluding any candidate and which candidate benefited from such an order. He also asked if the election judges were "overawed by the presence or menace of soldiers, so as to interfere with free suffrage, and a free and equal election." On September 3, Bramlette protested directly to Lincoln. "Without rebuke the military commandant issued an order directly interfering with the most important election then depending, and in open conflict with the constitution and laws of the State, and in dereliction of the most sacred rights of a free and loyal people." Kentucky's voters also bridled at Burbridge's interference; despite the removal of Duvall, the Unconditional Union candidate did not win the seat. Rather, a last-minute substitute whose name was telegraphed to the counties in the district by Conservative Union men on the morning of the election won by over four hundred votes.[38]

Contemporaries and historians alike viewed the August 1 elections as just a warm-up for the presidential election looming three months ahead. E. Merton Coulter asserted in 1926 that the "main purpose" of arresting Wolford was to keep him "from playing a part in the presidential campaign."[39] The arrests that Burbridge ordered in late July and early August—especially of the more prominent Sons of Liberty—likewise took out a number of administration opponents. Frank Klement, an historian who devoted much of his career to studying the Democratic opposition in the Midwest, argued that organizations like the Sons of Liberty were nothing more than fringe societies of the Democratic party that supported McClellan and that their alleged "conspiracies" were "legends and myths . . . based upon wartime political propaganda."[40] Certainly, in the case of the Sons of Liberty, the timing of their subsequent release seemed to betray a political motivation. Several of them, including Joshua Bullitt, the most prominent member of the Kentucky establishment to be caught up in Burbridge's sweep, were sent south to Memphis, where they were detained by General C. C. Washburn rather than being sent through the lines. Bullitt's mother wrote that she had heard from "a western man" that the whole Sons of Liberty "conspiracy" consisted merely of a compact among Democrats to vote. Most telling, on November 26, just a few weeks after the presidential election, Bullitt announced to his mother: "I am released unconditionally, with the other prisoners from Ky."[41]

Burbridge used his ample powers as commander in other overtly political ways as well. The *Frankfort Commonwealth* reported a speech by Burbridge on the Thursday before the election, for example, in which he told those assembled, "Now, gentlemen, you all want pay for your horses, and niggers, and corn, and your hogs. Be cautious what record you make." Since the federal government only promised compensation for property taken from loyal men, the clear implication was that a vote for McClellan was a mark of disloyalty that would jeopardize any chance of compensation. An account by a more biased observer—Confederate general William Preston, who evidently ventured into his home state of Kentucky during election season from his self-exile in Canada—depicted Burbridge campaigning in Georgetown in front of a sullen crowd, forced by soldiers to attend. He told those assembled that he knew they were all rebels at heart, that he represented the sword of the government, and that all those who did not vote for Lincoln would be treated as enemies of the government after the election.[42]

In October, Burbridge freely admitted to Judge Advocate General Joseph Holt that he had been working on Lincoln's behalf. "I deem it of the utmost importance for Kentucky's future that the State should be carried for Mr. Lincoln. I have used every means in my power to accomplish this end." He told Holt it would be a good idea to send claims commissioners into Kentucky who were charged with recompensing loyal slaveholders for their slaves who had joined the Union army. "The moral effect of this would be great, and would confirm hundreds in the faith who are now weak-kneed and doubting." He also said he had thrown some government patronage to "prominent influential men, who were not of doubtful loyalty, but of doubtful politics . . . —in other words, when I could by honorably bestowing favors make a vote for Mr. Lincoln I have done so."[43] Although such moves triggered howls of corruption from Democrats and Conservative Unionists, the use of government largesse to secure votes was a long-established—if not exactly officially approved—nineteenth-century political strategy.

The real concern was security. McClellan supporters worried that the deployment of soldiers at polling places would result in their being barred from the polls under accusations of being "disloyal." On October 17, Bramlette sent a long letter to election officials outlining who was allowed to vote and who was not, specifying that their qualifications were not to be determined by the military authorities. If any military officer should attempt to control or dictate to election officials, "you should treat the orders with indignant contempt, and scorn obedience which implies perjury and cowardice in you." Sheriffs were advised to arrest soldiers attempting to interfere, calling on citizens for assistance if needed. If they could not prevent military interference, Bramlette counseled, they should call off the election. "If you are unable to hold a free election, your duty is to hold none at all." Frank Wolford, as usual, was more direct: "The man dies," Wolford stated, who stood between him and the polls on election day.[44]

Burbridge and his Unconditional Union allies, meanwhile, feared that without a military presence, guerrillas and Confederate sympathizers would disrupt the election and prevent Union men from casting their ballots. A group of Unionists from Bowling Green telegraphed Burbridge a few days before the election to report that "our friends are systematically threatened with the destruction of their property if they vote for the president." In response, Burbridge ordered the arrest of a "Mr. Perkins, of Elkton, and every man in . . . [the] district who attempts to intimidate Union men from voting." He wrote to Holt in October that the rebels planned to disperse a large number of cavalry over the state "to interfere with the election," after which they would reunite and join Confederate general John Breckinridge in southwestern Virginia in preparation for a full-on invasion of Kentucky. This information came from letters received by Confederate sympathizers from their friends in the southern army, Burbridge told Holt. Meanwhile, most of his own troops had been ordered either to the East or to the South. "I deem it of the utmost importance to have a sufficient force thrown into the state, between this and the November election, to protect every exposed voting precinct, and to frustrate any contemplated raid. With a judicious disposition of the troops the State may be carried for Mr. Lincoln."[45]

Such statements, of course, merely increased the Conservative suspicion that the army meant to win Kentucky for Lincoln at the point of a bayonet. Various speakers in the anti-Lincoln ranks, including Governor Bramlette, began to call for McClellan voters to go armed to the polls to forcibly defend their right to vote. Burbridge sought to walk back their fears with General Order No. 7, issued on October 26, 1864. They were operating "under the false pretense that the military meditate illegal interference." By calling for their partisans to arm themselves, these speakers only incited the "large rebel element in our midst" to acts of violence and frightened civilians away from the polls. Burbridge went on to say that the military would be available to help election officials enforce state laws regarding the eligibility of voters. He then reprinted the state statute, which had been passed back in 1862, in full. The 1862 act stripped citizenship from those Kentuckians who took up arms on behalf of the Confederacy or against the armed forces of the United States, and from those who rendered aid and assistance to those who took up arms. The act further provided that those who attempted to exercise the rights of citizenship might be required to swear an oath that they had never taken up arms or supported those who did. Burbridge clarified that "aid and assistance" could come in the form of words as well as deeds. "It is perfectly easy for discreet and patriotic officers of the election to distinguish . . . legal from disfranchised voters," and it was those officers who had the authority to put questions to and judge the answers of those attempting to vote. His officers, Burbridge warned, would arrest anyone violating the state election law. Needless to say, General Order No. 7 did little to reassure the pro-McClellan camp.[46]

McClellan, of course, won Kentucky—one of only three states in the Union to go Democratic in 1864—outpolling Lincoln by a 2-to-1 margin. McClellan supporters blamed "intimidation by the army" for a sharp decline in voter turnout, but complaints from Lincoln supporters also flowed into Burbridge's headquarters. From Paris, Kentucky, a correspondent telegraphed Burbridge on election day that "nothing but out and out rebels voting for [McClellan]. Judges swearing none of them." A lieutenant in Frankfort told him: "There are men voting for McClellan and Pendleton who have given aid and comfort to the rebels."[47] An open letter to Burbridge from the pseudonymous "Union" published in the *Lexington National Unionist* declared that if Burbridge had "attended the polls at any of the voting places," he would have seen men who "but the other day, in a back room cast their votes for a member of the rebel Congress[;] . . . men who have sent sons . . . into the rebel army; men who voted for the rebel candidates in the State Legislature 1861; all casting their votes against the Union candidates."[48] The "discreet and patriotic" election officers Burbridge counted on to enforce the election law did not appear to be screening out many ineligible voters, at least in the eyes of Unconditional Unionists. Indeed, given the results of the two elections in which Burbridge was accused of direct military interference—both of them victories for candidates the general opposed—it does not appear that his interventions were very effective.

More than political gamesmanship was involved in the arrests, banishments, and military interference in elections; what was really in play was the definition of loyalty to the Union. And the question of loyalty in 1864 hinged to a large degree on the willingness to accept emancipation as a war aim. In his complaint written to Lincoln in September about Burbridge's actions, Governor Bramlette asserted that "in common with the loyal masses of Kentucky, my Unionism is unconditional." Without obvious irony, he then spent the next two paragraphs spelling out the conditions of his Unionism. "We are not willing to sacrifice a single life or imperil the smallest right of free white men for the sake of the negro. . . . We are for the restoration of our Government throughout our entire limits, regardless of what may happen to the negro." Bramlette represented Kentucky loyalty as consisting of agnosticism on the subject of whether slavery would be part of a restored Union. "We reject as spurious the Unionism of all who make the status of the negro a sine qua non to peace and unity. We are not willing to imperil the life, liberty, and happiness of our own race and people for the freedom or enslavement of the negro. To permit the question of the freedom or slavery of the negro to obstruct the restoration of national authority and unity is a blood-stained sin." In a similar vein, Lieutenant Governor Jacob predicted that the effort to end slavery in the South would only lead to "an everlasting war. When the people come back to the recognition of Southern rights, that moment the war will end." Like Bramlette, he felt the preservation or destruction of slavery was only "incidental" to the war effort and should not be made one of the goals of that effort.[49]

By September 1864, however, such agnosticism on slavery no longer defined loyalty to the Union. The ground had shifted under the feet of Kentucky's Conservative Unionists. Emancipation was not a mere policy; it had become a bedrock aim of the war. Unionism meant fidelity to the now-linked national military objectives: the crushing of the rebellion and the destruction of slavery.

This fundamental disagreement over the definition of loyalty helps explain Burbridge's actions after the election, when political partisanship could no longer suffice as a rationale. In the week following the election, Burbridge issued orders for the arrest and banishment behind southern lines of Kentucky legislator and Union veteran John B. Huston, *Louisville Journal* editor Paul Shipman, Lieutenant Governor Jacob, and Frank Wolford (again). Even more than the Sons of Liberty arrests, these moves sparked outrage among Kentucky's Conservative Unionists. Governor Bramlette protested anew to Lincoln. Huston's sole offense was "opposition to your re-election," Bramlette wrote, urging Lincoln to stay Burbridge's hand before he sank the entire Union cause in Kentucky. "You are doubtless re-elected," he told Lincoln, "but surely cannot sanction this ostracism of loyal men who honestly opposed you." Historian E. Merton Coulter blasted these November arrests as "one of the most tactless and insane moves made by the military regime."[50]

The November arrests triggered a final breach between Bramlette and Burbridge. Back in August, after the Sons of Liberty arrests, Bramlette had written to Burbridge "as your friend" warning him that unscrupulous politicians in Ohio and Indiana, particularly Indiana's Governor Oliver P. Morton, were putting Burbridge in a false position by urging him to "make arrests in Ky and permit the conspirators to go untouched where they are more extensively and dangerously organized." In September, Bramlette wrote that "it has ever been my opinion that your purposes were laudable." While he had not agreed with all of Burbridge's actions, he told the general, he attributed them to "good motives" and "when I was apprised of the fact that persons were machinating against you I have flanked them and defeated their movements against you. . . . I have believed that your views and my own harmonized more nearly than yours and those who are constantly urging extreme action." But the November arrests moved Bramlette into the ranks of the machinators.[51]

On November 9, he wrote to both Grant and Sherman requesting Burbridge's removal. Decrying Burbridge's "evil and mischievous acts," his "outrageous and indiscriminate arrests" of McClellan supporters, his "threatening and bullying of citizens," and his "menacing [of] the civil authorities . . . of the state," Bramlette wrote that only his own diplomatic skills had prevented open violence. "He keeps it up. Yesterday he arrested many citizens for no offense except the disloyalty, as they term it, of being opposed to Mr. Lincoln's re-election." Bramlette characterized Burbridge as the unwitting tool of extremists in the state who intended evil consequences. They "work upon his weakness through his vanity," Bramlette charged. "He is wholly unfit for any command where there is anything at stake which requires either intellect, prudence, firmness of purpose, justice, or the manliness of the soldier to accomplish." Grant forwarded Bramlette's note to Secretary of War Edwin Stanton with the notation that he had never favored Burbridge for permanent command in Kentucky, but that he did not know "how far Governor Bramlette ought to be conciliated."[52]

Bramlette's notion that Burbridge was a pawn manipulated by radical Republicans gained currency among Conservative Unionists. After Joshua Bullitt's arrest, his mother wrote to his younger brother that she had heard that prominent Unconditional Unionist and antislavery politician "Judge [William] Goodloe is at the bottom of his arrest" and that "private motives of interest and malice prompts the persecution" of Joshua. Burbridge, she had been informed, was just "a fool . . . clothed with authority."[53] Far harsher was the denunciation by Jacob published in the *Cincinnati Enquirer* in January 1865. Jacob charged that his arrest—like that of Shipman, Wolford, and Huston—had been an act of petty revenge perpetrated by Robert J. Breckinridge, probably the most prominent Unconditional Unionist in the state and a well-known Presbyterian leader, after Jacob had deigned to criticize him publicly. "Breckinridge, Burbridge! Master, tool!" Jacob thundered. Burbridge he depicted as a "pink cheeked . . . pretty fellow," in whom "with the most powerful microscope it would be impossible to detect the first ray of intelligence[,] under the complete control of inordinate vanity, whisky, and a broken down political preacher."[54]

Burbridge defended his actions against the storms of protest, insisting that the arrests pertained to the disloyal words and actions of the four men. When challenged by Lincoln, he wrote back that "Governor Bramlette is wrong. . . . Huston's influence and speeches have been of a treasonable character and he persisted in making the latter after several warnings" of the consequences. Nonetheless, he reported that he had allowed Huston to return to Lexington on the condition that Huston take the oath and give bond not to oppose the government again. "A vigorous policy against rebel sympathizers in this State must be pursued, and if I have erred I fear I have made too few arrests instead of too many." Jacob, Burbridge wrote, "advised armed resistance to the enrollment and enlistment of slaves, advised citizens to arm to resist military interference at the polls on election day, and generally his whole conduct and speeches have been wholly disloyal."[55]

Burbridge's response to Bramlette was both more substantive and more hostile. "When the civil authorities make no effort to suppress disloyalty, the military must and will," he told Bramlette when he got news of the governor's petition to Lincoln. A few days later, he angrily denounced the speeches made by "Wolford, Jacob, Huston, and others" for "endeavoring by their remarks to discourage enlistments, and thus weaken the power of the Government in its efforts to suppress the rebellion. This has been done not only without any interference on the part of the State authorities but, on the contrary, with their apparent sanction and approval." While making no "insinuation of dereliction of duty" by state officials, Burbridge continued, Kentucky would not be besieged by guerrillas and her loyal citizens would not live under constant threat of violence if he had received the cooperation of the state authorities that Bramlette had promised.[56]

Bramlette fired back. He resented Burbridge's lack of courtesy and "bullying tone," he said, and defended his administration's history of cooperation with the federal authorities, repeatedly putting the state troops at the disposal of the military when asked to do so. "In no single instance have the civil authorities failed to properly and earnestly aid, not only to support the military in '*maintaining the Government,*' but to aid . . . in enforcing the *measures* of the Administration . . . [r]egardless of our private judgment as to the policy or impolicy of such measures."[57] Bramlette's emphasis on state troops actually sidestepped the issue Burbridge may have been more concerned about: the enforcement of the act to punish treasonable practices by state authorities to shut down expressions of discontent. It was in this area where the military had to step in to quell the hostile declamations by prominent people like Wolford, Huston, and Jacob.

Bramlette also covered much of the same Conservative Unionist ground that Wolford had when replying to Lincoln. First, Bramlette stated that although he had only heard one speech by Wolford, Jacob, Huston, et al., "I know the men, and know them to be incapable of any disloyal speech or act." Second, he noted that the civil authorities, as well as the military authorities, "have no right . . . to interfere with the freedom of political discussions." He distinguished between the duty of the citizen to obey the "laws . . . of the constituted authorities" and the right of the citizen to "use all lawful and peaceful means to correct or reform such laws . . . as he may deem unwise." Third, the allegation of discouraging enlistments was "a shallow pretense . . . to afford a pretext for wreaking political vengeance upon them" for advocating McClellan's election.[58] Neither Bramlette nor Burbridge explicitly brought up black enlistment, but by November 1864 the charge of "discouraging enlistments" essentially amounted to code for opposing black enlistment. Conservative Unionists viewed black enlistment and the assault on slavery that it represented as a policy choice subject to political debate and electoral reversal; Unconditional Unionists viewed it as a principle of reunification and a primary military objective. On this difference of views rested the differing definitions of loyalty and disloyalty.

In addition to arresting Conservative Unionists and interfering in elections, Burbridge also used his power to interfere in the state's economy. This, too, embittered the state's citizens and led Kentucky politicians to decry his tyranny and call for his removal. In August 1864, shortly after the Sons of Liberty arrests and the local election, Burbridge issued General Order No. 63, which established a system of trade permits by which only those of "well known loyalty" would be allowed to ship goods within the state. When loyalty was in doubt, the applicant had to swear an oath. This oath took various forms, but the question of emancipation, again, was at the heart of determining loyalty or disloyalty. For example, in the Second Military District, General Hugh Ewing issued a circular to his officers with the specified loyalty oath. In Ewing's formulation, in addition to swearing to uphold and defend the Constitution and the Union and swearing to never have aided the Confederacy, the applicant had to promise to "faithfully support all acts of Congress passed during the existing rebellion with reference to slaves . . . , and faithfully support all proclamations of the President . . . having reference to slaves." Similarly, in his protest to Lincoln written in September, Bramlette enclosed the loyalty oath prescribed by a different officer. The applicant was to answer two interrogatories, as well as swearing that he had never "given the slightest aid and comfort" to the rebellion. The second interrogatory read: "Will you faithfully sustain all the measures of the United States Government to suppress the rebellion (including the enlistment of slaves in U. S. Army)?"[59] Clearly, emancipation and the definition of loyalty were linked.

Although the system of trade permits was hated and criticized by merchants whose businesses were jeopardized by being denied a permit,

Burbridge's greatest economic offense in the eyes of his critics was the "Hog Order" of 1864, or the so-called "Great Hog Swindle." The Hog Order asserted a prior claim by the government on farmers' surplus hogs (those not needed for family use) to provide salted pork for army rations. Government agents were to be sent out to purchase the hogs, and farmers would not be allowed to drive hogs to market without a permit. However, the government's offered price was 1 to 2 cents per pound less than the market price. Bramlette wrote to Lincoln on November 14—two weeks after the issuance of the order—that it had caused "considerable commotion" among hog packers and farmers. Lincoln responded to the complaint by ordering Burbridge to rescind the order, which he did on November 27. Although it had only been in effect for one month, it was widely viewed as an attempt to snatch farmers' hogs for below-market rates and then channel all the packing business to politically connected packing houses. "This scurvy attempt to make money in the name of the Government at the expense of the Kentucky farmers was long remembered and resented by the people," Coulter wrote.[60]

Bramlette raged against the $300,000 lost by Kentucky farmers thanks to the Hog Order, but a later historian's assessment found that there was in fact a real crisis in pork packing driven by speculation in the market and the influence of a few large packing houses. "The speculation was wholly at the expense of the government," wrote Palmer Boeger in the *Southern Historical Review.* Boeger found that a poor corn crop and hog shortage led to salt pork prices outrunning the price of gold during the first part of 1864, and that the Hog Order was more an attempt to save the government money and ensure the army had a supply of pork than it was an illicit and corrupt cornering of the hog market. Indeed, while Bramlette claimed $300,000 in damage to Kentucky farmers, the principal commissary officer behind implementation of the Hog Order claimed to have saved the government $200,000.[61]

Legitimate or not, the Hog Order added to Burbridge's litany of tyrannical acts in the eyes of his critics. The military's interference in elections, its suppression of speech, its arrests of dissenters, and its intervention in the economy all contributed to white Kentuckians' hatred of Burbridge. And, in fact, it is quite easy to sympathize with their complaints. Living in the post-9/11 era of the Patriot Act and extensive government surveillance—and knowing the long history of political oppression undertaken by the US government—makes it hard to view Burbridge's actions with equanimity.

It is more difficult to see through the rights-based language of Burbridge's opponents to determine the underlying cause of their animus toward the general. Much of that animus stemmed from the fact that the oppressions "loyal" Kentuckians had to endure were inflicted for the sake of African American emancipation. Unwilling to accept the destruction of slavery in their midst—an institution that many Kentucky Unionists had gone to war to preserve—they lost their enthusiasm for the Union cause. In the eyes of the administration—and those charged, like Burbridge, with enforcing its war policies—the loyalty of many Conservative Unionists was suspect as a result. "Men and public journals that once stood fairly out for the cause of the country have allowed secondary considerations to so influence them that to-day it is extremely doubtful whether they would now be the friends of the Union, under any circumstances," wrote the *Lexington National Unionist* in the wake of black enlistment. "[T]hey are giving all the support they dare to the enemies of the Union cause."[62] Urged on and supported by his superiors, Burbridge's job was to root out disloyalty and forbid its public expression. When he found that many Unionist political elites resisted and resented him for doing his job—and, in fact, viewed themselves as a staunchly loyal opposition—he redoubled his efforts to stamp out their disloyalty.

Dark and conspiratorial fears on both sides thwarted any hope of rapprochement. Bramlette was convinced that a cabal of Unconditional Unionists—men like Robert Breckinridge, William Goodloe, and Indiana governor Oliver Morton—controlled Burbridge. They urged extreme measures on him in the hopes of triggering a collision between federal and state authorities, basically daring the state to resist Burbridge's policies with violence. The result of such a collision would be the takeover of the state by federal authorities. Only Bramlette's subtle diplomatic skills, or so insisted Bramlette, had been able to keep the conflict at bay.[63]

Burbridge, for his part, believed that men like Wolford, Jacob, Bullitt, and the rest encouraged the South to hold out, to expect help from sympathizers in the North, and to believe that Kentuckians would rise up against the government if a Confederate army would invade the state. Indeed, Adam Johnson and his band of irregular troops in western

Kentucky envisioned just such an outcome. Such conspiracies were explicit in the case of organizations like the Sons of Liberty, but the same sentiments—and the same corrosive effects—were implicit in the speeches and actions of people like Jacob and Wolford, and in the tolerance of such speeches by Bramlette and the civil officers of the government. Confederate correspondence captured during Burbridge's third raid into southwestern Virginia reinforced his suspicions and he quickly dispatched them to Washington to buttress his case. One of the captured letters described a visit to Richmond by George B. Prentice, the editor of the *Louisville Journal.* The letter summarized a meeting between Prentice and Bramlette that had occurred before the editor had left. The governor had reportedly described the "great dissatisfaction" with the federal government among Kentuckians and predicted that "all the people would rise up if an army would go there."[64]

For Burbridge, such sentiments were obvious evidence of disloyalty; for Bramlette, the very same sentiments were evidence that the federal officers were mishandling the state. In the end, the Lincoln administration decided it was better to conciliate the elected government of a nominally loyal state than it was to back Burbridge's efforts to root out anyone of questionable sympathies. By the end of November, Grant and Lincoln were both batting around ideas about Burbridge's removal and his possible replacement. His reelection secured, Lincoln wrote to Bramlette that he was conferring with various people to "devise means for the pacification and harmony of Kentucky . . . now that the passion-exciting subject of the election is past."[65] On January 11, 1865, the War Department ordered Burbridge to Washington to report to the adjutant general. On February 8, General John M. Palmer was named commander of Kentucky and Burbridge was ordered to report to General George Thomas in Nashville for reassignment. "Thank God and President Lincoln," the *Louisville Journal* quipped.[66]

Burbridge's "tyranny" played a greater role in his removal than his "butchery." His interventions in the state's political and economic life alienated the Conservative Unionists who controlled state government. They remained largely silent during his tenure, however, on his executions of

Confederate prisoners. Conservative Unionists had already turned against the administration because of its policies of enlisting and emancipating slaves in Kentucky; Burbridge's actions to silence criticism of those policies and enforce the new standard of loyalty only drove them further away. It seems doubtful that a policy of conciliation, in which politically prominent men were allowed to speak openly of their contempt for Lincoln's policies and his mode of conducting the war, would have helped the Union cause any more than Burbridge's policy of repression. More likely, it would have earned Burbridge the ire of his superiors, who expected action against expressions of disloyalty. Bubridge took a political gamble—he bet that those who stood by the administration, whose Unionism was unflinching, would be rewarded after the war for being on the victorious side.

# 6

# Butcher

As commander of Kentucky, Burbridge directly ordered the executions of over sixty men and was indirectly responsible for the executions of dozens of others. However, as the previous chapter argued, it was not these deaths that cost Burbridge his command, especially as they came at a time when thousands were dying on battlefields across the South. Rather, the executions of prisoners blackened Burbridge's reputation *after* the war, earning him his alliterative moniker: "Butcher Burbridge." Once the conflict ended, returning Confederate veterans found welcome among the large number of white Kentuckians who had been alienated from the Unionist cause by the assault on slavery and by Burbridge's suppression of dissent. This alliance meant that pro-Confederate "Lost Cause-ism" dominated Kentucky's postwar political scene, and it was primarily these partisans of the Lost Cause who heaped contempt on Burbridge for the executions, branding them as "military murders" undertaken without cause, evidence, or legal process.

Burbridge defended his actions as legitimate countermeasures against the "irregular bands of armed men" who had waged continual violence against Union soldiers, civilians, and Kentucky's communications infrastructure. These attacks by pro-Confederate guerrillas and Confederate cavalry raiders typified Kentucky's wartime experience in the years after the Confederate defeat at Perryville in October 1862, and particularly after John Hunt Morgan's defeat by Burbridge's troops at Cynthiana in June 1864. Many of Morgan's men, fleeing from the Union mopping-up operation, did not follow their commander back to Virginia. Instead, they hid out in Kentucky and went on to wage irregular warfare. Kentucky's guerrilla war never quite achieved the prominence associated with Missouri's internal struggles, but it was widespread, ongoing, and unresolved by the end of the war.

There is no doubt that Burbridge's policies against guerrillas were harsh. General Order No. 59, issued on July 16, 1864, called for the public execution of "four guerrillas . . . selected from the prisoners in the hands of the military authorities" for every unarmed Union citizen killed in a guerrilla raid. In addition, General Order No. 59 mandated the arrest and banishment beyond the lines of any rebel sympathizer living within five miles of "any scene of outrage committed by armed men, not recognized as public enemies by the rules and usages of war," and the seizure of the property of such sympathizers to indemnify losses suffered during the attack.[1] Three months later, on October 26, Burbridge issued what was, in some ways, an even harsher order. General Order No. 8 declared that "hereafter no guerrillas will be received as prisoners" and any officer who extended to captured guerrillas the treatment accorded prisoners of war would be regarded as disobeying orders. General Order No. 8 essentially required field officers to shoot guerrillas on sight and to execute those captured.[2]

Harsh as these orders were, they largely fit the mold of Union policies aimed at curbing irregular warfare in the border states. In the West Virginia mountains in 1862, Union general Robert H. Milroy ordered his officers to appraise the value of Unionists' property destroyed by guerrillas and then make Confederate sympathizers in the area pay for the damages. If they did not pay up within twenty-four hours, they could be executed. In April 1862, after one of his foraging columns was attacked near the town of Williamsville, Milroy ordered the detachment sent to investigate the attack to burn the town if they found that its residents had aided the attackers, and to kill any irregulars they captured and "hang their bodies by the roadside as a warning."[3] In Missouri, the proving ground for much of the Union's guerrilla-fighting policy, each commander found himself adopting harsh punitive policies, including summary execution. In early August 1861, Major General John Fremont declared martial law in Missouri and promised to execute all persons "taken with arms in their hands" inside Union lines. His successor, Henry W. Halleck, ordered similar treatment for "insurgents and . . . guerrilla bands," declaring such marauders outside the laws of war. Union general John Schofield—who would later be Burbridge's commanding officer as head of the Department of the Ohio—issued General Order No. 3 in the summer of 1862, which punished "treasonable language," levied assessments on Confederate sympathizers for Unionist property damaged in guerrilla raids, and fined Confederates and sympathizers in their neighborhoods $5,000 for each Unionist citizen who was killed. Schofield wrote in his diary that guerrillas "were under my orders executed on the spot when captured, and hundreds of sympathizers banished or imprisoned." The culmination of antiguerrilla policy in Missouri was General Thomas Ewing's infamous General Order No. 11, issued August 25, 1863, which expelled all the inhabitants from three counties in Missouri and part of a fourth.[4] Frustrated by the guerrillas, their tactics, and their reliance on the sympathies of the local population, Union commanders throughout the border states—and, indeed, throughout the Union-occupied South—adopted policies of exile, collective financial retribution, and summary execution.

Burbridge's policies do stand out in one way, however. In other regions ravaged by irregular warfare, Union commanders gave orders to kill combatants in the field. Burbridge's General Order No. 59 ordered the execution of men already in Union custody. These men, held in military prisons in Lexington, Louisville, and at various smaller posts around the state, had been picked up by Union patrols or turned in by their neighbors and, in theory, had been subject to an examination by a military commission.[5] They had not been captured on the battlefield after a surrender, and thus they were not held as regular prisoners of war, who generally were moved through Kentucky to military prisons farther north.[6] General Order No. 59 presumed the guilt of those lodged in Kentucky's military prisons, but their presumed guilt was general, not specific to the outrage for which they might be executed. Put simply, General Order No. 59 targeted detainees, who were uniformly labeled "guerrillas" no matter what the specific reason for their detention. As a "guerrilla," any prisoner in Union hands partook of the guilt of all guerrillas active in the state.

This notion of general guilt betrayed some of Burbridge's thinking about irregular warfare. General Order No. 59 only makes sense if

Burbridge believed that the executions of prisoners would deter guerrillas in the field from attacking civilians. Therefore, he had to believe that the guerrilla bands were somehow connected and communicating. In other words, if Burbridge's policy was going to be effective, the guerrillas still roaming the countryside needed to acknowledge concern and responsibility for their compatriots facing execution and so refrain from their attacks to prevent those executions. In some cases, Confederate and irregular commanders did express their concerns to Burbridge about General Order No. 59 and threaten similar retaliation against Union soldiers that fell into their hands. But their concern was almost always for their own men in Burbridge's jails and not about the policy in general. In January 1865, for example, Confederate general John C. Breckinridge wrote to Burbridge regarding three officers "over whom is impending a threat of execution upon the occurrence of events which they have no power to control." He demanded prisoner-of-war treatment for the officers and threatened retaliation against "three Federal officers of equal rank under your command" currently held as prisoners if his men were not accorded POW status. Similarly, in August 1864, the irregular leader Adam Johnson sent an officer under a flag of truce to General Hugh Ewing, district commander under Burbridge, to "have a definite understanding in regard to prisoners captured."[7]

There is no indication, however, that the retaliation carried out under General Order No. 59 had any deterrent effect on irregular activity in the state. Most of the guerrilla units were too diffuse, too autonomous, and too loosely organized for General Order No. 59 to have its desired impact. Self-constituted groups striking targets of opportunity and operating only occasionally under a Confederate command structure could not be brought to heel by retaliation against other men that they likely did not even know. On the ground of effectiveness, therefore, Burbridge's policy has to be judged a failure. Burbridge's General Order No. 8, which targeted guerrillas in the field directly, may have stemmed in part from his recognition of the faulty logic behind General Order No. 59.

General John Palmer, who assumed command of Kentucky after Burbridge was relieved, reached a similar conclusion in his memoirs. Burbridge, Palmer wrote, "had attempted to terrify the guerrillas by hanging their friends. . . . I chose to pursue a different course, and made war upon the guerrillas personally" by chartering Union guerrilla hunters to hunt down their Confederate adversaries. Palmer treated the guerrillas much more like criminal gangs who shared little connection with each other and needed to be destroyed individually. When Palmer captured guerrilla leaders, they were hanged for atrocities they had carried out, expiating their specific and individual guilt on the gallows. While Palmer's course of action proved more effective than Burbridge's General Order No. 59 in ending guerrilla activity, Palmer also benefited from the fact that he assumed command only two months before Appomattox. The Confederate war effort, including its dreams of sparking an uprising of sympathizers in Kentucky, had largely sputtered and died. Palmer thus faced a different task than Burbridge; rather than having to subdue a broad-based insurgency supported by a significant proportion of the population, Palmer had to run to ground a ragtag group of hardcore dead-enders intent more on creating havoc than striking a blow for the Confederacy.[8]

The harshness of Burbridge's antiguerrilla policies, as well as the language he used in talking about the guerrillas, reflected the influence of the legal reframing of guerrilla warfare by Halleck during his time in Missouri. Halleck had tried to draw a line in Missouri between legitimate Confederate soldiers enlisted in the regular Confederate army and self-organized bands of pro-Confederate insurgents. But when the Confederate government in 1862 authorized the activities of such self-organized bands through the Partisan Ranger Act, essentially extending official "cover" to their guerrilla actions, Halleck's distinction went up in smoke. Although he protested to his Confederate counterparts that mere orders could not legitimize illegal acts, Confederate officials maintained their right to name as soldiers anyone they wished and to order them to fight in any way that proved effective. They demanded, in turn, that the Union recognize these combatants as legitimate soldiers entitled to prisoner-of-war status.[9]

When Halleck was promoted to general in chief in the summer of 1862, he asked the legal scholar Francis Lieber to prepare a report on the legitimacy of guerrillas under the international laws of war. Lieber responded with a six thousand-word memorandum that took Halleck's distinction between officially recognized and "self-organized" groups and expanded upon it. Legitimate soldiers, in Lieber's formulation, served in a regular army, were paid and provisioned by that army, operated as part of a durable military organization whose movements were dictated by a central command structure that could enforce discipline on the operational unit, and wore some kind of uniform or indicator of their status as belligerents. Under these criteria, an armed prowler or bushwhacker would not be entitled to the protection of the laws of war, would not be accorded POW status if captured, and could be tried and condemned by a military commission.[10]

Lieber's ideas on guerrilla warfare were incorporated into the so-called Lieber Code, which was issued as General Order No. 100 to the entire Union army in May 1863. Lincoln handed out the Lieber Code to Union officers, sent it to Confederate authorities, and had it published in newspapers across the country.[11] It is clearly under the umbrella of the Lieber Code that Burbridge's actions in Kentucky must be understood. The terms used by Burbridge in General Order No. 59 and General Order No. 8—like "irregular bands of armed men, disconnected from the rebel army," "lawless bands of armed men," "armed prowlers," and references to the "rules and usages of war"—echoed the language in the Lieber Code.[12]

Section IV of the Lieber Code dealt with irregular warfare. In Articles 81–85, Lieber reaffirmed the rules he had previously stated about who counted as a legitimate soldier. Article 81 defined "partisans" as those "wearing the uniform of their army, but belonging to a corps which acts detached from the main body for the purpose of making inroads into their territory occupied by the enemy." For the most part, this described Confederate cavalry raiders like Morgan and Forrest and the soldiers under their command. Such partisans were legitimate combatants and entitled to POW treatment. The remaining four articles described illegitimate combatants. Squads of men "without commission, without being part and portion of the organized hostile army, and without sharing continuously in the war, but who do so with intermitting returns to their homes and avocations . . . are not entitled to the privileges of prisoners of war, but shall be treated summarily as highway robbers or pirates." Scouts who operated on their own—disguised as civilians or as Union soldiers—"are treated as spies, and suffer death." Groups of "armed prowlers . . . who steal within the lines of the hostile army" or who attack communications infrastructure "are not entitled to the privileges of the prisoner of war." These provisions described many of the irregular forces operating in Kentucky, including the post-Cynthiana remnants of Morgan's command, who—even though they might be enlisted in the army or follow unit commanders—had ceased to be "part and portion of the organized hostile army." Finally, "war-rebels," whom Lieber described as those "who rise in arms against the occupying or conquering army . . . whether called upon to do so by their own . . . government or not," were not entitled to POW status. This provision described those civilians and militia members who threw in opportunistically with a group of Confederate raiders or guerrillas during a conflict.[13] These articles, therefore, especially the two aimed at "armed prowlers" and "squads of men [operating] without commission," put most of the irregular forces who operated in Kentucky during Burbridge's tenure as commander on the wrong side of the law of warfare, at least as the federal government understood it.

But Kentucky's place in the Lieber formulation was awkward, because the code talked more about areas occupied by a conquering army than about territory within the Union. It is important to remember that, despite its large portion of Confederate sympathizers and those disaffected with the Union cause, Kentucky never seceded, never constituted "enemy territory," but was always formally regarded as a loyal state. Thus, to understand Burbridge's policies, it is especially important also to understand the Lieber Code's treatment of "war-traitors." Under the Code, a traitor was any person "in a place or district under martial law who . . . gives information of any kind to the enemy, or holds intercourse with him." The traitor is always "severely punished," Lieber wrote. Betraying information to the enemy or voluntarily serving as a guide for the enemy were offenses punishable by death.[14] Burbridge clearly understood those who provided food, aid, and shelter to the guerrillas in Kentucky as war-traitors. This provision doubtless extended to the wives and families of guerrillas, but, unlike his predecessor, Boyle, who got into hot water for his arrests of women, Burbridge was not assailed by his critics for using coercive tactics to get wives to betray their husbands.

Burbridge's policies, which would be so harshly criticized after the war, thus partook of a certain logic within the contemporary Union understanding of legitimate warfare and allowable countermeasures. He believed the irregular bands operating in Kentucky violated the rules and usages of war, whether the men involved were technically enlisted in the Confederate army or not. Under the Lieber Code, these men who made war seasonally, who went home to their own beds and regular vocations between times, and who operated independently of any larger military purpose did not deserve to be regarded as legitimate combatants. Unable to apprehend these offenders directly because of his depleted troop numbers, his assigned mission to protect Kentucky's military and transportation resources, and his inflated concerns with the threat of Confederate invasion, Burbridge used retaliation—an accepted means of enforcement under international law—to try to bring the guerrillas to heel. The measures targeting civilians—including arrests for disloyalty, expropriation of resources, threats of banishment—were also allowable actions against war-traitors in a district under martial law.[15]

Burbridge's harshness also reflected the turn toward "hard war" exemplified in the wartime actions of his commanding general. It was Sherman, as Burbridge's commanding officer, who prodded him to up the ante against Kentucky's guerrillas in 1864. "The recent raid of Morgan and the concurrent acts of men styling themselves Confederate partisans or guerrillas call for determined action on your part," Sherman wrote to Burbridge. "Guerrillas are not soldiers but wild beasts unknown to the usages of war." Channeling Halleck and Lieber, Sherman then laid out the criteria by which to recognize legitimate combatants: men enlisted, armed, officered, uniformed, etc. by a "recognized belligerent," and if detached from the main force, "of sufficient strength, with written orders from some army commander, to do some military thing." Moreover, Sherman said that where the civilian administration was too weak or too unwilling to "protect life and property," it properly fell to the military to undertake the duty. "My own preference was and is that the civil authorities of Kentucky would and could do this . . . but if they will not . . . then we must." Two weeks later, Lincoln renewed the proclamation of martial law in Kentucky, and eleven days after that Burbridge issued General Order No. 59. As historian Daniel Sutherland concluded, "Sherman's directives changed the course of the war in Kentucky."[16]

There is no way to measure precisely the magnitude of the guerrilla war in Kentucky. Individual episodes are scattered in personal letters and diaries, in newspaper accounts and remembrances, and in a variety of official records. Historian Christopher Phillips, however, has suggested a preliminary method to get at an approximation of the number of guerrilla incidents in the western border states. Phillips searched the online edition of the *Official Records of the War of the Rebellion* for references to terms like "guerrilla" and "bushwhacker" to develop a preliminary chronology of the guerrilla conflict. In a 2015 essay, he reported finding 547 incidents in Missouri and Kentucky.[17] This number grossly understates the actual number of incidents, reflecting the selection biases of the editors of the *Official Records* and the reporting biases of Union officers. Still, it is a more precise estimate than terms like "countless" or "innumerable" to describe guerrilla activities. A similar review of the *Official Records* for Kentucky during Burbridge's tenure as commander—searching not just for these terms but for reports of the presence of guerrillas, unconventional Confederate forces ("marauds," as Sherman called them), and of clashes with federal troops—showed seventy incidents mentioned in the *Official Records.* Broadening the survey to include the months of Burbridge's tenure covered by Lewis and Richard Collins in their 1874 *Collins' Historical Sketches of Kentucky,* a year-by-year chronicle of events that the authors deemed interesting or significant in Kentucky's history, largely culled from newspapers, netted an additional seventy-one incidents (see Appendix A).

Again, this preliminary and approximate count derived from these two sources does not provide anything approaching a complete picture. The *Official Records* represent only a selection of federal records, and Lewis and Richard Collins's volume reflects the somewhat idiosyncratic choices of the authors. Moreover, each excludes incidents that never made the papers or involved federal troops, like the robbery of a former Hardin County sheriff by a "secesh" guerrilla band, recorded in March 1864 by diarist Samuel Haycraft, or the September 1864 attempt by a guerrilla group to recruit a young man in Amelia Winn's household in Hancock County. No doubt, there were dozens of local incidents like these all over Kentucky during Burbridge's year as commander.[18]

Nonetheless, if the 141 incidents recorded in these two sources can be taken to represent a minimum baseline of irregular activity in Kentucky during Burbridge's tenure, that still divides out to some kind of incident involving unconventional forces or the sighting of guerrillas every two to three days during Burbridge's command. Irregulars were obviously visible and active.

If those 141 incidents are charted chronologically, it shows a steadily growing guerrilla problem during the months of Burbridge's reign. In the first three months of his command, from mid-January to mid-April, there were but five attacks reported in either the *Official Records* or the Collins history. April 18, of course, was the date that Burbridge ordered the enlistment of black soldiers in Kentucky, and reports of raids and clashes with irregular forces begin to rise steadily after that date. In the three months following the order, there were twenty-four incidents. From mid-July to mid-October, these sources noted forty-five such events. And from mid-October until the end of Burbridge's tenure in February, there were sixty-seven reported incidents.

These numbers are merely suggestive without being conclusive. It seems arguable that black enlistment—and the turn in Kentucky toward emancipationist war goals—sparked some portion of the increased activity by irregular forces. Certainly the status of blacks played a role when Confederate officers tried to recruit in the state. In August 1864, for example, when Adam Johnson was trying to raise men in western Kentucky, he issued a proclamation on the iniquities of Union rule. "Mothers, can you realize an affiliation of your daughters with the African? Young men, can you expect to have any claim to manhood? Can you hope to share the smile or claim the love of the bright-eyed daughters of this famed land of beauty, while those gentle beings are subjected to the insults of Yankee hirelings and negro troops?"[19] These were the common tropes of those who could not accept black equality—the fear of interracial sexual union and the diminution of white manhood by the recognition of black manhood.

This conclusion meshes with Phillips's findings about the broader guerrilla war and its chronological relationship to the Emancipation

Proclamation. Of the 547 incidents that Phillips noted, 86 percent took place after January 1, 1863, leading Phillips to "argue for the centrality of slavery and emancipation in precipitating the fullest expression of . . . [guerrilla] warfare in Missouri and Kentucky."[20]

Emancipation was not the sole reason behind the increase in reported incidents in Kentucky, of course. Desperate efforts to rally Confederate support in Kentucky by sending in regular Confederate troops on cavalry raids accounted for a portion of the activity. A portion was also due to John Hunt Morgan's defeat at Cynthiana and the dispersal of the survivors, and another portion probably grew simply from opportunism on the part of guerrilla raiders as the number of federal troops declined in the state. Finally, dissatisfaction with Burbridge's policies of electoral interference, arrest, and the suppression of dissent also played a role. However, as argued in the previous chapter, since these policies were largely motivated by conservative Kentuckians' resistance to emancipation, it may only serve to reinforce Phillips's conclusions. The Unconditional Unionists certainly believed so. "The agitation in the State by violent partisans of the opposition against negro enlistments . . . has so far demoralized society as to present favorable opportunities for the organization of these [guerrilla] bands," the *Lexington National Unionist* theorized.[21]

Breaking down the 141 incidents by county shows how widespread such incidents were; fifty-eight of Kentucky's 120 counties were specifically listed in the reports. But few counties were actually left untouched. Federal leaders were primarily interested in protecting assets and areas of strategic importance, and for that reason reports of guerrilla activity highlighted these assets and areas. Areas deemed of little strategic value did not make it into federal reports and were offered little protection. What they did receive often occurred *after* a raid had taken place. Local communities frequently pleaded with federal commanders to retain squads of Union soldiers in their community. After the 52nd Kentucky Mounted Infantry attacked and dispersed a band of irregulars, for example, the residents of Hopkinsville and the surrounding area were dismayed to hear that the unit had been ordered to Lexington. "We beg you to reconsider your order and allow them to remain," they asked Burbridge. "The citizens have aided in repelling the rebels, and will now be left to their mercy."[22] A similar plea came from residents of

Williamstown, in Grant County, when they learned that a company of the 30th Kentucky Mounted Infantry was about to be recalled. They have been "doing good service is arresting guerrillas and sympathisers [*sic*], [restoring] confidence to the Union citizens." If allowed to remain, they continued, they would "effectively break up or drive off these thieving murdering bands." A collector of internal revenue in Warren County wrote to Burbridge that he had relocated to Bowling Green for safety because of the presence of federal soldiers there. "[N]ow [I] am told that the 25th Ky Regt . . . have marching orders, which will leave this place wholly unprotected and subject my office as well as myself to the tender mercies of guerrillas and thieving bands."[23]

Even Union commanders did not know what to do when they were ordered to leave an area where guerrillas were active to join a larger force for some other purpose. Lieutenant Colonel J. A. Morrison of the 13th Kentucky Cavalry was ordered in November 1864 to move from Lebanon to Cumberland Gap, where Burbridge was gathering forces for his expedition into northern Tennessee and southwestern Virginia. Morrison could scarce credit the command to depart from Lebanon. "The guerrillas are around here in several squads committing atrocious deeds of murder of citizens and soldiers. Thirteen citizens were murdered yesterday in the vicinity of Springfield."[24] In a similar vein, the colonel commanding the post at Bowling Green dispatched a note to General Schofield after the 26th Kentucky Infantry was ordered to Nashville. The order "leaves this post almost without troops," he reported. "Can the 26th Kentucky remain here?"[25] Higher-ups in the Union army did not have much sympathy for such pleas. "We cannot afford to maintain armies to protect people against guerrillas," Sherman said.[26]

One problem with throwing the local communities back onto their own resources for protection from guerrillas was that this exposed those who took up community defense to retaliation. A citizen of Monroe County, along the central border with Tennessee, gave voice to these difficulties in a letter to Governor Bramlette in June 1864. The county's efforts to raise a company of militia had thus far yielded only thirty-five volunteers, R. J. Maxey wrote. The main problem with recruitment was that the colonel planned to drill the men six days each month and then send them home. Many "say they would be living in danger all the time if at home for there are frequent small raids from . . . gurillers [*sic*] in the south portion of our county." The men wished to be kept together as a unit once organized, but the colonel told them that was not how the militia law worked. When D. W. Lindsey, Bramlette's adjutant general, responded, he backed up the colonel's interpretation of the law.[27]

Other local citizens asked for state-issued weapons for protection from guerrillas. But again the state militia law frustrated their desires. No arms were issued until a properly organized militia company was enrolled. John Sallee, county clerk of Wayne County, blamed the lack of weaponry for the lack of militia organization in his county. "It would be somewhat hazardous to attempt anything of the kind unarmed and without any ammunition and no chance to get any[.] Would be liable to a raid any day by Guerrillas." A similar lament came from a citizen of Shelbyville. A local captain said he could raise fifty men, if armed and equipped. Such a company would "soon releive [*sic*] the citizens of their fears" as the county now had "several squads of Guerrillas and horse thieves." Adjutant General Lindsey was unimpressed. "We have invariably found that if citizens are not willing to organize, in the simple way provided by law, to enable them to get arms, they are sure not to do so after arms are obtained."[28]

Another problem with relying on organized state forces was that a local company was liable to be called into federal service. Citizens from several counties wrote to Bramlette or Lindsey and asked permission to form an independent company. "We want to be detailed expressly for to [*sic*] defend our neighborhood," wrote an Ohio County veteran. From Meade County, John Stuart wrote to Lindsey that "our experience has been that as fast as a man gets under the control of general authority he is needed at Louisville or Lexington or on a Rail Road and that is the last that is seen of him until he is killed or dies or is discharged to come home and thereafter busy himself in dodging bands of neighborhood marauders." A similar complaint came from a group of residents of Smithland, in Livingston County. "Our portion of the state has raised near four Regiments that have been sent off to distant fields, while our district has received little or no protection. . . . We wish to be authorised to raise a Regiment to protect ourselves and our families." Reporting on complaints from residents of various river counties—susceptible to guerrilla activity because of Union boat traffic on the Ohio River—the *Louisville Daily Journal* wrote that these "counties . . . have sent about one third of their population subject to militia duty into the federal army, and they are now in the front with Sherman, Banks, and others . . . while their homes are left not merely unprotected, but inviting these rebel raids."[29]

A third and more fundamental problem also derailed attempts to rely on local forces to repel guerrillas: an underlying suspicion of the local troops' true loyalties, a suspicion felt by federal commanders toward state officials and by Kentuckians toward their neighbors. In December 1864, Halleck wrote to Grant that "loyal Kentuckians say that if Bramlette's militia are armed, a large portion of them will join the rebels."[30] Indeed, it was ultimately a clash between Burbridge and Bramlette over state forces that provided Lincoln with the excuse to get rid of Burbridge. Bramlette had called for the organization of a Home Guard to protect the state's residents from guerrillas. Burbridge, in February 1865, cited his authority under martial law to disband troops "organized, equipped, and maintained" under state authority to stop Bramlette's plan. Bramlette protested this "unwarranted assumption of power by an imbecile commander" to Stanton, who quickly slapped Burbridge down, saying his order was premature and ordering him to revoke it. Burbridge did so but told Stanton that the state troops raised by Bramlette in the last twenty days "are worse than useless. . . . [A]ll [are] more or less disposed to marauding and plundering; and the inducements held out to enlist in the State service are preventing enlistments in the U.S. Service." Burbridge's haste in lashing out at Bramlette's troops, however, resulted in Lincoln replacing him with Palmer. Ironically, the orders sent to Palmer by Stanton giving him command of Kentucky stated that the troops raised under Bramlette's authority for use within the state were "prohibited by law." So Burbridge was right, just at the wrong time.[31]

There was also a lot of suspicion among the people themselves about the true loyalties of those who volunteered to serve in the local forces. Robert Cochran of Spencer County initially reported favorably on the Unionist loyalties of those enrolled in the county's organized guard, but in August 1864 he wrote to Lindsey that he had been mistaken. "The best and most loyal citizens" of the county, Cochran wrote, were against the company being organized and armed. Some of the enrollees had ties to the guerrillas. The captain of the company was alleged to have served under Confederate general Sterling Price in Missouri, then later joined and deserted from a Union cavalry regiment.[32]

But a more common accusation against the local troops was that they preyed upon the citizens themselves, particularly by forcibly requisitioning ("pressing") horses and occasionally making away with slaves. A slaveowner in Greenville, in Muhlenberg County, complained to Bramlette that the county's Home Guards had come to his house, treated his wife disrespectfully, took his wagon after loading it with corn, took his manservant, and raped his female slave. But just a few weeks earlier, the Muhlenberg County constable had written to Bramlette to praise the very same unit. "For guriller [*sic*] hunters tha [*sic*] cannot be beat." Recently, he had heard rumors that the unit was to be disbanded and he protested to Bramlette that it would leave the county unprotected.[33] In September 1864, Burbridge confessed that it was "humiliating in the extreme" to hear that local Home Guards were preying upon citizens, as were some squads of federal soldiers. "That the traitorous guerrilla robbers and thieves do this is to be expected," but not those "armed in the cause of Union and Law," he wrote in General Order No. 3, commanding vigilance against such activity by his officers.[34]

One of the most active and effective militia units in the guerrilla war, the Hall's Gap Battalion commanded by John Bridgewater, came under similar suspicion. Spencer County judge Jonathan Davis laid out an entire case against Bridgewater's oppressive practices to Adjutant General Lindsey in December 1864, with numerous affidavits from citizens alleging that Bridgewater had made off with their horses, slaves, or other property. "I have never known Captain Bridgewater to capture any rebel or his horse but I have known him to capture noncombatants and particularly their horses," wrote one aggrieved citizen. Immediately after sending off the affidavits to Lindsey, Judge Davis reported that Bridgewater had hunted him down in the streets of Taylorsville and charged him "with being a scoundrel[,] a liar[,] and a thief."[35]

Underlying these charges and countercharges were fundamental ideological and political differences. By complaining to state authorities about abuses committed by state troops or federal troops, those who sympathized with and supported the Confederate cause could hamstring military efforts to suppress Confederate irregulars. "I understand that I . . . am soon to be arrested for pressing horses from citizens," wrote one Ohio County officer to Lindsey. "It may be rong [*sic*] to press horses but I am thoroughly convinced that we can accomplish nothing unless we press horses when our horses give down." At least one citizen agreed: the officer's "opposers are Secesh and copperheads or union men with wooll [*sic*] in their teeth."[36] When the turn toward emancipation cleaved Kentucky Unionists into Conservatives and Unconditionals, those who opposed emancipation dreaded military authority being given to their former allies, whom they now regarded as dangerously radical. From Mercer County, a citizen complained to Bramlette about the two men who were proposing to raise an independent company to help fight guerrillas in the county. "[T]hey will treat many men in this county cruelly," he warned the governor about granting them a commission. "[T]hey are both strong for Lincoln, and will be the cause in the ensuing election to intimidate many from voting for McClelland [*sic*]. . . . They are not the kind of men that should have power. . . . I am astonished at our provost marshal for encouraging them."[37]

State troops distrusted alternately by federal officers and by their own citizens, federal troops spread too thin to stop attacks on citizens, and an energetic guerrilla insurgency that found ample support from the local population all combined to render any military response to the guerrilla problem largely ineffective. These issues were largely outside of Burbridge's control and he had to look for alternative strategies to curb guerrilla activity, especially with a commander like Sherman telling him to get tough with the guerrillas and their citizen supporters.

Burbridge's response, as indicated earlier, was to introduce a kind of quasi-judicial terror to deter guerrilla attacks: General Order No. 59. Issued in mid-July, at least five executions took place under its auspices by the end of the month. Just over half of the roughly sixty recorded victims of General Order No. 59, however, died between November 2 and November 19, at a time when guerrilla violence was also peaking (see Appendix B). After November, the public retaliatory executions virtually stopped, replaced by the take-no-prisoners ethic of General Order No. 8. As previously described, General Order No. 59 prescribed that for every Unionist citizen killed in a guerrilla attack, four prisoners were to be removed from the military prisons and publicly shot to death near the scene. The prisoners, presumed to have been adjudged guerrillas by a military commission, were to pay the ultimate price for a crime committed by others.

Prisoners were chosen by random draw, according to postwar accounts. In 1876, the *Midway Sun* printed "A War Reminiscence" that described the execution of four men for a guerrilla attack in Woodford County. The four were selected by lots cast among a large group of prisoners being held in Lexington. Local historian Bryan Bush, describing one set of General Order No. 59 executions carried out in September 1864, wrote that "the prisoners were unlucky to draw black beans from a box containing hundreds of white beans." A Louisville tobacco factor recalled in an 1896 reminiscence that he "drew the bean twice," but was spared execution through the intervention of some Union officers.[38]

The postwar criticisms heaped upon Burbridge's executions focused on four main issues: First, critics charged that those shot had not received any form of hearing or trial. In 1882, a newspaper dispute between Burbridge and Congressman Joseph Blackburn, a former Confederate officer, gave rise to several scathing commentaries on Burbridge's reign in Kentucky. John Neal, a former Confederate, remembered being taken to "the butcher pen" in Louisville, where he was ordered to be shot without any trial. (He, too, was saved by timely intervention from a Union officer.) A *Courier-Journal* article stated simply that "Gen. Burbridge murdered forty or fifty Confederates and private citizens in the State without trial even by court-martial." The *Frankfort Yeoman* attributed Kentuckians' hostility to Burbridge in part to his "bloody record in executing, without form of trial or authority of law, civil or military, numbers of Confederate soldiers and other prisoners." Basil Duke, who had served under John Hunt Morgan during the war and who rose to prominence after the war as a corporate lawyer and spokesperson for the Lost Cause, wrote in February 1882 that "I firmly believed, and I still believe, that he murdered in cold blood, without trial or any pretext even of retaliation, very many citizens and prisoners of war."[39]

In his attempts to push back against these criticisms, Burbridge maintained that all the men who were executed had been tried and condemned by a military commission. A pro-Burbridge article from the *Philadelphia Press* that appeared during his feud with Blackburn stated that "the simple facts, when fully and fairly presented, . . . completely exonerate the general," going on to conclude that "in all cases, when men were taken prisoner by Gen. Burbridge's troops, they were tried by court-martial. No prisoner was ever shot under Burbridge without trial." In one of Burbridge's responses to Blackburn, published in the *Courier-Journal* in January 1882, Burbridge wrote, "As I informed you in my previous letter, not a man was put to death by my order, without having first been tried and convicted by a regularly organized court-martial."[40]

Burbridge's detractors demanded the proof. If courts-martial were held, where were the records? Referring to the execution of four men near the town of Midway, a *Courier-Journal* letter writer asked, "Can Gen. B [*sic*] produce any recorded proofs of a court-martial or any lawful tribunal which condemned these unfortunates to such a horrible death? He certainly can not, as they were unconscious of their terrible fate until a few moments before their death."[41] Another letter writer during the public controversy between Blackburn and Burbridge wished to hear from "some of the honorable citizens of Kentucky, who Burbridge says sat on the court-martial which tried these men, to sustain his assertion that not a man was shot by his order without having been first regularly tried and condemned."[42]

Burbridge never publicly produced the court records, though he defended himself by publishing the orders and endorsements from Sherman, Stanton, Lincoln, and others demanding that he crack down on Kentucky's guerrillas and applauding his efforts.[43] In addition, there are fragmentary records of military tribunals in various sources. During the summer of 1864, the *Louisville Daily Journal* published several stories about the capture of "guerrillas" or "bushwhackers" with the accompanying note that they were being forwarded to Lexington for trial by a military commission. "From the number of prisoners forwarded to Lexington, we should judge that the military courts there are doing good work," the paper stated.[44] In addition, some of the communications between Burbridge and his officers collected in the *Official Records* indicate that investigations occurred and evidence was gathered on guerrillas who were apprehended and imprisoned. "The evidence in Goulder's case is positive," Burbridge's adjutant wrote to General Hugh Ewing in July 1864. "[T]he execution of his sentence, 'to be shot to death,' to be at once carried out."[45] The language of "evidence" and "sentence" clearly indicate there was some type of judicial proceeding in Goulder's case. (Some confusion attended Goulder's fate, however. Three days later, Burbridge telegraphed Ewing again, asking, "Have the men been shot that I ordered? If not, have them shot at once, except Goulder. Send him to Lexington."[46]). Similarly, a report on a clash between federal troops and guerrillas "claiming to belong to Morgan" that resulted in the capture of eighteen prisoners noted that the prisoners would be forwarded "as soon as depositions are taken."[47] Depositions are an evidence-gathering process; what cannot be known is whether the evidence was used in a subsequent trial or whether the taking of depositions constituted the only legal proceeding before the prisoners were sent on to Louisville or Lexington.

None of this clears Burbridge of the charge that some of the prisoners executed in retaliation for guerrilla actions did not receive a legal hearing. Military commissions were supposed to keep written records of their proceedings and forward them to the commanding officer for approval, who was then supposed to send them to the judge advocate general in Washington for final review. In fact, historian Mark Neely marveled at the existence of "careful records of trials by military commission," which he considered an "anomaly . . . in the context of the other hopelessly incomplete records of civilians held by military authority" during the war. Neely found, however, that even these careful records included "only a handful of Kentuckians." Since the vast majority of names of Burbridge's victims do not appear in the registers for the records described by Neely, it seems highly unlikely that all the men in Kentucky's military prisons underwent such formal proceedings or that the proceedings to which they were subject were always captured on paper and forwarded through the appropriate chain of command. In any event, the complete set of transcripts never materialized.[48]

Most likely many of these investigations did not even merit the title of military commission. In the journals kept by General Hugh Ewing, commander of the region west of the L&N Railroad, for example, he refers to numerous instances where he arrested, examined, and either released or sent on to Louisville numerous civilians on his own initiative, absent the formal structure of a military commission and without written records of the proceedings.[49] Arriving at the prison, it is possible that these prisoners were simply assumed to have already gone through a more stringent legal process. Such rudimentary examinations, falling far short of basic standards of due process, would not have quieted Burbridge's critics, but they do undercut the idea that Burbridge merely executed innocent men with no evidence. Moreover, in his communications with his subordinates, Burbridge was clear: He wanted "all captured guerrillas to be held for trial by military commission."[50]

When the charges and countercharges were flying between Burbridge and Blackburn in 1882, a newspaper reporter looked up one of the "honorable citizens" who Burbridge mentioned as sitting on the military tribunals and asked him about the truth of Burbridge's statements. John Mason Brown had been a brigade commander in Kentucky during the crucial months of 1864. In 1882 he was a prominent lawyer in Louisville. Burbridge had said that Brown had sat on the courts-martial of two men who were executed: Ferguson and McGrew. In his response, Brown tried to distance himself from Burbridge, but at the same time confirmed a portion of the general's account. Brown had, he said, no knowledge of the Ferguson case, but as to the McGrew case (referred to as McGill in Burbridge's letter, but who was actually named McGee[51]), he "was arrested within the lines of my brigade as a spy" whose "principal object" was "the assassination" of a regimental commander in Brown's brigade. "McGrew was tried by a drum-head court"[52] composed of Brown and two other officers, "convicted as a spy, and . . . executed as such." Brown mentioned no records or transcripts or approvals by higher-ups before the sentence was carried out.[53]

It is interesting to note that McGee/McGrew was executed as a spy, as was Walter Ferguson, the other man mentioned by Burbridge. Although both men are included in the list of those Burbridge had executed, the accusation of spying puts them into a different category than those who were executed under General Order No. 59, who were shot in retaliation for guerrilla actions.

The hanging of Walter Ferguson was one of the most controversial of the executions Burbridge ordered, both because of Ferguson's youth and because several members of Ferguson's family and a delegation of Lexington women made personal pleas to Burbridge to spare him. "Does not the ghost of Walter Ferguson haunt Burbridge? Can he forget the appeals the ladies of Lexington made to him in behalf of his youth?" editorialized the *Cynthiana News* in 1867.[54] Years later, Kentucky's US senator (and former Confederate general) John Stuart Williams told reporters that Ferguson's killing "would forever damn [Burbridge]."[55]

Ironically, given the charge that Burbridge's victims were killed without trial or other legal proceeding, the Ferguson case did generate a full transcript. A Lexington native, Walter Ferguson had joined the Confederate army when he was just fifteen, had ridden with John Hunt Morgan, and had been cut off from the command after Cynthiana. He then shed his Confederate uniform, made his way to Louisville, where he lodged for eight days at the St. Cloud Hotel under the name Walter Carroll, and searched for a way either to get to Canada or to locate the beaten and scattered remnants of his regiment. On July 5, 1864, someone alerted the head of the federal police force in Louisville of Ferguson's true identity. Accosting Ferguson on Jefferson Street, the detective arrested him and sent him under guard to the provost marshal's office, where he was examined preliminarily and held for trial by military commission. The commission, made up of five Union officers and a judge advocate, met in Lexington in August. Ferguson was defended by Lexington lawyers Richard H. Prewitt and James C. Morris.

Both prosecution and defense relied on the Lieber Code during the proceedings. The prosecution cited Lieber's paragraph 83, which stated that a single soldier in civilian dress found within enemy lines was to be treated as a spy. The defense cited Lieber's paragraph 88, which more specifically defined a spy as "a person who secretly, in disguise or under false pretence, seeks information with the intention of communicating it to the enemy."[56] In twenty-two closely written pages, Morris argued that the prosecution had not proven Ferguson's intention to act as a spy, that Ferguson's effort to conceal himself by trading his uniform for civilian dress and going under an assumed name was just common sense, and that Ferguson's mere presence in Louisville was not sufficient evidence that he was a spy. In just four pages of rebuttal, the judge advocate declared such objections irrelevant. A Confederate soldier in civilian dress within enemy lines was, *pace* Lieber, a spy. Before the commission could pronounce sentence, however, Ferguson escaped. The escape seemed only to confirm his guilt and, reapprehended, he was hanged on November 15 at the Lexington fairgrounds.[57]

Ferguson's case highlighted a second criticism leveled by Burbridge's enemies. In addition to the lack of due process, they charged that many of those killed had not been guerrillas at all, but—like Ferguson—legitimate Confederate soldiers entitled to prisoner-of-war status. "Gen. Burbridge says no regular Confederate soldier was shot," stated one letter published in the *Courier-Journal.* "Now these four men shot here in Midway in retaliation for the murder of old man Adam Harper were regular Confederate soldiers."[58] Senator John Stuart Williams told the newspaper, "Why, there are monuments up in the graveyards in Kentucky that such and such a Confederate soldier was murdered by Burbridge."[59] The stain of such accusations lingered. Two years after Burbridge's death, the *Courier-Journal* reviewed his policy of retaliatory killings and concluded that they were "not executions of marauders, who provoked no sympathy, but of brave soldiers of the regular Confederate armies."[60] And in 1910, at a reunion of Confederate veterans in Georgetown, the reporter proclaimed that "on this historic site Gen. Steve Burbridge ordered Confederate soldiers to be shot."[61]

It is true that of the sixty-one men listed in Appendix B, roughly half were enlisted in the Confederate army. John Neal, one ex-prisoner, wrote that he was a member of Captain Bob Logan's company in Colonel J. Warren Grigsby's regiment when he was granted leave to come home to Kentucky. He was captured en route and narrowly escaped execution.[62] One correspondent culled accounts of Burbridge's various executions from *Collins' Historical Sketches* to demonstrate Burbridge's atrocities. Among these he cites the execution of Lindsey Duke Buckner, a Confederate captain in Colonel James Chenoweth's regiment, Thomas Hunt, a Confederate enlistee captured while traveling to join his regiment, and a party of four captured while on their way to join the Confederate army.[63]

This accusation goes to the heart of who was considered a legitimate combatant during the Civil War. Several historians have attempted to parse those who participated in irregular warfare and fit them into a typology of categories, ranging from the legitimacy of the "partisan ranger" to the illegitimate "bushwhacker," with the "guerrilla" falling somewhere in between. Robert Mackey, for example, distinguished between partisans—"elite conventional forces given an unconventional role"—and guerrillas, whom he described in Lieber-esque terms as "self-constituted sets of armed men . . . [that formed] [n]o integrant part of the organized army." John Hunt Morgan and John Singleton

Mosby he considered partisans, while the Bands of Ten called into existence by General Thomas Hindman in Arkansas he considered to be guerrillas. Mackey noted that, for the most part, "Partisans, when captured in gray uniforms, were normally treated as combatants, while guerrillas were not."[64]

These writers admit that the typologies are not perfect, that the lines are blurry, and that men could conceivably fit into one category at a certain point in the war and into a different category at another point in the war. In reviewing the early career of Adam Johnson, who was eventually a commissioned officer and received authority from Richmond to form a partisan ranger band in Kentucky, Scott Tarnowieckyi concluded that Johnson "slid along [the] continuum," at different times a bushwhacker, a guerrilla, and a partisan.[65] The same might be said of officers who operated in the state after Morgan's defeat. Lieutenant Colonel George Jessee was a regular Confederate officer cut off from Morgan's retreat who sought refuge in Owen County. He had orders to gather the scattered remnants of Morgan's command, but he also led periodic in-state raids against Union targets.[66] These raids were not continuous, and some of the men associated with Jessee returned to their homes between raids. So, while he was a regular officer, some of his activities in Kentucky met Lieber's definition of a guerrilla. Moreover, if the men he commanded were picked up off the battlefield—in ones and twos—could they claim POW status simply by the fact that they had joined the Confederate forces at some point? Under the terms of the Lieber Code, the validity of such a claim would be highly questionable.

Burbridge's critics took the position that all who enlisted and wore the Confederate uniform at any time were at all times legitimate Confederate soldiers, and therefore entitled to prisoner-of-war status. They did not accept that enemy soldiers behind the lines of the army, detached from any unit, and without orders or capability to achieve any military objective had no legitimate military reason to be in Kentucky. In contrast, by Halleck's terms (who had complained that Confederate commissions could not pardon guerrilla actions in Missouri), by Lieber's terms (who insisted that legal combatants had to be under orders from a military chain of command), and by Sherman's terms (who told Burbridge that legitimate soldiers were officered, uniformed, and capable of accomplishing some military purpose), these men were not entitled to prisoner-of-war status. Thus, Burbridge's actions regarding men captured off the battlefield in Kentucky were within the laws of war as articulated by the federal government.

Adam Johnson recognized and resented this assertion by federal officials. "Already thousands of our gallant [Kentucky] sons have armed themselves . . . and are determined to strike a blow for liberty," he proclaimed in a local newspaper. "All such are branded by the Lincolnites as guerrillas. I can assure you . . . that all who are now enrolled under me are recognized by the Confederate government." In August 1864, in fact, Johnson traveled to New Albany, Indiana, and sent a message to General Hugh Ewing, the Union commander in Louisville, requesting clarification of General Order No. 59. What soldiers would be defined as guerrillas? Were all Confederate soldiers to be held responsible for the acts of all lawless men? Although Johnson signed the note as the commander of Confederate troops in southern Kentucky, Ewing rejected the overture, telling Johnson he was "distant from Confederate lines, with a small force composed of irresponsible men, and, no proof existing to the contrary, he should be regarded as acting on no authority but his own."[67] For Ewing—and for Burbridge—what mattered was not Johnson's self-conception as a legitimate combatant but the "Lincolnite" definition.

Thirdly, critics of the executions ordered by Burbridge under General Order No. 59 pointed out that the men selected had no connection to the atrocities for which they were being forced to suffer the penalty. When a man named Adam Harper was shot down by a guerrilla band under Sue Mundy, four prisoners were selected to be taken and shot near Midway, where the attack occurred. According to an account published in 1882 during the controversy with Blackburn, Harper's relatives begged Burbridge to relent and spare the men chosen. "Every sensible man and woman in the country knew that they were not responsible and were innocent."[68] Basil Duke, weighing in on Blackburn's side, wrote that Burbridge "knew, and his advisers, aiders, and abettors well knew[,] that these unfortunates were guiltless of the crimes for which they were made to suffer."[69]

While punishing the "guiltless" violates standard civilian due process, reprisals against enemy personnel in order to prevent violations of the laws of war are allowed even to this day. In Burbridge's understanding,

General Order No. 59 retaliated against men held in Union custody for acts in violation of the laws of war committed by guerrillas who were not in Union custody. As Halleck wrote in 1864, the law of retaliation sought "not primarily the punishment of the individual offender, but to deter others from a like crime." Thus punishment might fall upon "a city, an army, or an entire community . . . for the illegal acts of its . . . individual members." In an 1865 article, Lieber wrote that "the terrible character of retaliation in war" was that "it strikes those who are not or may not be guilty of the outrage we wish to put an end to." Article 27 of the Lieber Code stated that "the law of war can no more wholly dispense of retaliation than can the law of nations. . . . A reckless enemy often leaves to his opponent no other means of securing himself against the repetition of barbarous outrage." Article 59 stated simply that "all prisoners of war are liable to the infliction of retaliatory measures." Given that, as "guerrillas," Burbridge's prisoners were not viewed even as prisoners of war, the infliction of retaliatory measures against them—even if they were not implicated in a specific guerrilla attack—could hardly have been interpreted, on the federal side, as a violation of the laws of war.[70]

Finally, Duke and others also accused Burbridge of corruption, specifically that he used threats of random execution to extort cash payments from the prisoners. Those who paid up were spared. "[I]n numerous instances, blood-money was demanded and paid, which S. G. Burbridge shared; and many innocent men were shot to terrify others into buying their lives," Duke charged. James Blackburn, brother of the congressman with whom Burbridge clashed, told a newspaper reporter that Burbridge "was not acting even under a mistaken or fanatical patriotism. . . . He has had men selected to be shot, and then UPON PAYMENT OF MONEY would take the one who was able to purchase his life from among the victims and supply his place by some other prisoner." A writer in the *Courier* in 1868 asked, "If a man was so bad he endangered the safety of the Union, and it became necessary . . . to put him in prison, how much was our Union cause promoted by letting some favored gentleman pluck him out of $500 or $1000 and then let him out to run at large?"[71]

It seems likely that there was corruption in the military prison system in Kentucky. Corruption was endemic in nineteenth-century America, and almost every prison system is warped by some degree of corruption. In October 1864, Schofield wrote to Sherman from Louisville that "there seems to have been criminal looseness, and, in some instances, gross corruption in the administration of military justice [in Kentucky]. Public enemies of the worst character have received their liberty by payment of large fees to lawyers having personal influence with the commanding officers." Schofield, who was no fan of Burbridge, ordered an investigation into the "transactions of the police and provost-marshals" and had some of the offenders arrested. He was not investigating Burbridge, he said, "who has been acting in reference to the arrest and disposition of disloyal persons under direct orders from your [Sherman's] headquarters." Nonetheless, he added, "the charges relative to corruption in the release of prisoners involve the official character of Brevet-Major-General Burbridge."[72]

It is very difficult to establish the historical truth or falsity of such a charge, since corruption by its nature was meant to be hidden from public view. Regarding Burbridge, a federal grand jury empaneled in Kentucky after the war to "look into the conduct of all Federal officers" cleared Burbridge of participating personally in corrupt practices. One of the grand jurors wrote to Burbridge in October 1865 relating the proceedings. "After a protracted session of sixteen days and the examination of a large number of witnesses we found no shadow of grounds for the charge against you," he stated. Witnesses "gave it as their opinion that no man dare approach you with an offer of a bribe and if he did they thought it would be at the peril of his life." In addition, most of the postwar accusations of corruption were notably vague as to the names of the officers who arranged the payoffs. When a specific person was mentioned—as was Colonel Marcellus Mundy in an article in the *Maysville Eagle* in January 1868—other outlets equally hostile to Burbridge leapt to the defense of the accused officer. The *Eagle* charged Mundy with being Burbridge's "*receiver,* and upon payment of a large sum of money the Colonel engaged to secure the release of the condemned guerrilla." The next day the *Louisville Courier*—no friend to Burbridge—defended Mundy, pointing out that the colonel had by 1864 resigned from the army and was working as a lawyer in Louisville. "When he is called the 'receiver for Burbridge's blood money,' injustice is certainly done him. . . . Mundy procured the release of many of those that were arrested, by becoming personally bail for them. . . . It is hardly reasonable for any one to blame the lawyer for taking a fee for a successful defense of a criminal."[73]

Money thus definitely changed hands, but the nature of those payments is less than clear. Loyalty oaths and bonds for good behavior earned the release of some accused of disloyalty; lawyers were retained and legal fees evidently paid by some of those who could afford it; bail was posted and some prisoners emerged from jail as a result, while others—too poor or too bereft of friends and acquaintances to raise the funds—faced the cruelty inherent in random executions. In the minds of those who denounced Burbridge after the end of the war, all this became "blood money." As commanding officer, Burbridge must rightly bear responsibility for any bribes that were taken by the officers under his charge, but the charge that prisoners were systematically fleeced to unjustly enrich Burbidge was largely a fiction in the service of the ideology of the Lost Cause in Kentucky.

Burbridge must also bear responsibility for the inescapable conclusion that General Order No. 59 did not reduce guerrilla activity. In addition to their other criticisms, Duke and other anti-Burbridge writers did not hesitate to point this out. Writing of those who were executed under Burbridge's order, Duke wrote that "their deaths in no wise curbed the conduct of the guerrillas."[74] Retaliation had no impact because the guerrillas obeyed no central command. Too focused on coordinated invasion by a Confederate force, Burbridge misunderstood the guerrilla threat for much of his tenure. Viewing them as "wild beasts," as Sherman termed them, while at the same time expecting retaliatory measures to bring them to heel—whether by eroding their local support or by motivating the Confederate government to call them home—was inherently contradictory.[75] By October 1864, Burbridge evidently recognized the contradiction and hoisted the black flag in the form of General Order No. 8.

General Order No. 8 made no pretense of retaliation; it was intended to be punitive. Field commanders were ordered to execute summarily guerrillas captured in the field and were forbidden from taking any as prisoners. General Order No. 8 marked a shift toward a guerrilla-hunting strategy from General Order No. 59's reprisal strategy, and presaged the policy that John Palmer, Burbridge's successor in Kentucky, would follow. There was not a clean break between the two approaches, however. Retaliatory executions of prisoners continued after the issuance of General Order No. 8 and, in fact, summary executions in the field had been tacitly allowed before its formal issuance. In August 1864, for example, John Mason Brown asked his divisional commander for clarification on Sherman's mandate to treat guerrillas "as wild beasts." The response: "You are directed to shoot well-known guerrillas anywhere and at any time and will be doing a service to the citizens and the army."[76]

Burbridge issued General Order No. 8 in the aftermath of his first expedition to Saltville. It is interesting to speculate about whether the murder of black troops the day after Saltville and the subsequent murders of convalescing soldiers by Champ Ferguson influenced Burbridge's decision. Perhaps he was so appalled by the massacre of the wounded that he opted for the more severe tactic of summary execution in the field rather than for the niceties—however sparse—of military commissions. Again, because Burbridge left behind so little regarding his personal motivations, the answer to this question remains unknowable. Available evidence does show, however, that he remembered Saltville's aftermath with bitterness and regarded Ferguson as beyond the pale of civilized treatment. In an exchange of letters with Basil Duke in early 1865, Duke charged that Burbridge was unjustly holding Duke's men responsible for the outrages at Saltville. Burbridge replied that Duke's information "that I propose to hold your command responsible for the murder of negro soldiers . . . at Saltville . . . is incorrect. I have ascertained what troops are responsible for the outrages . . . and should the opportunity occur, I shall hold them to a strict accountability." He also told Duke that should Champ Ferguson or any of his band "fall into the hands of U.S. forces they will not be treated as prisoners." Shortly after the war, Ferguson was arrested, tried for crimes committed both during and after the war, and was hanged in Nashville on October 20.[77]

General Order No. 8 also showed that, in spite of his continuing fear of a Confederate invasion of the state, Burbridge evidently felt confident enough by October 1864 to devote more troops to antiguerrilla activities. He may have also felt—though there is no direct evidence of this—that a more visible federal guerrilla hunting effort would help reassure Unionist voters in the upcoming presidential election. After the second—and climactic—battle at Saltville, most of Burbridge's orders to his field commanders focused on countering guerrillas. By February 1865 he had announced a new policy of stationing troops in every county to suppress guerrilla activity, and his adjutant could write to a concerned citizen of Hartford, Kentucky, that "there being now no danger of an invasion of the State by the enemy, the whole force under his [Burbridge's] command will be employed in active efforts to exterminate these thieving bands."[78] February, of course, was too late for Burbridge, as orders had already been issued for his replacement by Palmer.

Kentucky was subject to "marauds," as Sherman called them, throughout the war, both from Confederate cavalry and from guerrillas banded together into larger units (and sometimes from combinations of the two). In December 1864, Confederate cavalry under General Hylan B. Lyon rode into the state, attacking Hopkinsville and conscripting men for the Confederate forces. Also in December, a force under George Jessee attacked various Kentucky river towns.[79] More common, however, and occurring alongside these larger-scale confrontations, were ongoing local conflicts. Localized guerrilla bands—or sometimes just one or two guerrillas in the neighborhood—would pull off a raid or an attack on a group of Unionist citizens or soldiers, a squad of soldiers would be detached, and a gun battle or escape or execution would ensue.

An example of how General Order No. 8 was put into practice came in Henderson County in 1864. A posse of armed citizens captured five men who had committed depredations around the town of Henderson. The captured men at first claimed civilian status and asked that they be turned over to the civil authorities. The citizens did so, but the local military commander—citing General Order No. 8—demanded that they be turned over to him. The men had at different times claimed to be Confederate soldiers separated from their command, and the colonel commanding the local army post ordered them executed. A squad of black soldiers marched them to the execution spot, where the colonel "informed the trembling victims that the office of an execution was not a pleasant one, but that the order was mandatory upon him, and that they obviously came under its provisions."[80]

Another example of how General Order No. 8 worked at the local level was revealed in a postwar court case in the autumn of 1866. Cyrus W. Farris had served as provost marshal for Gallatin County during the war. In 1866, he worked as a federal mail agent, delivering mail via steamboat to the various small river towns along the Ohio. In September, as the *General Buell* pulled into the town of Ghent, Farris was pulled off the ship by the Gallatin County deputy sheriff, who had a warrant for Farris's arrest for the murder of John James Morrow and John W. Baker during the waning years of the war. The *Buell's* crew resisted the sheriff's demand and proceeded upriver to Warsaw. There the deputy—a former Confederate soldier and the brother of John James Morrow—had rallied ninety to one hundred townsmen (all guerrillas and former rebel soldiers, the newspapers said) and threatened to open fire on the *Buell* if the crew did not surrender Farris, who was arrested and held for examination in Warsaw.[81]

Such postwar legal actions were not uncommon. As mentioned above, at least one federal grand jury in Kentucky investigated wartime actions by Union military personnel. According to congressional testimony by Representative Samuel McKee, over three thousand of "those who had been loyal to the Union during the Civil War" faced prosecution in Kentucky for their wartime actions. McKee told his House colleagues that as soon as a Confederate soldier returned to the state, "he at once seizes upon the first opportunity to harass in the courts of the State those who during the war have been engaged in defending the flag."[82] The prosecution against Farris was eventually dropped, but Farris's forcible abduction caught journalists' attention, and the subsequent investigation showed how General Order No. 8 functioned.

The incident for which Farris was arrested occurred in 1864. As provost marshal, Farris testified, "it was necessary for me to enroll and recruit negroes. . . . The fact of my recruiting negroes in Gallatin County rendered me obnoxious to the citizens of that county." Farris learned that Morrow—"a deserter from both armies . . . and a guerrilla for all intents and purposes as decided by the authorities"—threatened to kill him for recruiting two of his mother's slaves. Farris alerted Lieutenant William Johnson, commanding a squad of the 45th Kentucky Infantry stationed at Warsaw, of the threats. Johnson's squad was charged, according to Farris, "with carrying out Gen. Burbridge's order, regarding guerrillas and those harboring them." As Farris explained upon questioning, General Order No. 8 required—upon penalty of dishonorable dismissal—soldiers to "shoot down all guerrillas and all persons harboring them."[83]

The next morning, Farris accompanied the soldiers as they rode out to locate Morrow. Forcing a reluctant neighbor to lead the soldiers to the woods where Morrow was hiding out, the troops formed a skirmish line and began moving through the woods. Morrow was raised at the far right of the line, disobeyed an order to halt, and was shot, the bullet entering his back and exiting just above his pubic arch. He pleaded with Farris, who was also a doctor, to save him. "I remarked to him that that was a nice appeal to come from him then, when it was hardly cold from his lips that he was secreted in the country . . . for the purpose of taking my life."[84]

Lieutenant Johnson questioned the dying Morrow about who had fed him while he was hiding out, insisting that he wanted the truth so that the army's punishment would not fall upon an innocent man. Morrow revealed that John W. Baker "had fed him for a week or 10 days." Johnson then dispatched a detail of ten men to apprehend Baker and execute him. That evening, when the soldiers returned to Warsaw, Farris learned that Baker had been shot.[85]

The Farris case revealed a few notable things about General Order No. 8. The first was its broad definition of "guerrilla." It included not just those who engaged in irregular combat, but those who merely threatened hostile action against federal officials and those who provided aid and comfort. Farris's statement that Morrow was a guerrilla "for all intents and purposes as decided by the authorities" reflects that "guerrilla" was an umbrella term for all those who harbored hostile intentions toward the government or any government official. This was in line with the Lieber Code and with Union policy in pacified areas of the South. Another element of General Order No. 8 was its lack of any pretense of legal investigation or examination of the accusation that someone was a guerrilla. The emphasis on military commissions and official sanction had been tossed aside in favor of a policy based on the judgment of commanders in the field. Finally, the executions under General Order No. 8 were generally not public affairs, designed to send a message to other guerrillas and to their civilian sympathizers. They were intended to eliminate enemies of the federal war effort. They did so at the cost of breeding ongoing bitterness between community members, as evidenced by the fact that Farris felt compelled to move his family to Cincinnati after the war to keep them safe and by the former provost marshal's abduction and arrest.

And yet General Order No. 8 produced far less outcry after the war than General Order No. 59's policy of retaliatory executions. Not that Burbridge's postwar enemies lauded General Order No. 8, but they rarely gave it prominence when reciting the litany of Burbridge's sins. The casting of lots, the 4-for-1 inequity, the lack of due process, the failure to acknowledge the legitimacy of Confederate soldiers, the punishment for crimes committed by others—these elements of General Order No. 59 were repeated and rehashed whenever Burbridge's reputation needed to be blackened anew. The memory of General Order No. 59 focused Kentuckians' postwar ire on Burbridge; the responsibility of field commanders for determining who would die under General Order No. 8 seemed too diffuse to serve the ideological needs of Kentucky's postwar political order. That ideology sought to delegitimize the later aims of the war, especially emancipation, and the postwar objectives of the Republican party. In doing so, it made Burbridge a pariah in Kentucky.

7

# Pariah

It has long been noted by historians that Kentucky embraced the Lost Cause soon after the war. The Lost Cause vision of the war valorized those Kentuckians who fought for the Confederacy, viewed emancipation as unconstitutional, arbitrary, and mistaken, and saw the Confederacy's loss as evidence of northern brutality rather than as a defeat of the cause that the Confederacy represented.

The result was that rather than relish the rebel defeat, many white Kentuckians chose not to celebrate the state's role in the Union victory, and postwar culture and politics worked mightily to disguise the fact that the state had been on the winning side. On July 4, 1865, the first Independence Day after the close of hostilities, one diarist wrote that "the citizens [refused] to make any demonstrations whatever." Another wrote, "Where are our liberty poles, where are our fireworks?" Newly free African Americans held one of the few celebrations, a "grand jubilee" at Camp Nelson, while returned Confederates in Clark County proposed to celebrate July 5, the day two years before when John Hunt Morgan had ridden into the town of Lebanon.[1] The Lost Cause phenomenon was summed up pithily by historian E. Merton Coulter in 1926 when he wrote that Kentucky "waited until the war was over to secede from the Union."[2]

Coulter and others who followed him argued that it was federal heavy-handedness (especially under Burbridge) that drove Kentucky into the arms of the postwar South. Federal control in Kentucky looked too much like "military occupation," Coulter wrote, which made comparisons with their fellow Union states to the north "exceedingly odious. While Kentucky was suffering almost the rigors of a conquered territory, other loyal states were experiencing little inconvenience: as Kentuckians soon came to see and bitterly resent."[3] Writing fifty years after Coulter, historian Ross A. Webb explained Kentucky's postwar behavior as being justifiably driven by "the excesses of Federal military occupation, the disruption of Kentucky's labor supply by the military, and the imposition of the Freedmen's Bureau on a 'loyal' state." Webb distinguished between these justified grievances of white Kentuckians and the "revival of the 'Lost Cause' in Kentucky." Kentucky's pro-Confederate turn was, Webb argued, a "protest against the infringement of what most Kentuckians considered to be their rights and privileges under the Constitution."[4]

Cultural historians of a more recent vintage take issue with Webb's divorce between the cultural embrace of the Lost Cause and the "real" issue of the defense of state sovereignty. These historians argue that the two are inextricably linked; that is, Confederate identity justified opposition to the federal government, and such opposition reinforced Confederate cultural identity. This was especially so because much of the federal policy that caused resentment among white Kentuckians had to do with the granting and protection of equal rights for blacks.[5]

In addition, these cultural historians argue that the adoption of the Lost Cause narrative was neither an accident nor an inevitability. In her book *Creating a Confederate Kentucky*, historian Anne Marshall argued there was "no *one* memory of the war in Kentucky but rather divergent memories belonging to many Kentuckians, which competed with one another over time for cultural primacy." While "white Confederate memory dominated the historical landscape of postwar Kentucky on the surface," it achieved that dominance by marginalizing or silencing Unionist and emancipationist memories of the war. It took a good deal of cultural work, in other words, to make a Confederate Kentucky. In Marshall's view, historians who see Kentucky's postwar Lost Cause-ism as a natural evolution that came easy have focused too much on results and not enough on process. She quotes approvingly W. Fitzhugh Brundage's view that "historical narratives do not simply construct themselves, but are . . . the products of 'the active labor of selecting, structuring, and imposing meaning on the past.'"[6]

The demonization of Burbridge—and the resulting black legend that grew around his reign—was an important part of that "active labor." This does not mean that, absent Burbridge, Kentucky would not have adopted its postwar neo-Confederate ideology. Rather, focusing on their sufferings under Burbridge and continually rehashing tales of his cruelty and injustice readily justified white Kentuckians' embrace of the Lost Cause. Burbridge was the foil character against whom those

Kentuckians who fought for the South, who criticized Union war policies, and who fell under the strictures of martial law defined themselves and their cause. This process of vilification emerged most plainly during public occasions of remembrance and memorialization, during postwar political campaigns, and whenever Burbridge sought some sort of federal appointment or patronage position.

As numerous historians have demonstrated in works about the postwar South more generally, the Lost Cause was memorialized in marble and cast in bronze. Twenty-first-century political controversies have recently brought the numerous memorials to the Confederate dead and the statues of Confederate heroes that dot the southern landscape back into public consciousness. Kentucky's cemeteries, courthouse lawns, and public squares are no exception. Kentuckians erected sixty-three Civil War monuments and memorials between 1862 and 1933, fifty-three of which memorialize the Confederacy. As with monuments in the South generally, the early years (pre-1890) of monument building generally focused on remembering the dead and were placed in cemeteries; the later monuments (after 1890) aimed more at vindication of the southern cause and education of the public and so were placed on courthouse squares and in public areas. Thirty-seven of Kentucky's monuments went up after 1890.[7]

Among Kentucky's Confederate memorials are several "martyrs' monuments," erected in memory of some of the men put to death under Burbridge's General Order No. 59. The first of these was put up in 1864 in the cemetery at St. Joseph, Daviess County, to honor Charles Thompson and Pierman Powell, who were executed July 22, 1864, in retaliation for the murder by guerrillas of James Rankin of Henderson.[8] A simple double tombstone, the inscription reads:

Charles W. Thompson    Pierman Powell
Confederate Soldiers,
Executed In The City Of Henderson Ky.
July 22, 1864.
By Order Of Gen. Burbridge.
C.S.A.

Martyrs' monument, St. Joseph, Kentucky. An early monument to two men killed under Burbridge's General Order No. 59. (C. Bedford Crenshaw.)

More of a grave marker than an actual Confederate memorial, the St. Joseph monument nonetheless reminded residents of the injustice of the execution by labeling the men legitimate Confederate soldiers—a status denied them by General Order No. 59—and ensured that the man responsible for the injustice was publicly named.

A second "martyrs' monument" was erected in the town of Eminence, Henry County, in 1866. Although placed in the town cemetery, this monument was more than just a grave marker. In the case of Powell and Thompson, the army had released the bodies to friends of the two men for burial. In the Henry County instance, the bodies of three men were dug up from where they had been buried after the execution and then reinterred in the Eminence cemetery. "The ladies of Henry County have made arrangements for the erection of a handsome monument over their remains, the cornerstone of which will be laid on that day with appropriate remarks," noted the newspaper announcement of the event. "A large attendance is solicited and expected to attend the event." The "handsome monument" was a seven-foot-high white marble obelisk sitting atop a white marble base. A ten-line inscription reads:

> Three CSA soldiers who
> were shot Nov 3 1864, at
> Pleasureville by order of Gen
> Burbridge in pretense of
> retaliation of two Negros that
> were killed near Port Royal.
> Sleep on ye braves for you have got
> our sympathy to our latest breath.
> We would not have thee change thy lot
> with him who caused thy death.

Like the Thompson and Powell monument, this one emphasized the illegitimacy of the execution, characterizing the dead as legitimate Confederate soldiers and noting that there was only a "pretense" of retaliation. Likewise, the news article announcing the event reminded its readers that the men killed were not the guilty parties and were legitimate POWs.[9]

As often happened when Burbridge's name surfaced in the newspapers, additional letters came in denouncing his misdeeds and recalling his victims. The day of the Henry County reinterment, for example, brought forth a note from "Voyageur." The writer reminded readers that a fourth man, William Long, had also been executed on that day in 1864, but that his body had been removed by relatives soon after the execution. "I write this in order that not the name of a single victim of despotism may be forgotten by the people of Kentucky and of the South. Why should one of these martyrs be forgotten?" Voyageur thus linked the fate of Kentucky and the South, explicitly laid the mantle of martyrdom on those executed, and characterized Burbridge's reign as despotic. He went on to herald Long's patriotism and the cruelty of the killing. "Taken from a loathsome prison to the fatal spot and chained with his companions to a towering oak, . . . he yielded up his life a sacrifice upon the altar of his country. We cannot forget that we have lived under the iron rule of a military upstart, nor should oblivion blot from our memory one single victim of his cruelty."[10]

Martyrs' monument, Eminence, Kentucky. Victims of a Henry County execution were reburied with a marker indicting Burbridge for their deaths. (C. Bedford Crenshaw.)

The years did not dull the impulse to rehash Burbridge's wartime actions. In 1878, the *Eminence Constitutionalist* ran an article on the monument, commenting that "many are the persons who stop and read the inscription, and remember the cold-bloodedness of 'him who caused their death.'" All who saw the monument felt sympathy for the dead, the article stated, for they were not guilty of the crime for which they were executed, "viz. the killing of a negro." Four years later, in a similar vein, the *Courier-Journal* featured a profile of the monument at Eminence. "It is said that the scene of the shooting of these Confederate soldiers was most heart-rending, but they stood as firm and as cool before their unrighteous death as the cold-blooded chieftain who gave the command to fire."[11]

Reburials like the one in Henry County were common occurrences in both North and South as the bodies of Civil War soldiers were brought home from distant battlefields and buried in local cemeteries. In the years after the war, hundreds of Kentuckians—both Union and Confederate—were retrieved from the battlefields where they had fallen and brought back to the state. Some were quietly reburied by family or by local residents; others received great attention and public outpourings of grief. The transfer of John Hunt Morgan's body from Virginia back to Lexington Cemetery in April 1868, for example, brought out hundreds of mourners.[12]

In 1870, three more bodies of men executed by Burbridge's order were exhumed and reburied, this time in Frankfort's cemetery. Although not approaching the magnitude of the Morgan ceremonies, this was not intended as a private reburial, but rather as a public affirmation of the dead men's martyrdom and condemnation of Burbridge's injustice. The governor proclaimed a day of mourning for the reburial. The *Frankfort Yeoman* called it "the largest and most interesting [funeral] ever witnessed in this city." An escort of 250 men, including cadets from the nearby Kentucky Military Institute, accompanied "a beautiful white funeral car, adorned with evergreens and white flowers," that carried the three coffins. "All the streets were crowded with citizens on foot and in vehicles," the *Yeoman* reported, "and when the procession moved to the cemetery the city was almost entirely deserted." A prayer was offered, and the KMI cadets fired three volleys over the graves. "This demonstration had no semblance of a political character," the *Yeoman* continued. "It was a simple act of justice to the memory of three innocent men—whose lives were taken without trial, and without the authority of any Christian law or precedent!"[13]

The disavowal of politics was telling and typical of such cultural condemnations of Burbridge. The embrace of returning Confederates, the repeatedly expressed desire not to inflame the passions of the war, the emphasis on simply doing justice to the dead—all these expressions of political neutrality could only heighten the negative comparison with Burbridge and with Union war policy in Kentucky. Against his pettiness, they were magnanimous; against his cruelty, they were merciful; against his tyranny, they were freedom-seeking.

By 1890, the Lost Cause in Kentucky had successfully pushed rival interpretations of the war—ones that heralded the saving of the Union or that celebrated the end of slavery—to the side. Nationally, reconciliation between North and South, with the consequent acceptance of the legitimacy of the southern cause and the patriotism of Confederate soldiers, was the rallying cry. The claims of African Americans fell increasingly on deaf ears as segregation ordinances bloomed in Kentucky and across the South, and the federal government abdicated its role as protector of black rights against assaults by the states.[14]

The most faithful transmitters of the Lost Cause—Confederate veterans—were dying off, however, so if the values of the Cause were to be held dear by generations to come, education of the public was key. Thus monument building began to migrate out of cemeteries and into public spaces, and southern heritage organizations like the United Daughters of the Confederacy and the Sons of Confederate Veterans assumed the mandate to educate the public about the war and vindicate the cause of their ancestors. This was the era when a seventy-foot-tall memorial to the Confederacy was erected in Louisville.[15]

It was also a time that called forth new memorials to honor those executed by Burbridge. In 1890, four men who had been executed in 1864 in retaliation for the murder of Adam Harper by guerrillas were exhumed and reburied in the Midway city cemetery, in Woodford County. These men had already been reburied once—taken from the shallow trench where they fell after their execution and buried by Midway citizens with a large grave marker inscribed with the word: "Retaliation." But by 1890, local Confederate heritage enthusiasts felt that more public attention needed to be given to these martyred men. The 1890 reburial was the opening point for a four-year fundraising campaign by the "ladies of Midway and vicinity," whose objective was to erect a monument to the "four gallant Confederate soldiers."[16] In 1894 a fifteen-foot-tall obelisk made of granite was located on the site. The inscription listed the names of the dead men—M. Jackson, J. Jackson, C. Rissinger, and N. Adams—over which read the words "Rest Soldiers Rest Thy Warfare Oe'r." Underneath the names, the inscription reads, "Shot by order of Genl. Burbridge Nov. 5, 1864 in retaliation," and the base of the obelisk laments "Our Confederate Dead." While more funerary in tone than most monuments of the post-1890 era, this marker—like other martyrs' monuments—makes sure to mention Burbridge by name and to bestow Confederate military legitimacy upon the dead men, with the height of the obelisk calling attention to the significance of the grave.[17]

In June 1904, a martyrs' monument went up in Jeffersontown, near Louisville, with "elaborate and appropriate exercises, under the management of the Albert Sidney Johnston chapter [of the] United Daughters of the Confederacy." The monument was a simple granite headstone with the names of the four dead men on the back—Wilson Lilly, Sherwood Hatley, Lindsay Duke Buckner, and M. Blincoe—and the inscription "Being Dead Yet Speaketh." The front side of the monument spoke to the Lost Cause themes that the ceremony reinforced. It listed Lilly's and Hatley's names again and read in part "Robbed of the glory of death on the field of battle by Stephen G. Burbridge who ordered them shot without cause or trial." In large letters at the base of the stone was inscribed "MARTYRS." As with all the monuments, it was important to name Burbridge specifically, to reinforce the injustice of the proceeding, and to testify that the deaths were not forgotten but served a larger cause. As the newspaper coverage announcing the event stated, the goal of the UDC in buying the monument was to "keep fresh the memory" some three and a half decades after the execution took place.[18]

The UDC coordinated with the streetcar company to run two cars together to handle the crowd. It asked Major William J. Davis, a veteran

Martyrs' monument, Midway, Kentucky. The "ladies of Midway" raised funds for four years to erect this obelisk after the reburial of four men executed under General Order No. 59. (C. Bedford Crenshaw.)

of Morgan's cavalry, to be the master of ceremonies, and arranged for two local pastors to deliver an address and a prayer. In his address, the Reverend E. L. Powell "bitterly condemned the Union General Stephen G. Burbridge . . . and prayed that God would have mercy on his soul. 'Let us have only a cloak to hide him in, for we would not mention his name. The bitterness of our indignation is a testimony that there is no honor in infamy.'" The UDC also found an aging eyewitness to the event, Mrs. J. Burton Jones (née Miss Pink Snyder), "to relate what I remember of . . . the circumstances connected with that dreadful tragedy." She remembered watching the squad of soldiers march four men in irons to the hillside and be "placed in a position to be shot." Later it was found, she recalled, that the manacles were riveted so tight that it took a blacksmith to remove them. After the execution, the dead men were "thrown into a trench with hardly enough dirt to cover them," and the citizens were warned not to move them. Nonetheless, the bodies of Buckner and Blincoe were taken by their friends and family, and Snyder and her friend secured permission from the Louisville provost marshal to bury the other two bodies. The women "collected funds in Louisville and Jeffersontown to give the dead men a Christian burial in the cemetery at Jeffersontown," Snyder recalled. There they remained, "unwept, unhonored, and unsung," until the UDC made the decision forty years after the execution to memorialize their deaths and erect a new monument. Newspaper coverage of the event noted that the graves of Lilly and Hatley "were completely hidden in flowers" following the ceremony. If the other two graves could be located, it reported, the UDC planned to put monuments on them, too.[19]

Taken together, the martyrs' monuments are a small proportion of the total number of Confederate monuments in Kentucky, but they served a very particular purpose. Whereas other Confederate statuary honored and glorified those Kentuckians who fought and died for the South, these monuments reminded those who had stayed home and not joined the Cause as soldiers that they, too, had suffered. By remembering those who died under Burbridge's policy of retaliation, they "kept fresh the memory" of the other oppressions of federal war policy: the "Hog Order," the crackdown on dissent, and—though it remained an unspoken subtext—the destruction of slavery and the enlistment of former slaves into the federal army. Invoking the "despotism" of Burbridge

Martyrs' monument, Jeffersontown, Kentucky. Years after Burbridge had left Kentucky, monuments were erected that recalled the executions. (C. Bedford Crenshaw.)

kept alive the resentment felt by many white Kentuckians over the way the war had played out in the state.

Postwar Kentucky politics were remarkably fluid and complex, but they essentially developed into a tripartite division of loyalties, which soon became a duality. After the war, many white Kentuckians held firm to the banner of the Democratic, or Conservative, party, which had been the majority party in the state prior to the war and led the opposition in Congress to postwar policy. On the other side were the Republicans, also known as the Unconditional Union, or just simply Union, party. While more moderate than the Radical Republican faction that dominated the party nationally, they nonetheless extolled the outcome of the war and encouraged Kentuckians to accept that a new legal and racial order had been born. In the middle, and in play, was the so-called Conservative Union party. Also known as Union Democrats, they represented a middle ground between, on the Republican hand, accepting the outcome of the war and the policy of Reconstruction, and, on the Democratic hand, cozying up to former Confederates and secessionists.

In the first elections after the war, white Kentuckians' political leanings were already clear. They sent five Conservative congressmen to Washington (out of nine) and a Conservative majority to the state legislature. Under Conservative control, the General Assembly refused to ratify the Thirteenth Amendment, which abolished slavery in the United States, and it lifted the wartime proscriptions on political participation by those who had fought for the Confederacy. The Conservatives believed they could build their strength by forgiving the former Confederates, under the mantle of healing wartime divisions, and bringing them into the party. Instead, what they found was that former Confederates soon came to dominate their party, and wartime service in the Confederacy became a virtual prerequisite for running for state office.[20]

Under the leadership of ex-Confederates, the revived Democrats, emboldened by electoral victory, moved to isolate the Republican party by picking off weak-kneed Conservative Unionists. By 1867, the Conservative Union party had crumbled and numerous prominent former Unionists made their political bed with the Democrats.[21] One of the Democrats' most effective weapons was to tar Republicans and Conservative Union candidates with associations with Burbridge.

One of the first electoral contests in which the "Burbridge strategy" came into play was the 1866 election between Alvin Duvall, the Democratic candidate, and former Union general Edward Hobson, who was backed by both the Republicans and the Conservative Union party. The election was only for clerk of the Court of Appeals, but it brought out the full rhetorical arsenal on both sides. Duvall had previously served as an appellate judge, but in 1864 Burbridge barred him from running for reelection because of his southern sympathies. Fearing arrest, Duvall had fled the state and only returned after the war. Hobson had been a divisional commander under Burbridge and had helped bring John Hunt Morgan to bay. Inattentive voters, however, might have been surprised to learn that Hobson was Duvall's opponent, since much of the Democratic newspaper coverage branded the election as a choice between

Duvall and Burbridge. Hobson was hardly mentioned. "The issue will be between the people and Judge Duvall on one side, and Burbridge and his apologists on the other," summarized a Louisville newspaper.[22]

The people of Kentucky "were not allowed to vote for him [Duvall] by the intervention of bayonets, but thank God we have no Burbridge now to dictate to, and rule over us," the *Courier* wrote in endorsing Duvall. "We once more begin to breathe the pure and refreshing air of liberty." A few weeks later in the campaign, it asked whether the people had already forgotten the humiliations to which they were subjected by this "petty military satrap." The election was the chance for the people to send a message: They can "register their detestation of the tyrants who trampled upon their rights and insulted their persons." A vote for Duvall would be an act of both revenge and justice against Burbridge, the *Courier* concluded.[23]

Dr. Joseph R. Buchanan, who had been arrested by Burbridge during the crackdown on the Sons of Liberty, attacked a pro-Hobson speech by John Marshall Harlan in which the prominent Republican had labeled the Democrats the party of secessionists. "The election will turn upon the relative merits of Burbridge and Duvall," Buchanan wrote, "of the upright and able Judge on the one hand, and on the other a military satrap, whose crimes would be atoned for in prison were they not shielded by the legislation of the Satanic party in Congress."[24] A few weeks later, Buchanan spoke out again, this time attacking Richard T. Jacob, the former lieutenant governor banished by Burbridge but who held onto his Conservative Unionist identity after the war. "In the great case of Burbridge vs. Duvall," Buchanan warned Jacob, "it will look very badly to see your name on the Burbridge side of the case."[25]

Not only was Hobson submerged under the black cloak of Burbridge, but Burbridge's wartime policies were linked to Radical Reconstruction in a seamless way. Anyone who supported Hobson supported the Radical party, wrote the *Lexington Observer and Reporter,* and "we have experienced the tender mercies of this same party. We have had 'Boards of Trade,' military commissions, hog orders, horse stealings, our elections conducted by military officers . . . ; our prisons full of innocent citizens guarded by negro soldiers; our best men exiled or imprisoned; almost innumerable of our sons and neighbors shot or hung under the convenient charge of 'guerrilla.'" The *Courier* wrote that the supporters of Hobson included "every Burbridge man; . . . every Freedmen's Bureau man, every Civil Rights Bill man; every man who is for the pending negro-equality [14th] amendment."[26]

There was some pushback, but the politicians tarred with the Burbridge brush tended to run away from Burbridge rather than trying to defend or justify his wartime policies. Thus Jacob wrote that it was wrong to characterize Hobson as a radical; true, he had voted for the Thirteenth Amendment, Jacob wrote, "but it was only when slavery was destroyed. . . . He voted for McClellan and resisted the iniquities of Burbridge when it cost something to resist." Somewhat later, a newspaper correspondent wrote that Hobson had always despised Burbridge, "who was his superior in grade but his inferior in every quality of the officer and the man." Similarly, when a northern Democratic newspaper lauded Duvall and lumped Governor Bramlette in with Burbridge, a Louisville writer saw fit to disagree. Bramlette "is far above the sphere of such brutes as Burbridge, and, while that blood-stained tyrant lorded it over our people, was one of his bitterest foes. . . . We are not advised that they are on friendly terms even now."[27]

His political identity subsumed in the hatred of Burbridge, Hobson did not stand a chance. Duvall won convincingly, taking 95,979 votes to Hobson's 58,035. Kentucky's Democratic party had found an effective political strategy. It linked criticism of current Republican policies aimed at protecting black rights through federal intervention in the former slaveholding states (including Kentucky) to the hated memory of Burbridge and his wartime policies that struck down slavery and muzzled critics. Then it hung those twin millstones around the neck of almost any Republican candidate.[28]

Looking forward to the gubernatorial race in August 1867, the *Courier* began to plump Joseph R. Buchanan in December 1866. The paper lauded as one of his major attractions the fact that, like Duvall, he had been a target of Burbridge's crackdown. He will gain the support of the "ostracized and proscribed," the paper predicted, because like them he suffered under the arbitrary power of Burbridge. Similarly, in January 1867, the *Kentucky Gazette* put forward Jefferson Brown as candidate for attorney general, characterizing him as a Democrat so outspoken that he was forced to flee the state during Burbridge's reign. Similar endorsements soon came in for Frank Wolford and for Henry Kalfus

General Edward Hobson. Hobson's service as Burbridge's divisional commander sabotaged his political prospects, as he could not escape his association with "the most hated man in Kentucky." (Library of Congress, Prints and Photographs Division.)

for governor and treasurer, respectively, because they both had been arrested by Burbridge. To elect Wolford, one correspondent wrote, "will be a rebuke to the tyrants."[29]

As it turned out, none of these early names ended up the nominee for governor. That fell to John Helm, a man twice arrested by federal authorities and who lost one of his sons, a Confederate general, during the war. It was a three-way race, with the Conservative Union party putting forward their own candidate, who only got 13,167 votes, compared to the Republican's 33,939 and Helm's 90,225. The lopsided result spelled the end of the Conservative Unionists as a third party. Helm, however, died just five days after taking office and was replaced by his lieutenant governor, John Stevenson, who soon provided more evidence of the efficacy of the Burbridge strategy in sabotaging political opponents.[30]

The so-called Burbridge Imbroglio began early in 1870, when a rumor began circulating that Kentucky senator Thomas McCreery had, along with Representatives James Beck and Jacob Golladay, endorsed Burbridge for a federal position as internal revenue commissioner. In March, McCreery denied that he had done so, and soon accused Governor Stevenson, who was challenging McCreery for his Senate seat, of spreading such a "vile invention." Governor Stevenson confessed that he had believed the story when he first heard it and had told other people, but that he had accepted McCreery's denial and no longer believed the senator had done anything to favor Burbridge. But the damage was done: McCreery lost the seat to Stevenson, who resigned the governorship in 1871 to go to Washington, and McCreery blamed the scandal caused by the rumor for his defeat.[31]

Golladay, one of the other congressmen caught up in the imbroglio, had actually fended off his own set of accusations regarding Burbridge two years earlier. In 1868, Golladay issued a spate of denials that he had ever supported a Burbridge bid for a federal appointment. To support his denials, he even published a letter and telegram from Burbridge stating that the two were only friends, not political allies. "The military administration of Gen. Burbridge has made him so odious to the people of the District that, if this charge could have been sustained, it would have made even Mr. Golliday [*sic*], the strongest man, weaker than the weakest," a newspaper correspondent explained. Friendship alone evidently did not tarnish Golladay, for despite his acquaintance with Burbridge he won the seat.[32]

Others did not fare so well, as Burbridge's political toxicity persisted well into the postwar period. Kentucky's white politicians and their supporters could invoke his name and rely on his infamy to derail anyone who sought his favor or recommendation. This was the source of the public spat between Burbridge and Joseph Blackburn, which captivated the political press for several weeks in early 1882, even sparking rumors that there would be a duel between Burbridge and Blackburn to settle the controversy. The press hyped the possibility of a duel because the hostile tone of the letters seemed to leave no other way for the men to defend their honor. But Blackburn stated publicly that he did not regard Burbridge as a gentleman and thus would feel no compunction to reply to a challenge, even if one were offered.[33]

The root of the disagreement rested in the familiar ground of political appointments and recommendations. Dr. W. T. Owsley visited Burbridge at his office in Philadelphia late in 1881 and asked Burbridge to recommend him to Blackburn for a federal clerkship. Burbridge told Owsley that he and Blackburn did not speak with each other, but assured the doctor that if he presented himself to Blackburn, he was certain the congressman would do right by him. After all, Owsley was a fellow Kentuckian and Blackburn, Burbridge said, was a gentleman. Instead, when Owsley went to Blackburn's office, all he had to do was mention that he was acquainted with Burbridge, and Blackburn threw him out. "If Gen. Burbridge endorses you, I don't. That's enough for me," Blackburn reportedly told Owsley. "My district is dotted all over with graves of soldiers he had murdered during the war. He knows what Kentucky people think of him, and he doesn't dare come back to the district."[34] Blackburn's disdain for Burbridge had manifested itself six years earlier when he turned down an invitation to visit Burbridge at his Philadelphia home shortly after Burbridge's second marriage, stating that he neither knew Burbridge nor desired to know him.[35] As a Kentucky politician, Blackburn knew that to seem friendly to Burbridge or to do a favor for one of his acquaintances was to short-circuit one's political career. Owsley's error lay in mentioning that he even knew Burbridge, which he then compounded by admitting that he had solicited a recommendation from him.

Burbridge accused Blackburn of trying to reopen the wounds of the war by using Owsley to inflame the passions of Kentuckians outraged by Burbridge's policies during the war. He also pushed back against the idea that graves dotted the countryside. Executions were "hardly sufficiently numerous," Burbridge noted. Moreover, the occupants of said graves were not peaceable citizens or Confederate soldiers, but "nondescript[s], whose trade was rapine and murder."[36] In a letter sent a week after the original audience with Owsley, Blackburn denied the charge of inflaming wartime passions, saying he had never spoken "unkindly of any officer of the United States army, unless his act put him beyond the pale of civilized warfare, in the twilight of barbarism."[37]

There were further exchanges of letters. Basil Duke, as previously mentioned, weighed in on Blackburn's side, and the affair unleashed another wave of anti-Burbridge reminiscences in the press. "A son of Judge W. H. Hunt of Maysville was shot in south Frankfort," the *Courier-Journal* told its readers shortly after the fracas with Blackburn began. One of the prisoners, described as "an old man, and harmless citizen," broke away from the guard and "ran to the residency of Miss Sallie Jackson, nearby, and asked her 'for God's sake to protect him.' He was dragged away, however, and brutally murdered while crossing a stone fence on the way to the place . . . selected for the execution." A self-proclaimed Union man and staunch Republican wrote in to condemn the executions at Midway. "My only desire is that all the coming ages of eternity may still hold a tyrant responsible for the commission of this bloody deed." Another letter writer recalled that Burbridge put the executions at Midway under the charge of a "drunken Lieutenant, who wanted every one in the village, male and female, to witness the execution. Unfortunately, my little brother did witness it, and the vision never left him until the day of his death." An article in the *Frankfort Yeoman* by former Confederate officer and Louisville historian J. Stoddard Johnston reprinted the accounts of each execution ordered by Burbridge from *Collins' Historical Sketches of Kentucky*.[38]

This round of anti-Burbridge press, like the martyrs' monuments, "kept fresh" the memory of Kentuckians' sufferings. They justified Blackburn's disdain for Burbridge and his rebuke of Owsley, and they hit on familiar anti-Burbridge themes: his cruelty; his lack of respect for the sentiments of women, the elderly, and children; and his dishonorable conduct during the war. His victims, by contrast, had been upright and honorable soldiers, innocent and ignorant of the misdeeds for which they were killed.

There was opposition, especially in the immediate postwar years. The Republican party in Kentucky occasionally featured Burbridge at its conventions, as it struggled to rally Union men—black and white—to its banner. In February 1867, Burbridge told the crowd that he was gratified to see so many "who are disposed to stand by the Government under all circumstances." However, as Republicans realized the direction of the political winds in Kentucky and the joy with which the Democratic press tied them to Burbridge, they backed away from him. That 1867 appearance, for example, led the *Courier* to proclaim that "Gen. Burbridge was unquestionably the representative man of the Radical party. . . . This fact is sufficiently indicative of the character, wishes, and feelings of that body." In 1868, the *Courier* reported that the convention had sent a resolution to thank Burbridge for his service during the war to the Committee on Resolutions, from which it was expected not to emerge. "It seems the Radicals are a little ashamed of Burbridge and negro equality," the paper noted.[39]

Burbridge also solicited and received support from former comrades during the war. One of the most outspoken of these was James Brisbin, who worked under Burbridge's command to enlist black troops and, after the war, black voters for the Republican party. In the immediate postwar years, when blackening Burbridge's reputation was a priority for a newly revived Democratic party, Brisbin published several letters in the *Cincinnati Commercial,* a Republican outlet, that extolled Burbridge. In Brisbin's telling, Burbridge "acted wisely while in command in Kentucky, and never committed acts of tyranny, violence, or fraud, as has been so often charged . . . by the rebel press of the state." He defended the Hog Order, General Order No. 59, the banishments and arrests of dissenters. In fact, he criticized Burbridge for a "sickly sentimentality"—common to Kentuckians—about his "native state" and its people. Because of this misplaced sentimentality, Burbridge "frequently failed to do his duty." A truly unbiased commander would have "cured" Kentucky "of her rebellion."

Brisbin also solicited tales from Union soldiers of "murders and outrages committed by rebel soldiers and citizens" in Kentucky. "I desire not only to exculpate Gen. Burbridge from the unjust charge made against him, but to show to the people that many murders, rapes, arsons, and thefts were committed by the rebels."[40]

Besides Brisbin, other former Union officers also defended Burbridge from the imprecations of the resurgent ex-Confederates in Kentucky. J. Bates Dickson, Burbridge's adjutant, wrote that "a purer patriot or more loyal soldier never lived. His steadfastness to the Government ruined him in property and position at home."[41] General Sherman also came to Burbridge's defense, stating that Burbridge was obeying his orders. "I alone am responsible," Sherman wrote, "and I have no fear but my orders were right and appropriate." He called Kentuckians "foolish" for blaming Burbridge for acts undertaken because of Sherman's orders. "Some of them should be thankful that you [Burbridge] were too lenient."[42]

As the years went by, however, Burbridge increasingly found himself having to advocate in his own defense through periodic forays in the press, most notably in the disputes with Blackburn and then Duke in 1882, but sporadically in the years before and after. His comrades moved on to other phases of their lives, and his fellow Kentuckians continued to widen the distance between him and them. But the basic outlines of his defense were developed in these early years and remained consistent throughout the postwar decades: he was following orders; he adhered to military law; if anything, he was too lenient given the extent of guerrilla activity and Confederate sympathy in the state; and he was the victim of a vindictive rebel element that had seized control of postwar Kentucky.[43]

Few white Kentuckians bought it. Denunciations of his actions followed whenever Burbridge tried to defend himself. Active hatred of Burbridge also emerged whenever he sought a position with the federal government. White Kentuckians demanded that Burbridge receive no appointment or patronage position as a reward for his wartime service.

Like many who had fought on the Union side during the war, Burbridge expected to reap some benefit from backing the victor. Brisbin, after all, went on to become a full colonel in the regular army, serving as commander of various infantry regiments and army posts throughout the western United States. Burbridge's successor John Palmer served as governor of his home state of Illinois and as a presidential candidate in 1896. His predecessor Jeremiah Boyle, went on to head the L&N Railroad. John Marshall Harlan, another prominent Union military man and Republican politician, was named to the US Supreme Court. As historian James Klotter wrote of Burbridge's advisor Robert Breckinridge, "His world seemed upside down. At the moment of triumph, . . . he should be receiving rewards and honor. Instead, a majority of his fellow citizens labeled him a black abolitionist, a bloodthirsty Radical Republican, an outcast."[44] Burbridge doubtless felt the same way; hamstrung by Kentuckians' resolute opposition to him, he was regularly disappointed in his efforts to secure a federal patronage position.

Before the development of a professional civil service, appointment to a federal job depended on a complex calculus of personal ties, political networking, and partisan advantage, as well as to some degree on competence and qualifications. One of the main advantages of the presidency for the president's political party was the appointment power, which was used to reward party loyalists, build the party in the local area, and thwart political rivals.[45] Aspirants to these positions, moreover, were not shy about making a claim on a position based on these considerations. Burbridge, for example, amassed several dozen letters of recommendation from Republican party leaders, prominent Kentucky Republicans, military leaders, federal judges, and legislators to bolster his case for an appointment. Sometimes these letters touted him for a particular position; other times they merely touted him as someone who deserved an appointment—any appointment. "A large portion of the Republicans of this place [Frankfort] and vicinity would be gratified if General Burbridge should be appointed to some suitable mission," wrote James Halchitt, the president of the Frankfort Republican Club, to President Grant in 1870. Because of Burbridge's service to the state during the war and the hatred that he had engendered among Democrats since the end of the war, Halchitt wrote that Republicans were "anxious that he should be recognized and properly rewarded by your administration." When it seemed at one point that Burbridge was close to an appointment, a group of Bowling Green Republicans wrote to him to say that they were pleased that the president had signaled a willingness to "repay you for your losses during the war."[46] This notion of repayment or reward—for his service during the war and for his loyalty to the Republican party afterward—runs throughout Burbridge's accumulated letters of recommendation.

In April 1869, the Washington correspondent for the *New York Herald* described what the actual process of appointment looked like. Believing assurances that the president had "sent their names in," aspirants crowded the Senate chambers to buttonhole Senators and make final pitches for confirmation. "The jam of people at the door to the main entrance of the Senate Chamber resembled the crowd that gathers around a dog fight in the street. . . . If a Senator happened to show his face, . . . he was immediately besieged by the crowd." Everyone believed they would be named to a position. Even when there were "a dozen applications for the same place, . . . there was no diminution of this strange sanguine enthusiasm," the correspondent wrote. In this instance, the journalists present—tired of being pumped for information by the aspirants—concocted a false list of nominations as a practical joke on the multitude of office seekers. One of the false names read was Stephen G. Burbridge for minister to Brazil. While his friends huzzahed, others—now anxious to make his acquaintance—elbowed their way toward him to congratulate him. "He was found on the outskirts of the crowd and hastened himself to feast his eyes on the list." Alas for Burbridge, the practical joke proved to be just another letdown in a lengthy catalog of federal appointments he did not secure.[47]

A partial list of the positions that Burbridge sought and for which he solicited recommendations included diplomatic minister to Brazil (1866), sergeant of arms in the Senate (1867), commissioner of internal revenue in Philadelphia (1868), US marshal in the District of Columbia (1868), receiver in the Land Office of Humboldt, Kansas (1869), diplomatic minister to Denmark (1870), US marshal in Kentucky (1870), surveyor general in Colorado (1870), district assessor in Covington, Kentucky (1871), commander in chief of the Centennial Guard (1876), diplomatic minister to Belgium (1877), governor of the Utah Territory (1878), and a second try at diplomatic minister to Brazil in 1881 after the election of James Garfield. Obviously diffuse in his ambitions and agnostic as to location, Burbridge scattered letters across the federal departments of State, Interior, Treasury, and Justice. All these efforts came to naught.[48]

Burbridge did serve as a special agent of the Treasury Department in St. Louis in 1869, investigating and collecting excise taxes on whiskey, a rare postwar success at obtaining a federal position. The appointment was short-lived, however, and Burbridge found himself back in Washington angling for a new and better appointment when a federal indictment was handed down charging him with bribery during his time in St. Louis. Burbridge decried it as a ploy by his political enemies to derail his quest for a federal posting and, indeed, he was never formally charged and the US prosecutor was instructed to drop the case less than a year later.[49]

While the bribery allegations could not have helped his chances, it was really the resolute opposition of Kentucky's congressional delegation and the public outcry that accompanied any rumor of a Burbridge appointment that stymied his ambitions. In September 1866, for example, word spread in Kentucky that Burbridge had been granted a commission as a lieutenant colonel in the regular army. The *Louisville Courier* pronounced the commission "an outrage upon the feelings of the people of Kentucky." It was willing to remain silent so long as Burbridge was willing to retire from public view, it stated, but if he wanted a government appointment, then the paper would hasten to refresh the public memory of "our plunderer and the murderer of our innocent citizens." A month later, Burbridge's commission was rescinded by President Andrew Johnson, who said the secretary of war had made the appointment behind his back while he was out of Washington, D.C. Johnson, at the time busily alienating the Radical wing of the Republican party through his policies of Presidential Reconstruction and trying to shore up his support among Conservative Unionists and War Democrats, was open to the hostile representations made against Burbridge. The *Courier* credited Governor Bramlette and former General Edward Hobson with persuading Johnson. Hobson, of course, contesting against Duvall, would have had ample incentive to distance himself from Burbridge, with whom he was being linked during the campaign. Bramlette apparently denounced Burbridge as "destitute of the ability of an officer, the courage of a soldier, or the principles of a gentleman."[50]

Given the politics of the Johnson administration, Burbridge clearly believed his chances were better under President Grant, for he pushed harder for an appointment and for higher offices during the Grant years. As Robert Breckinridge wrote in his recommendation of Burbridge, "it is utterly inconceivable that such an administration as that of Genl Grant with its avowed determination to recognize and sustain and reward the heroes and patriotic men" who served the Union cause "can find no shelter, no security, no honor, no reward for this man [Burbridge]."[51]

Several of Burbridge's letter writers made note of the black legend growing up around his reign thanks to the relentless attacks upon him by the Democratic press reinvigorated by a politically dominant Lost Cause ideology. "The disloyal and their sympathizers have ever born [*sic*] Genl Burbridge the most intense hatred and have heaped upon him the bitt[er]est abuse," one group of Lexington Republicans wrote to Grant: "You may ask why he is more unpopular than other gallant soldiers from Ky. It is this: 1st He was required as military commander of Ky to execute rigidly an order of retaliation against Rebel guerrillas. . . . 2d He began the work of recruiting Negroe soldiers . . . and this was an unpardonable sin in Ky. 3d He began the attack on slavery in Ky by giving Negroes free passes. These are the acts for which he has suffered so severely."[52]

However, while Kentucky Republicans initially supported Burbridge's gambits for federal office, it soon became clear that gaining an appointment for Burbridge would not help them build the party in the state and their support became more tepid. With a Democratic congressional delegation and a local party struggling to get out from under the infamy of Burbridge, the political benefits of a Burbridge appointment dwindled rapidly. By 1870, attacks were circulating that a Burbridge appointment would "injure the Republican party and weaken General Grant's administration with the loyal people of Kentucky," a local Covington Republican informed Burbridge. He wrote that he was disappointed that the party could not set aside its "dissension and divisions," noting ironically that "after the late Waterloo"—meaning the widespread Republican losses in the most recent Kentucky elections—"the party is not in a condition to be much hurt." The best he could do for Burbridge, though, was to wish him brighter prospects in the future.[53]

In March 1872, Burbridge attended the Kentucky Republican Convention in Louisville as a delegate from Kenton County. He called out the chairman of the convention in the press for refusing to recognize him when he legitimately sought the floor. "The discourtesy was so marked," Burbridge wrote, "that it was generally observed and it particularly attracted the attention of my fellow delegates." The chairman responded via the newspapers a few days later: "In view of the dishonored position which Burbridge occupies before the people of Kentucky, I am under no obligation to make any explanation whatever to him." He then denounced Burbridge as "a nuisance" to the Republican party whose "previous history and general reputation furnish abundant material for the just application to him of almost every epithet." He asked the pity of "every reputable man . . . for being compelled to come into as close contact with him [Burbridge] as I do in writing this statement."[54]

As with those seeking elected office, those Kentuckians seeking appointments themselves also could be tainted by Burbridge's political toxicity. Burbridge's nemesis Joseph Blackburn, for example, initially supported the application of John K. Goodloe for a federal job. He filed an application on Goodloe's behalf and promised to support his bid politically. Then Blackburn learned that Goodloe had signed a letter endorsing Burbridge and spoken of "Burbridge's excellent conduct during the war." He promptly withdrew Goodloe's application and renounced his support.[55] In Kentucky's postwar political climate, supporting Burbridge's aspirations did little to help one's party or one's own career.

There were other factors besides Burbridge's tenure as commander of Kentucky that pushed the state's political culture toward an embrace of the Lost Cause and Confederate returnees; the alienation of Conservative Unionists caused by black enlistment, emancipation, and postwar policies aimed at providing civil and political equality to African Americans all played a role. But it is equally true that critics of those wartime measures and postwar policies found Burbridge to be a convenient cudgel with which to pummel their political opponents. By refreshing the public memory repeatedly through memorialization, reinterments of the dead, and retellings of Burbridge's actions in office, they ensured that he would find no public role in his native state. By cultivating a black legend around those actions and tying it explicitly to the Republican party, they helped delegitimize the party in the state and consign it to the political wilderness for the next three decades. And by consistently opposing any effort by Burbridge to seek a patronage "reward" for his actions, they reminded ambitious men that there would be little forgetting and less forgiveness toward those who disrupted the prevailing racial and social order in Kentucky.

8

# Exile

It was often asserted by those who railed against Burbridge after the war that he never set foot in the state again after April 1865 "for fear of popular vengeance." This was not entirely correct, for Burbridge did return to the state several times for Republican political gatherings, to testify before the state legislature, and to visit acquaintances.[1] And for two or three years, from about 1870 to about 1873, he resided in Covington, Kentucky, while working as a claims attorney. However, it is true that he never again resided in Scott County, where his ancestral home was located, or Logan County, where he had lived during his early adulthood. He came, from the early 1870s until his death in 1894, to be something of an exile from his native state, shunned by most white Kentuckians of both political parties. The loathing felt toward Burbridge by the majority of white Kentuckians severely limited his social and economic prospects in the state and credibly threatened his life. This fact actually became a sort of recommendation as he sought federal office. Robert Breckinridge wrote, for example, that those "two parties [Democrats and Conservatives] unitedly joining two thirds of our population . . . [have] render[ed] his abode in his native state unsafe" and this made Burbridge deserving of an appointment from the Grant administration. Another group of prominent Kentucky Republicans recommended Burbridge for a position because he had been "driven from this state by the hatred" of the "disloyal and their sympathizers. . . . Even his little children are insulted by the cruel hate of rebels."[2]

The threat of violence was all too real in postbellum Kentucky. The end of the war did not restore peace and unity to the residents of the state, and the rise of the Lost Cause ideology and its advocates sparked defensiveness among Unionists and desires for retaliation among former Confederates. African Americans were the targets of first resort by groups of whites opposed to any assertion of black rights and, increasingly, any black presence in their communities at all, and Kentucky's black citizens suffered far more from postwar violence than any other group. White Unionists, especially if they were prominent or vocal supporters of the postwar constitutional order, also felt the hatred of their neighbors. Much of the violence in eastern Kentucky that came to be labeled "feuds" in the postwar era could be traced to wartime cleavages between Confederate sympathizers and Unionists, which morphed into battles between political partisans for control of local governments.[3]

Given the violent postwar environment in Kentucky, Burbridge had justifiable grounds for fearing for his life. Evidence abounded of revenge being taken against Union men generally, and in some cases against men associated with Burbridge's policies specifically. The forcible kidnap and arrest of C. W. Farris, described in a previous chapter, provided one example. A few months after that incident, in late October 1866, the *Lexington Observer* reported an assault upon a person named only as Mr. Oldham. He had been "in some way connected with Burbridge's administration during the reign of terror," the newspaper reported. A Cincinnati resident named Shackleford blamed Oldham for having caused his arrest by Burbridge's troops. While Oldham was "sitting quietly in front of the Phoenix Hotel" in Lexington, Shackleford approached him and stabbed him in the face. Oldham stumbled away from his assailant, who pulled a gun and fired after him, but the shots missed.[4] In early 1867, a man named Timberlake ran across Burbridge himself in a Covington hotel. Timberlake had been arrested as well, and now he accosted Burbridge for the cost of his bail, threatening to kill him if he was not repaid.[5]

Burbridge's extended family also fell victim to the violence of the postwar years. On October 13, 1867, Burbridge's elder brother Thomas died from a gunshot wound suffered during an altercation with a neighbor in Russellville. In reporting his death, the press was careful to note that Thomas "was quite a different order of man" from his brother, sparing him perhaps some of the hatred felt toward Stephen. According to press accounts, Thomas Burbridge held a mortgage on Richard Lyles's farm and had been attempting to foreclose, and was also suing B. E. Mitchell to regain possession of some stock that Mitchell was holding on Thomas Burbridge's behalf. Mitchell told Lyles that Thomas had been spreading "damaging reports" about his behavior during the war, to wit, that Lyles "has stolen horses and robbed Negroes." Mitchell and Lyles confronted Thomas face to face in Russellville. He denied spreading the reports, but Mitchell called him a liar. Thomas Burbridge then assaulted Mitchell and knocked him down. At that point, someone cut Thomas on the head with "a sharp instrument" and shot him just above the hip. Suspicion fell upon Lyles as the assailant. Thomas died from his wounds four days later, and Lyles fled the county to avoid arrest.

The conflict was almost immediately cast in political terms, as Lyles had served in the Confederate army during the war and Thomas Burbridge was a staunch Unionist. The *Cincinnati Commercial,* a Republican paper, branded the attack a "cold-blooded plan to murder another Union man." The *Louisville Courier,* for its part, decried the *Commercial*'s conclusion that "if two men in Kentucky have a quarrel and one is killed, the reason is *always* politics." It accused the *Commercial*—and the northern press generally—of "pervert[ing] and misrepresent[ing] all they see" in order to stimulate prejudice "against our people and furnish pretexts with which to justify Radical policy."[6]

The conflict that ended in Thomas Burbridge's death cannot be reduced solely to wartime differences, but neither can the politics of the affray be dismissed out of hand. If the northern press had, as the *Courier* accused, an incentive to see Kentucky as a land of unreconstructed rebels bent on wreaking vengeance on wartime Unionists, the Kentucky press's incentive was to adopt a "nothing-to-see-here" attitude toward the violence in the state. "Almost every 'outrage' committed anywhere in the state was followed by the insistence of white Kentuckians . . . that the state's troubles had nothing to do with the obviously racial/political riots" that occurred elsewhere in the South, concluded one recent historian of violence in postwar Kentucky.[7] In Thomas Burbridge's case, while personal issues may have been the kindling for the conflict, allegations about wartime behavior provided the spark. Moreover, those allegations involved two of the most contentious issues from the war, the expropriation of property (horses) and the treatment of blacks. If Thomas Burbridge's death was not a simple case of a rebel shooting down a Union man, it did show how wartime cleavages could cause insults and economic disagreements to erupt into lethal violence.

Just over a month later, Stephen Burbridge's other brother, Oscar, was also involved in a gunfight—this one explicitly over political differences and the dim view taken by Conservative Unionists of Stephen Burbridge's actions. The *Cynthiana News* printed an article describing Stephen as "lying upon his sickbed . . . crying piteously for mercy," then proceeded to attack him for not extending mercy to those he had executed "for no other cause than that they were rebel soldiers." Now he has been brought low by God, the newspaper thundered, "the man who contrary to all military as well as civil law, murdered so many Kentuckians." This was pretty standard Lost Cause editorializing, but Oscar Burbridge took umbrage at the attack on his brother and confronted the editor of the Cynthiana paper, A. J. Morey, at the Planters House Hotel in Covington. The editor denied writing the article, telling Oscar he would meet him at a later date and reveal to him the author. Morey then borrowed a pistol and walked the streets of Covington asking after Oscar's whereabouts. When the two met again, the conversation restarted and quickly grew heated. Morey called Oscar a liar, Oscar caned Morey, Morey went for the pistol but Oscar drew his own gun first and wounded Morey, who fled into the hotel. Oscar Burbridge was arrested, released after posting a $1,000 bond, and eventually was acquitted of the charge of shooting with intent to kill.[8]

In this case, it was the Democratic press who amped up the politics of the conflict. A reporter from the *Paris Kentuckian* interviewed Morey, who was not dangerously wounded, and several of the editor's friends, and by their account Oscar Burbridge had been much more aggressive. Oscar "denounced the whole Democratic fraternity in the style of Brisbin, saying that he intended to put a stop to such slanderous abuse of Gen. Burbridge." After shooting Morey, he allegedly shouted "exultingly, 'I've given you your dose.'" At the bail hearing, the prosecutor reportedly said that every Conservative and Democrat would have to be shot if all who disapproved of Stephen Burbridge's "reign of terror 'received their dose.'"[9] The shooting of Morey showed how divided Kentucky's Unionists had become over Burbridge's wartime policies, for Morey characterized himself and Oscar Burbridge as "warm political and personal friends" before the war. The implementation of black enlistment, the hard antiguerrilla policies, and the broad suppression of dissent had resulted in Kentucky's Conservative Unionists feeling more at home with returned Confederates and anti-Reconstruction Democrats than with the Republican party as defined by its national leaders and viewed as the party of Stephen Burbridge by white Kentuckians.

If violence provided a push factor to keep Burbridge out of Kentucky, his brother Oscar kept the lure of postwar opportunity in front of him, urging him to seek his fortune outside the state. On May 1, 1865, just a few months after Stephen had been relieved of command in Kentucky, Oscar wrote to him from Memphis about the lumber business. "It is to be the bigest [*sic*] thing known in this country." Oscar worried that it would take more up-front capital than anticipated, so he urged Stephen to round up some investors. All the "rebel farmers" were returning, intent on rebuilding, and every mill within two hundred miles of Memphis had been destroyed. Oscar told his brother that he had seen Secretary of War Stanton's order for a reduction in the size of the army now that the war was over, and "[I] suppose you will soon be ready to go into business. I want you here. We can rise with Memphis. In one year we can be able to buy a nice place for our families and live here. I intend to quit Ky."[10] Oscar's own credit was not solid, so he needed Stephen to bring in outside money. "I am doing all I can to work out of our difficulties and feel as if I could never show my face in Ky until I am prepaired [*sic*] to return independent."[11]

By July, Oscar's focus of enthusiasm had shifted. "I think Texas is the place at present." He told Stephen he had found an investor who would put $15,000 into "cattle, cotton, hides and wool." Then within the space of a paragraph he changed gears again, telling Stephen that he had met General Francis Herron, who was planning to go to Washington, D.C., to secure a federal appointment as commissioner to the Indian Territory. "He wants you to go with him and assures me we can make as much money as we want."[12] A week later, though, he was lambasting Herron as a "scoundrel" and "one of the most unmitigated d_____d rascals I ever knew."[13]

A store, a riverboat, a plantation—there were, Oscar enthused, lots of business opportunities to be had in the postwar South. One could even buy government vouchers at 20 percent of their value on the open market and then redeem them with the quartermaster for cash. It was all just a matter of obtaining the capital. "If Clay [a potential investor] was here with money now we could double it in two weeks," Oscar gushed.[14] Oscar eventually ended up as a federal government appointee, working as a special supervising agent for the Treasury Department in New Orleans, with authority over title disputes involving thousands of bales of cotton in Louisiana, Texas, and Arkansas.[15]

Evidently, Stephen bought into the vision suggested by his brother's first proposed venture, and he opened a sawmill in Tennessee. A July 1867 article for the *Cincinnati Commercial* entitled "A Strange Story" suggested that the venture was not going well. The former general had "applied more than once to the Government for some small office," the paper noted, "but his applications have not been noticed." The sympathetic tone of the article—the *Commercial* was a Republican-friendly paper—depicted Burbridge as being down on his luck and unrewarded for his service.[16] Indeed, in a letter written by Judge William Goodloe, one of the Republican leaders in Kentucky, urging a federal appointment for Burbridge, it described the general as having "been compelled to live from hand to mouth since the close of the war. He is poor and has been poor since the close of the war."[17]

Indeed, in May 1868, Burbridge filed for bankruptcy, taking advantage of a federal bankruptcy statute that had been passed in 1867. The 1867 law was intended to help indebted southern farmers and merchants get out from under prewar debts that had been largely secured by the value of slaves and by southern land values, which had plummeted after the war.[18] Somewhat ironically, it now helped Burbridge get out from under debts held by other Kentuckians (although not just Kentuckians), many of whom doubtless shared the majority's antipathy toward him and toward federal policy generally. Among his thirty-five unsecured creditors, Burbridge listed twenty-seven from Kentucky, to whom he owed just over $15,700—or 84 percent of his total unsecured debt. Most of this debt had been extended on open account or on the signing of a note by Burbridge, and most dated from 1864 onward; Burbridge had clearly been borrowing liberally to pay his expenses in the waning years of the war and afterward. Also included among his unsecured creditors was a farmer named James Green from Fulton,

Tennessee. Green held a lien on Burbridge's Tennessee sawmill for unpaid rent. Green had foreclosed on the lien, taking possession of the mill, but the sale price of the mill was not sufficient to pay the debt. Under the terms of the bankruptcy law, most of these creditors would not receive any repayment of their loans.[19]

More significant from a financial point of view than Burbridge's unsecured debt was the $74,716 he owed on mortgage notes for a number of town lots in Keokuk, Iowa. Most of these notes dated from the mid-1850s, when many felt that Keokuk, located just below the falls on the Mississippi River, was destined to become the head of Mississippi River navigation, providing a riverine link to St. Louis for the Upper Midwest. Outflanked by railroad connections between Chicago and other river towns like Davenport and Dubuque, Iowa, however, Keokuk's land boom was short-lived. "Keokuk advanced from a local market town to the status of secondary regional entrepot and then fell back to its former status all between 1852 and 1858," concluded one historian of the region's economic history.[20] Unfortunately for Burbridge, he bought at the peak of the boom. Many of the mortgage notes dated from early 1857, just months before the Panic of 1857 would lead to a nationwide collapse of land values and an economic depression. In his bankruptcy filing, Burbridge listed the value of his Keokuk assets at $34,700, less than half what he owed on them. The only other assets Burbridge listed were $900 in wearing apparel for him and his family. The court discharged his debts on September 18, 1868, and Burbridge was left, quite literally, with little more than the shirt on his back.[21]

It was during this period that Burbridge really began to push in earnest for a government appointment to help make ends meet. Most of his applications date from the 1868–1870 period, and he is listed as living in Washington, D.C., in the 1868 city directory. With the failure of those bids for office, he began working as a claims attorney in Covington sometime in 1870. There is no entry for him in the 1870 census, but he is listed in Covington city directories for 1871 and 1872. His brother Oscar was also living in Covington during this same time period.[22]

Burbridge had briefly read law in the office of Garrett Davis as a young man, but he had never practiced, so his value as an attorney probably stemmed more from his former army connections and his reputation within the ranks of the national Republican party. As a claims attorney, he handled the paperwork for loyal Kentucky citizens whose property had been appropriated or destroyed by federal forces during the war. Claimants had to document both their loyalty during the conflict and substantiate their property losses; claims attorneys like Burbridge guided them through this process, as well as exerting lobbying pressure in Washington to expedite the payment of the claims. The attorneys then took a percentage of any successful claim as their compensation. Such a system incentivized the filing of claims and sparked competition among attorneys, who boasted of their influence within the federal government and their success rate at getting claims paid.

The temptation for fraud was huge. Each claim was investigated by an agent of the department to whom the claim was submitted, who was supposed to be independent of the claimant and of the attorneys presenting the claim. This was not always the case. For example, Weden O'Neal, a Burbridge associate and fellow claims attorney in Covington, boasted that his warm relationship with the claims investigator from the Quartermaster Department meant that the claims he submitted almost always received a favorable report. The investigator stridently denied that O'Neal had any influence over him and called out O'Neal publicly in the press. Indeed, friction between O'Neal and Burbridge over O'Neal's boasting almost resulted in a duel between the two men.[23]

In 1871, Burbridge found himself the butt of similar rumors when the *Cincinnati Gazette* reported that he was about to be prosecuted for complicity in submitting fraudulent claims. In a letter to the editor, Burbridge denied wrongdoing and explained that his role in the claims process was more of a gatekeeper than an investigator. He received claims petitions from all over Kentucky from people with whom he had no acquaintance, he wrote. "Not one of these claims is audited until an agent of the department has personally investigated it and reported upon it. . . . It is impossible for me, in the amount of business I do, to personally inspect every claim offered me for collection; nor do I feel required to do so, unless there is palpable evidence of fraud, knowing that, before payment, the case will be rigidly examined by an agent of the Government specially detailed for that duty." He could only conclude that rumors about his prosecution had been circulated out of "the implacable malice of my enemies in this State, who, for my zeal and fidelity to the Government during the rebellion, have been hounding me ever since," seeking "my utter disgrace and ruin."[24] In other words, rumors that he was a fraudster were meant to ruin his business by discouraging claimants from seeking him out. Whatever substance there was to these rumors, no prosecution was ever instituted.

Fraud allegations, a bankruptcy, a murdered brother, and lack of a political reward for his wartime services—to all these blows was added one more personal during the Covington years: the death of his wife, Lizzie. She died sometime in February of 1872, but that date—like most other details of her death—is uncertain. She may have died in March 1871; the different dates are given in different affidavits in Burbridge's Civil War pension file, which was compiled decades later.[25] A search for a contemporary record of her death yielded no results. By the early 1870s, Burbridge kept a fairly low profile, and the press largely ignored him unless he tried to apply for a government position or an excuse came around to recall the executions and imprisonments that had occurred during his time as commander. His wife's death apparently passed unnoticed by the papers.

Shortly after his wife's death, Burbridge left both Kentucky and the establishment Republicans. In 1872, he joined the reformist Republican insurgency known as the Liberal Republicans. The Liberal Republican movement brought together a diverse coalition of party loyalists, businessmen, lawyers, and journalists in favor of free trade, sound money, and a smaller government. They were sharply critical of the corruption within the Grant administration, the Reconstruction governments that had been formed in the South, and the urban political machines that controlled many large cities. In a letter to the *Cincinnati Commercial,* which had attacked his bolt to the Liberals, Burbridge wrote that the Grant administration was riddled with nepotistic appointments and staffed by unqualified men who had the Senatorial connections to get through the appointment process. It was a common critique made by Liberal Republicans: Corruption kept the "best men" out of office. Burbridge no doubt saw himself as one of the "best men" who had been passed over during the appointment process. It was yet another irony in Burbridge's life that after earning a reputation in Kentucky as a black Radical Republican who would stop at nothing to enforce Lincoln's misguided efforts against slavery, he would join a movement that effectively advocated for "home rule" in the South, with the federal government playing little to no role in the protection of blacks' civil and political rights.[26]

Burbridge left Kentucky to move back to Washington, D.C., soon after his wife died. There he met a young widow named Sarah Willits Ridgway Magarge, whom he married in 1875. After his marriage, he closed up his Washington, D.C.-based claims practice and moved to her hometown of Philadelphia. The couple then took a long sojourn in Europe, staying abroad for at least two years.[27]

Sarah was nine years Burbridge's junior and had excellent family connections. The Ridgways were one of the first families of Pennsylvania; their ancestor Richard Ridgway predated William Penn's arrival in the colony by three years. Sarah's grandfather Jacob Ridgway was said to have been one of the two richest men in Philadelphia. Her father, Thomas Ridgway, was president of the Girard Life Insurance Annuity and Trust Company. And her brother John Jacob Ridgway held the lucrative government post of surveyor of customs at the Port of Philadelphia and was president of the Real Estate Investment Company.[28] After Burbridge returned from Europe, John named him secretary of the real estate company, from which came one of the more misbegotten chapters of Burbridge's life.

In early 1882, just after his highly publicized newspaper feud with Joseph Blackburn, Burbridge and some other investors bought "a large tract of infertile land" just below Mays Landing in southern New Jersey, about twenty miles west of Atlantic City. They built some frame houses and recruited Russian Jewish refugees to settle there on fifteen-acre farming plots. They called the settlement Estelville. According to an account in the *New York Herald,* the plots and homes were priced at \$500; the emigrants each received \$150 for a down payment from the Hebrew Emigrant Aid Society, then they were to pay Burbridge the balance over the next ten years. There were about a dozen such Jewish agricultural settlements established in southern New Jersey during this time period. Some were private speculations like Burbridge's, but the more successful ones were sponsored by philanthropic organizations and were provided with continuing aid for the years it took the colony to get established. Burbridge and his associates offered little in the way of ongoing support; for example, the first eighty-six colonists arrived too late to get in a crop before winter, and Burbridge had made no provision to keep them fed. Many took work where they could find it and appealed to Jewish philanthropies for aid. Estelville was considered such an undesirable place to be that when some of the settlers at another colony rebelled against the local authorities, they were banished and sent to Estelville. They returned a few months later "nearly naked and almost starved."[29]

Burbridge was generally unsympathetic and blamed the settlers' work ethic. He was quoted in the *Herald* saying that American families given the same opportunity would "have taken advantage of it and have developed the resources of that section." The Hebrew Emigrant Aid Society disagreed. "[T]he colony is so badly off [because] he [Burbridge] has no resources at his command. . . . [H]e is too poor to carry it on, and has failed."[30] Estelville limped along for another few months before a fire in August killed one family and led the others to abandon the settlement and seek better fortune elsewhere.[31] The debacle at Estelville did, however, finally land Burbridge a government appointment; he was appointed postmaster of the small community in March of 1883.[32]

He spent the last half of the 1880s in Saratoga Springs, New York, possibly seeking relief from his worsening rheumatism and other health problems. In 1891, he filed a Civil War-related disability pension claim with the Federal Bureau of Pensions, claiming "general debility and disease of kidneys," and enjoyed his usual luck when applying for relief from the federal government: he was rejected. Although he continued to have business connections in Philadelphia, some years before 1894 he and Sarah moved to Brooklyn. He died there on November 30, 1894, from what the physician listed as cardiac valve disease and cardiac syncope. He was buried in Arlington National Cemetery.[33]

Burbridge's exile from Kentucky extended into the next generation. At the time of their mother's death, the four Burbridge children ranged in age from ten to sixteen. They most likely lived with their father in Covington for the first few years after Lizzie died. By 1875, Burbridge's oldest daughter, Margaret, at eighteen years of age, had married a Kentuckian named Daniel Hatch and had borne him a daughter (whom she named Lizzie, after her mother). By 1880 they were living in Washington, D.C., where Daniel worked as a clerk in the Treasury Department.

Stephen Gano Burbridge. After his first wife's death, Burbridge married a rich widow and lived for several years in New York. (National Archives.)

When Margaret died in her ninety-fifth year, she lived in Detroit. Her older brother Albert was also married and living in Washington, D.C., in 1880, but soon thereafter he moved to Los Angeles, where he lived until his death in 1932. Burbridge's younger daughter Lillie, who was only about thirteen when her mother died, met and married Edward Butler in Washington, D.C., in 1900 and the couple eventually relocated to Grosse Pointe, Michigan. Oscar, the baby of the family and the namesake of Stephen's brother, lived with his father in Philadelphia in 1880, but by the time of his father's death had followed his older brother west to California. When his youngest son was born in 1896, Oscar named him Stephen in honor of his father.[34]

Burbridge's passing occasioned another burst of newspaper attention to the details of his time as commander of Kentucky. "Dead Man Was Hated By Many Kentuckians," headlined the *Louisville Courier-Journal,* running a story about the brother of a local resident who was executed, republishing the text of the "Hog Order," and rehashing the charges of corruption in Burbridge's military prisons. Burbridge's death had caused "a small stir" in Kentucky, the newspaper wrote, but "generally very little attention has been attracted by the departure from life of a man who, among a large part of the Kentucky population, was . . . the most cordially hated man in existence." The *Courier-Journal* writer explained the lack of attention by the fact that the passing years had "softened the bitterness of war," and noted the fact that the younger generation "had not heard much about Gen. Burbridge."[35]

The softening of the "bitterness of war" represented, at a broader level, the emphasis in national culture on reunion and reconciliation between North and South. This reconciliationist urge in many ways symbolized the triumph of the Lost Cause narrative of the war. Good and valiant men had fought for both sides, the reconciliationist narrative went, and both sides had believed in the rightness of their cause. In deference to southern ideologues, the reconciliationist narrative muted the idea that slavery had been the root cause of the war, downplayed the roles of black soldiers and African Americans, and transformed Lee, Jackson, and the Confederate soldiery from rebels into southern patriots. It equally acknowledged the greatness of Lincoln, Grant, and Sherman, of course, and lauded the preservation of the Union as the prerequisite for the growth in power and prestige of the United States in the decades after the war, but much of the critique of secessionism, slavery, and southern leadership that had marked earlier interpretations of the war was shorn away. In this context, Burbridge—especially now that he was dead—could move from being actively hated to being vaguely despised and mostly forgotten.[36]

But not entirely forgotten. Indeed, one of the animating anxieties of Lost Cause organizations like the United Daughters of the Confederacy and the Sons of Confederate Veterans was exactly the phenomenon that the *Courier-Journal* had noticed: the younger generation was increasingly ignorant of the southern cause and the sacrifices of their forebears. As historian Anne Marshall noted, "the UDC considered instilling veneration of the Confederacy into future generations one of its most important tasks."[37] Thus came the renewed emphasis on the erection of Confederate memorials and monuments after 1890, including the "martyrs' monuments" in Midway and Jeffersontown. As late as 1922, the UDC was still sending Confederate flags to place on the graves of those "martyred" by Burbridge and planning to hold memorial services at "these sacred mounds." In 1904, a decade after Burbridge's death, the Albert Sidney Johnston chapter of the United Daughters of the Confederacy in Louisville appointed a committee to collect information on Burbridge's time as commander in the state, "in order that a correct history of his career in Kentucky may be given."[38]

Interestingly, a similar project was undertaken by Burbridge's friends shortly after his death. A group proposed compiling "a history of the life and war record" of Burbridge to send to "all the Southern papers, . . . with the idea of vindicating the general's memory in respect to charges against his war record while commander in Kentucky in 1864."[39] The project evidently never came to fruition, but it was symbolic of Burbridge's exile from Kentucky that the report was proposed by a group of his "Washington admirers," while the UDC's alternate version was proposed from the Louisville Hotel. Even after his death, his home state was closed to him, his memory and legacy there serving the purpose of glorifying the cause against which Burbridge had fought during the war and in all the years thereafter.

# Conclusion

One of the acknowledged risks of biography is that the author will fall in love with the subject and lose the critical distance necessary to evaluate fairly the subject's life and career. In the case of Stephen Burbridge, the risk of falling in love with the subject is minimal.

First, Burbridge does not reveal much of himself in the papers he left behind, so it is difficult to know the man behind the Union officer. Moreover, the Union officer who is revealed can be prickly, defensive, and both self-exculpatory and self-congratulatory. He could also be courageous and honorable, but even in those moments he maintained an official distance that, as Louis de Falaise acknowledged in his review of Burbridge's career, makes it difficult to know the inner man.[1] Of course, Burbridge also had a wife, children, and an extended family who loved him and defended him, but precious little in what he left behind disclosed anything about this more human side of his life. So the picture that we have of him is inevitably partial and incomplete.

Second, many of the actions he undertook during his time as commander of Kentucky strike modern readers as repugnant. The executions of guerrillas with little regard for the formalities and protection of due process, the clampdown on civil liberties and free speech, and the interference in the electoral process call up visions of present-day autocrats and dictators, not to mention the darker corners of the American past with its surveillance and suppression of dissenters. It is easy, therefore, to understand the outrage of Kentuckians who lived through Burbridge's reign.

However, because it is easy to understand, it is all the more important to appreciate the context in which Burbridge's actions—and the reactions of his opponents—took place. When Burbridge's opponents invoked their rights and liberties as citizens, they did so with a particular vision of "citizen" in mind. When they defended their opposition to the emancipatory thrust of Lincoln's wartime policies using the language of free speech and political liberty, this language was aimed at denying those same rights to African Americans. White Kentuckians' anger over Burbridge's suppression of civil liberties was real and sincere, but the ultimate goal of that anger was the continued suppression of black aspirations to freedom. As Ira Katznelson argued in a different context, "the relationship between race and democracy has been a pressing question ever since the United States was founded."[2]

A possibly apocryphal story from Boyle County, Kentucky, reflects the slaves' clear-eyed perception of the notion of freedom contained in the Conservative slogan "the Union as it was, the Constitution as it is." After black enlistment began in Kentucky, the master on one plantation worried that his slaves might flee and enlist, so he went to his slaves and asked their intentions. The slaves reportedly told the master that they had talked a good deal about the war and they asked the master what he thought the result of the war would be. The master said he supposed all the colored men would be free by the end of the war. The slaves said, "We think if the war is going to make us free, we ought to fight; but if it is for the Union and the Constitution as they was [*sic*], we think, massa, you ought to fight."[3]

Wolford, Bramlette, Jacob, Bullitt, and the dozens of others that Burbridge arrested, banished, or jailed fought for a constitutional order that would uphold Kentucky's prewar racial hierarchy. They fought for it on the battlefield—many of them on the Union side—and then they fought for it rhetorically and politically. They believed that the postwar status of black people in Kentucky should be exclusively a discussion—or an argument—among white men. Burbridge's role as commander of Kentucky was not to facilitate such a discussion; rather, he was charged with implementing the administration's directives regarding the enlistment of slaves. It was not a policy that was to be litigated at the ballot box and implemented only if a majority of white Kentuckians agreed. Burbridge's opponents decried his assault on the principles of political liberty, but they believed that those principles should only undergird a regime built on slavery and white supremacy.

Burbridge's harsh tactics against the guerrillas that afflicted Kentucky can also cause modern readers to cringe. It is hard not to have some sympathy for the victims of killings that seemed to happen too quickly and too randomly to be fair. But placing Burbridge's policies toward the guerrillas in the context of 1864 Kentucky helps to clarify and legitimize those policies, despite their apparent cruelty. Guerrilla activity spiked in the wake of black enlistment; the attempt to overturn Kentucky's racial order inspired some men to take to the bush and inspired even more to sympathize generally with their objectives. Too under-resourced to effectively occupy the whole state, Burbridge used the tools provided by the Lincoln administration's new vision of warfare—as articulated and practiced by men like Halleck, Lieber, and Sherman—to combat the irregular forces sowing chaos in Kentucky.

In the eyes of his Lost Cause critics after the war, almost every man executed by Burbridge's order had been a regular Confederate soldier who should have been granted POW status, not treated as a common brigand. These critics accused Burbridge of violating the laws of civilized warfare because he refused to recognize as legitimate combatants those men whom the Confederate government had labeled as partisan fighters. That he refused to do so was true. By the time Burbridge took command in Kentucky, the Union did not view un-uniformed men operating independently of the command structure and executing small hit-and-run raids as legitimate combatants just because they had enlisted or had at some point served in the Confederate army. That the Confederate government said they were did not make it so, and it would have been insubordinate for a Union commander to accept the Confederacy's version of who counted as legitimate soldiers.

A vocal group of returned Confederates and Lost Cause ideologues nurturing and amplifying Kentuckians' hatred of Burbridge after the war strove successfully to divorce Burbridge's actions from their context. They framed his actions as a simple choice between freedom and tyranny, between fair play and butchery, with a weak-willed and vain Burbridge choosing tyranny and butchery at every turn. If the question of African American freedom entered into the equation, it was only to show that the cruelty endured by Kentuckians at Burbridge's hands had all been in pursuit of a foolish and vengeful policy of emancipation. Burbridge bore the blame for the war's outcome with which the majority of white Kentuckians disagreed.

Yet this is the final irony of Burbridge's life: he was not at heart an emancipationist or antislavery in his outlook. Burbridge's animating principle was devotion to the Union, and to his duty to preserve and defend the Union. He undertook black enlistment and dealt the death blow to Kentucky slavery not out of principled opposition to the peculiar institution itself but out of the conviction that these measures were necessary to subdue the rebellion and salvage the Union, including Kentucky's place in the Union. In an age that distrusts nationalism, the motivating force of Unionism has been lost to memory, even though it was a common sentiment among white northern soldiers. As Gary Gallagher has noted, there are few modern Civil War films or other forms of cultural production that extol Unionist sentiment.[4]

The story of Burbridge's life—or more specifically the year in which he commanded Kentucky—lands just at the intersection of history and historical memory. His actions can be understood only by looking at the historical context of a Kentucky whose civilian leadership was desperately trying to swim upstream against the prevailing current of emancipation and whose civilian population was being ravaged by guerrilla warfare. Yet Burbridge's standing as "the most hated man in Kentucky" cannot be understood by simply looking at his actions; rather, his actions had to be remembered in a specific and terrible way to serve the political and ideological purposes of Kentucky's postwar neo-Confederate power elites. Recast in the form of a black legend, Burbridge's actions as commander could feed Kentuckians' need for grievance against Republicans and stoke their dissatisfaction with the way the war turned out. As the man who had done his duty toward the Union in full, Burbridge became the perfect scapegoat for Kentucky's Lost Cause.

# Acknowledgments

This book would not have been possible without the support and assistance of Jim Prichard, formerly of the Kentucky Department of Libraries and Archives and now with the Filson Historical Society, and Lindsey Apple, longtime professor of history at Georgetown College. Sometime before I began this project, Jim and Lindsey had decided on their own that it was time for a scholarly biography of Stephen Burbridge that would look beyond the Lost Cause-inflected image of him. But for reasons both personal and professional their project stalled. When I reached out to them to express my interest in writing such a biography, both of them were exceedingly generous with their time, their expertise, and their existing research.

Lindsey handed me a file folder of records on Burbridge from the National Archives and introduced me to Sandra Baird, archivist at the Georgetown College library, who provided some much-needed information on Burbridge's (and his wife Lizzie's) educations. Jim gave me two file boxes of Kentucky records and newspaper articles (often sorted by subject) dealing with Burbridge and graciously offered to read an initial draft of the manuscript. These two men embody the scholarly ideals of collegiality and collaboration in the pursuit of knowledge.

In addition to Sandra Baird, archivists at the Filson (including Jim), the Kentucky Historical Society, the Kentucky Department of Libraries and Archives, Duke University's Rubinstein Library, and the University of Kentucky Library were all very helpful and accommodating to my requests. Brandon Slone at the Kentucky Military History Museum aided my understanding of the relations between Kentucky's state forces and US forces and provided much-needed assistance with the state military archives. At the University Press of Kentucky, I was fortunate to work with Patrick O'Dowd, who was unfailingly supportive of the project and secured two excellent readers for the manuscript. The comments of Aaron Astor and the second anonymous reader strengthened the book and caught several errors. Of course, any errors that remain are solely my responsibility.

Finally, I have to thank my family for their support and encouragement. My children, now grown up, are constantly pushing me to think in new ways, ever-present reminders that the historical categories and interpretations we take as given today can and will change in the future. My wife, Sue, has always been my first reader and most faithful supporter. I cannot possibly repay her for the love and encouragement she has given me over the years.

*Appendix A*

# Retaliatory Executions of Guerrillas per Burbridge's General Order No. 59

The following list of men executed per Burbridge's order is mostly composed of those condemned by General Order No. 59, which instituted the official policy of retaliation. However, some men included in the list were condemned under other provisions; because they are commonly included in the list of Burbridge's victims, I have included them here. If a CSA affiliation is noted, it indicates that at some point the person had been part of the Confederate army. It does not indicate that they were captured on the battlefield during a military engagement and hence entitled to treatment as prisoners of war. The notes indicate the guerrilla offense that triggered the execution, not offenses allegedly committed by those executed. This list does not include those killed under Burbridge's later General Order No. 8, which demanded summary execution of guerrillas by field commanders.

Sources are listed as follows: "Source number (page number)." Source numbers are as follows:

1. Bryan Bush, *Butcher Burbridge: Union General Stephen Burbridge and His Reign of Terror Over Kentucky* (Morley, Mo.: Acclaim Press, 2008).
2. Lewis and Richard Collins, *Collins' Historical Sketches of Kentucky,* vol. 1 (Covington, Ky.: Collins and Co., 1874), https://archive.org/details/collinshistorica01coll.
3. J. Winston Coleman, *Lexington in the Civil War* (Lexington, Ky.: Commercial Printing Co., 1938).

4. Byron Crawford, "Two Executions in Kentucky Aided Neither Union nor Unity," *Louisville Courier-Journal*, May 2, 1980.
5. James Head, *The Atonement of John Brooks: The Story of the True Johnny Reb Who Did Not Come Marching Home* (Geneva, Fla.: Heritage Press, 2001).

| **Date** | **Name** | **CSA affiliation reported** | **County of execution** | **Notes** | **Source(s)** |
|---|---|---|---|---|---|
| 22July64 | John P. Powell | Yes | Henderson | For attempted killing of James Rankin and outrages around Henderson | 1 (123–126), 2 (136), 4 |
| 22July64 | Charles W. Thompson | Yes | Henderson | " " " " " " | 1 (123–126), 2 (136), 4 |
| 27July64 | B. Grisley Wooten | 2nd Kentucky Cavalry | Scott | For killing of Mr. Robinson | 1 (126–127), 2 (137) |
| 27July64 | William Woods | Yes | Scott | " " " " " " | 1 (126–127), 2 (137) |
| 29July64 | Harvey Thomas | 2nd Kentucky Cavalry | Logan | For killing of Mr. Porter | 1 (127–128), 2 (137), 5 (200) |
| 12Aug64 | "Four Guerrillas" | | Henry | Few details | 1 (134), 2 (138) |
| 15Aug64 | George W. Wainscott | Company E, "Mounted Rifles" | Grant | For killing of Joel Skirvin and Andrew Simpson | 1 (137), 2 (138) |
| 15Aug64 | William Lingenfelter | Company E, "Mounted Rifles" | Grant | " " " " " " | 1 (137), 2 (138) |
| 15Aug64 | John W. Lingenfelter | Company E, "Mounted Rifles" | Grant | " " " " " " | 1 (137), 2 (138) |

Retaliatory Executions of Guerrillas per Burbridge's General Order No. 59

| Date | Name | CSA affiliation reported | County of execution | Notes | Source(s) |
|---|---|---|---|---|---|
| 15Aug64 | Richmond Berry | Colonel Hollis's Regiment | Nelson | For killing for J. R. Jones | 1 (137), 2 (138), 5 (200) |
| 15Aug64 | May Hamilton | 7th Cavalry | Nelson | " " " " " " | 1 (137), 2 (138), 5 (200) |
| 20Aug64 | J. Bloom | | Simpson | For killing of Harvey Travelated by the "notorious scoundrel Harper" | 1 (137), 2 (139), 5 (200–201) |
| 20Aug64 | W. B. McGlassin | | Simpson | " " " " " " | 1 (137), 2 (139), 5 (200–201) |
| 4Sept64 | John Brooks | 8th Kentucky Infantry | Meade | For killing of David Henry by Thomas DuPuyster's men | 1 (138–139), 2 (140), 5 (152–153) |
| 4Sept64 | Robert Blinco | Yes | Meade | " " " " " " | 1 (138–139), 2 (140), 5 (152–153) |
| 4Sept64 | Frank Holmes | Yes (recruit) | Meade | " " " " " " | 1 (138–139), 2 (140), 5 (152–153) |
| 4Sept64 | Julius Bradis | 2nd Kentucky Cavalry | Meade | " " " " " " | 1 (138–139), 2 (140), 5 (152–153) |
| 13Sept64 | William LaMaster | 14th Kentucky Cavalry | Lawrence | For murder of a Union citizen | 1 (141), 5 (202) |
| 13Sept64 | John Lancaster | | Lawrence | " " " " " " | 1 (141), 5 (202) |

| Date | Name | CSA affiliation reported | County of execution | Notes | Source(s) |
|---|---|---|---|---|---|
| 25Oct64 | Wilson Lilly | 1st Missouri Volunteer Infantry | Jefferson | For shooting of a Union solider by Sue Mundy's guerrilla band | 1 (152–153), 2 (144), 5 (217–218) |
| 25Oct64 | Sherwood Hatley | | Jefferson | " " " " " " | 1 (152–153), 2 (144), 5 (217–218) |
| 25Oct64 | Lindsey Buckner | Colonel Chenoweth's Regiment | Jefferson | " " " " " " | 1 (152–153), 2 (144), 5 (217–218) |
| 25Oct64 | William Blincoe | 2nd Kentucky Cavalry | Jefferson | " " " " " " | 1 (152–153), 2 (144), 5 (217–218) |
| 26Oct64 | James Brewer | Volunteer aide to General John C. Breckinridge | Christian | Few details | 1 (153), 5 (203) |
| 26Oct64 | Thomas Bassett | 1st Kentucky Cavalry | Christian | Few details | 1 (153), 5 (203) |
| 2Nov64 | S. Thomas Hunt | Yes | Franklin | For killing of Robert Graham by William Marshall's guerrilla band | 1 (157), 2 (145), 5 (204) |
| 2Nov64 | Thornton Lafferty | | Franklin | " " " " " " | 1 (157), 2 (145), 5 (204) |
| 2Nov64 | Elijah Horton | 10th Kentucky Cavalry | Franklin | " " " " " " | 1 (157), 2 (145), 5 (204) |
| 2Nov64 | John Jones | Yes | Franklin | " " " " " " | 1 (157), 2 (145), 5 (204) |

Retaliatory Executions of Guerrillas per Burbridge's General Order No. 59

| Date | Name | CSA affiliation reported | County of execution | Notes | Source(s) |
|---|---|---|---|---|---|
| 2Nov64 | William Long | | Henry | For killing of two black men | 1 (157–158), 2 (146), 5 (205) |
| 2Nov64 | William Tithe | 4th Kentucky Cavalry | Henry | " " " " " " | 1 (157–158), 2 (146), 5 (205) |
| 2Nov64 | William Darbrow | 4th Kentucky Cavalry | Henry | " " " " " " | 1 (157–158), 2 (146), 5 (205) |
| 2Nov64 | Dick Yates | Yes | Henry | " " " " " " | 1 (157–158), 2 (146), 5 (205) |
| 5Nov64 | M. Jackson | | Woodford | For murder of Adam Harper by Sue Mundy's guerrilla band | 1 (158), 2 (146), 5 (205) |
| 5Nov64 | J. Jackson | | Woodford | " " " " " " | 1 (158), 2 (146), 5 (205) |
| 5Nov64 | G. Rissinger | | Woodford | " " " " " " | 1 (158), 2 (146), 5 (205) |
| 5Nov64 | N. Adams | | Woodford | " " " " " " | 1 (158), 2 (146), 5 (205) |
| 5Nov64 | Tingle (?) | | Nelson | Shot while trying to escape | 1 (158), 5 (205–206) |
| 5Nov64 | Parkhurst | | Nelson | " " " " " " | 1 (158), 5 (205–206) |
| 5Nov64 | Warford | | Nelson | " " " " " " | 1 (158), 5 (205–206) |

| Date | Name | CSA affiliation reported | County of execution | Notes | Source(s) |
|---|---|---|---|---|---|
| 8Nov64 | Richard Cheney | | Hart | For murder of James Murray, Union soldier | 1 (158), 2 (146), 5 (207) |
| 8Nov64 | J. Peters* | | Hart | " " " " " " | 1 (158), 2 (146), 5 (207) |
| 9Nov64 | James Hopkins | | Nelson | For murder of two black men | 1 (158–159), 2 (146), 5 (207) |
| 9Nov64 | John Sipple | | Nelson | " " " " " " | 1 (158–159), 2 (146), 5 (207) |
| 9Nov64 | Samuel Stagdale | | Nelson | " " " " " " | 1 (158–159), 2 (146), 5 (207) |
| 13Nov64 | Horton brother | Hollis's Regiment | Henderson | For murder of a Union soldier | 1 (168), 2 (148) |
| 13Nov64 | Horton brother | Hollis's Regiment | Henderson | " " " " " " | 1 (168), 2 (148) |
| 13Nov64 | Horton brother | Hollis's Regiment | Henderson | " " " " " " | 1 (168), 2 (148) |
| 13Nov64 | Tom Forrest | Hollis's Regiment | Henderson | " " " " " " | 1 (168), 2 (148) |
| 13Nov64 | Moore | Hollis's Regiment | Henderson | " " " " " " | 1 (168), 2 (148) |
| 13Nov64 | John Fry | Hollis's Regiment | Henderson | " " " " " " | 1 (168), 2 (148) |
| 15Nov64 | Captain McGee | Yes | Fayette | Hanged as a spy | 1 (168), 2 (148), 3 (48) |

Retaliatory Executions of Guerrillas per Burbridge's General Order No. 59

| **Date** | **Name** | **CSA affiliation reported** | **County of execution** | **Notes** | **Source(s)** |
|---|---|---|---|---|---|
| 15Nov64 | Walter Ferguson | 2nd Kentucky Cavalry | Fayette | Hanged as a spy | 1 (168), 2 (148), 3 (48) |
| 19Nov64 | Lycurgus Morgan | Yes | Green | For murder of 2 Union soldiers | 1 (169–170), 2 (148), 5 (208) |
| 19Nov64 | W. B. Dunn | | Green | " " " " " " | 1 (169–170), 2 (148), 5 (208) |
| 19Nov64 | John Henn | | Green | " " " " " " | 1 (169–170), 2 (148), 5 (208) |
| 19Nov64 | W. T. Thornton | | Green | " " " " " " | 1 (169–170), 2 (148), 5 (208) |
| 19Nov64 | Jacob Baker | | Green | " " " " " " | 1 (169–170), 2 (148), 5 (208) |
| 19Nov64 | A. B. Tudor | | Green | " " " " " " | 1 (169–170), 2 (148), 5 (208) |
| 20Jan65 | Nathaniel Marks | | Jefferson | Condemned as guerrilla by military commission | 1 (183), 2 (153), 5 (209) |

* Aka McDonald, Aka Jones.

*Appendix B*

# Actions Involving Irregular Forces in Kentucky, 1864–1865

The following table shows the date and the location of actions recorded in the *Official Records* and in *Collins' Historical Sketches of Kentucky* that involved forces variously reported either as "guerrillas" or "rebels," and sometimes as "bushwhackers" or "thieving bands," which occurred during Burbridge's tenure as commander (March 1864–February 1865). The actions included cavalry raids by uniformed CSA troops (such as those led by Forrest and Lyon), attacks and skirmishes involving forces best termed "irregulars," not being uniformed or necessarily under Confederate military orders even if officered by commissioned CSA officers such as George Jessee and Adam Johnson, and actions by and against—as well as sightings of—small bands of armed men. Union officials were not consistent in the labels they applied to the forces involved in these actions, using "rebel" and "guerrilla" without distinction, although the use of the term guerrilla increased in frequency as time passed.

The objective in presenting this information is to provide a sense of the frequency and widespread nature of irregular military actions in Kentucky during Burbridge's tenure as commander. While presented separately here, each event is not necessarily a discrete occurrence. In other words, a band of men might have been sighted in Bardstown and then the same band attacked two days later in Spencer County. The table below records that as two separate events, even though both involved the same group of men. Source citations for the *Official Records* are in the following format: *O.R.*, volume #-part #, page #. All citations are from Series 1. The format for citing *Historical Sketches of Kentucky* is: Collins, page #. All citations are from volume 1.

| *Date* | *County* | *Location* | *Source* |
|---|---|---|---|
| 28Mar64 | Nelson | New Haven | *O.R.*, 32-3, pp. 172ff |
| 29Mar64 | Lyon | Eddyville | *O.R.*, 32-3, p. 181 |
| 13Apr64 | Johnson | Painstville | *O.R.*, 32-3, p. 358 |
| 14Apr64 | Cumberland | Burkesville | *O.R.*, 32-3, p. 360 |
| 15Apr64 | Owsley | Booneville | Collins, p. 133 |
| 5May64 | Breckinridge | Sinking Creek Bridge | *O.R.*, 39-2, p. 130; *O.R.*, 39-1, pp. 12, 29 |
| 6May64 | Lewis | Vanceburg | *O.R.*, 39-1, p. 882 |
| 16May64 | Pike | Rockhouse Creek | *O.R.*, 39-1, p. 14 |
| 18May64 | Clinton | Wolf River | *O.R.*, 39-1, p. 17 |
| 1June64 | Powell | Stanton | Collins, p. 134 |
| 12June64 | Harrison | Cynthiana | *O.R.*, 39-1, pp. 20ff |
| 15June64 | Garrard | Paint Lick | *O.R.*, 39-2, p. 120 |
| 17June64 | Henry | Smithfield | *O.R.*, 39-2, p. 127 |
| 17June64 | Owen | Owenton | *O.R.*, 39-2, p. 128 |
| 17June64 | Spencer | Taylorsville | *O.R.*, 39-2, p. 128 |
| 18June64 | Trigg | Cadiz | Collins, p. 135 |
| 19June64 | Nelson | Bardstown | *O.R.*, 39-2, p. 128 |
| 21June64 | Clay | Big Creek Gap | *O.R.*, 39-2, p. 136 |
| 21June64 | Meade | Brandenburg | Collins, p. 135 |
| 25June64 | Pulaski | Somerset | *O.R.*, 39-2, p. 146 |
| 26June64 | Pulaski | Camp Burnside | *O.R.*, 39-2, p. 146 |
| 27June64 | Grant | Crittenden | *O.R.*, 39-2, p. 148 |
| 30June64 | Grant | Lusby's Mills | *O.R.*, 39-2, p. 154 |
| 30June64 | Owen | Owenton | *O.R.*, 39-2, p. 154 |
| 11July64 | Hardin | Elizabethtown | Collins, p. 135 |

| *Date* | *County* | *Location* | *Source* |
|---|---|---|---|
| 11July64 | Henderson | Henderson | Collins, p. 135 |
| 15July64 | Logan | Russellville | *O.R.*, 39-2, p. 172 |
| 15July64 | Shelby | near Bagdad on Six Mile Creek | *O.R.*, 39-2, p. 172 |
| 21July64 | Ohio | Rough Creek | Collins, p. 137 |
| 22July64 | Hart | West of the RR | *O.R.*, 39-2, p. 199 |
| 22July64 | Scott | 11 miles from Georgetown | *O.R.*, 39-2, p. 199 |
| 22July64 | Scott | Eagle Creek | Collins, p. 137 |
| 23July64 | Green | | *O.R.*, 39-2, p. 201 |
| 23July64 | Nelson | New Hope | *O.R.*, 39-2, p. 201 |
| 27July64 | Owen | Lusby's Mill | *O.R.*, 39-2, p. 209 |
| 6Aug64 | | Cumberland River | Collins, p. 138 |
| 7Aug64 | Livingston | Salem | Collins, p. 138 |
| 13Aug64 | Union | Ohio River | Collins, p. 140 |
| 13Aug64 | Oldham | Westport | Collins, p. 138 |
| 14Aug64 | Union | Uniontown | *O.R.*, 39-2, p. 250 |
| 20Aug64 | Campbell | | *O.R.*, 39-2, p. 273 |
| 20Aug64 | Warren | Woodburn | Collins, p. 139 |
| 20Aug64 | Union | Morganfield | Collins, p. 139 |
| 21Aug64 | Caldwell | Princeton | Collins, p. 139 |
| 23Aug64 | Carroll | Jax's Landing | Collins, p. 139 |
| 23Aug64 | Trigg | Wallonia | Collins, p. 139 |
| 26Aug64 | Shelby | Shelbyville | Collins, p. 139 |
| 27Aug64 | Daviess | Owensboro | Collins, p. 139 |
| 28Aug64 | Henderson | Henderson | Collins, p. 140 |
| 29Aug64 | Carroll | Ghent | *O.R.*, 39-2, p. 323 |

| *Date* | *County* | *Location* | *Source* |
|---|---|---|---|
| 29Aug64 | Carroll | Lock No. 1, Kentucky River | Collins, p. 139 |
| 30Aug64 | Grant | Williamstown | *O.R.*, 39-2, p. 321 |
| 31Aug64 | Union | | Collins, p. 139 |
| 1Sept64 | Henry | New Castle | *O.R.*, 39-2, p. 335 |
| 1Sept64 | Warren | Near Bowling Green | *O.R.*, 39-2, p. 335 |
| 1Sept64 | Meade | Brandenburg | *O.R.*, 39-2, p. 339 |
| 1Sept64 | various | | Collins, p. 139 |
| 2Sept64 | Clinton | Albany | *O.R.*, 39-2, p. 338 |
| 3Sept64 | Shelby | Shelbyville | *O.R.*, 39-2, p. 341 |
| 4Sept64 | Scott | Georgetown | *O.R.*, 39-2, p. 345 |
| 5Sept64 | Oldham | LaGrange | Collins, p. 140 |
| 10Sept64 | Gallatin | Sparta | *O.R.*, 39-2, p. 367 |
| 10Sept64 | Henderson | Henderson | Collins, p. 141 |
| 7Oct64 | Mercer | Harrodsburg-Nicholasville | *O.R.*, 39-3, p. 159 |
| 10Oct64 | Christian | Hopkinsville | *O.R.*, 39-3, p. 201 |
| 11Oct64 | Fayette | near Lexington | *O.R.*, 39-3, p. 220 |
| 11Oct64 | Fayette | Lowe's Station | Collins, p. 142 |
| 13Oct64 | Lyon | Eddyville | *O.R.*, 39-3, p. 284 |
| 13Oct64 | Estill | Irvine | Collins, p. 143 |
| 13Oct64 | Meade | Brandenburg | Collins, p. 143 |
| 13Oct64 | Bath | Bethel | Collins, p. 143 |
| 14Oct64 | Mercer | Shakertown | *O.R.*, 39-3, p. 283 |
| 15Oct64 | Breckinridge | Hardinsburg | Collins, p. 143 |
| 17Oct64 | Harrison | Lair's Station | *O.R.*, 39-3, p. 355 |
| 18Oct64 | Meade | Brandenburg | *O.R.*, 39-3, p. 355 |

| *Date* | *County* | *Location* | *Source* |
|---|---|---|---|
| 18Oct64 | Henderson | Rock Spring, 8 miles from Henderson | *O.R.*, 39-3, p. 355 |
| 19Oct64 | Bath | Mudlick Springs | Collins, p. 143 |
| 20Oct64 | Hart | Munfordville | Collins, p. 146 |
| 23Oct64 | Fleming | Tilton | Collins, p. 144 |
| 25Oct64 | Fleming | Flemingsburg | Collins, p. 144 |
| 25Oct64 | Jefferson | Jeffersontown | Collins, p. 144 |
| 26Oct64 | Fleming | Hillsboro | Collins, p. 144 |
| 28Oct64 | Henry | | *O.R.*, 39-3, p. 491 |
| 28Oct64 | Franklin | Peak's Mills | *O.R.*, 39-3, p. 491; Collins, p. 145 |
| 28Oct64 | | Kentucky Central RR | *O.R.*, 39-3, p. 492 |
| 31Oct64 | Nelson | Bloomfield | Collins, p. 146 |
| 1Nov64 | Grant | Williamstown | Collins, p. 145 |
| 2Nov64 | Nelson | Bardstown | *O.R.*, 39-3, p. 612 |
| 2Nov64 | Woodford | Midway | *O.R.*, 39-3, p. 612; Collins, p. 146 |
| 3Nov64 | Henry | Pleasureville | Collins, p. 146 |
| 4Nov64 | Laurel | Black Water | *O.R.*, 39-3, p. 638 |
| 5Nov64 | Lawrence | Peach Orchard | Collins, p. 146 |
| 5Nov64 | Christian | Hopkinsville | Collins, p. 146 |
| 7Nov64 | Breathitt | Middle Fork, Kentucky River | Collins, p. 146 |
| 11Nov64 | Breathitt | Holly Creek | Collins, p. 147 |
| 13Nov64 | Henderson | Henderson | Collins, p. 147 |
| 19Nov64 | Green | Oceola | Collins, p. 148 |
| 19Nov64 | Hart | Munfordville | Collins, p. 148 |

| *Date* | *County* | *Location* | *Source* |
|---|---|---|---|
| 20Nov64 | Taylor | Campbellsville | *O.R.*, 45-1, p. 983 |
| 27Nov64 | Marion | Lebanon | *O.R.*, 45-1, p. 1131 |
| 28Nov64 | Marion | Raywick | *O.R.*, 45-1, p. 1130 |
| 28Nov64 | Breckinridge | Stephensport | Collins, p. 149 |
| 4Dec64 | Bath | Owingsville | Collins, p. 149 |
| 13Dec64 | Henry | New Castle | Collins, p. 150 |
| 17Dec64 | McLean | Ashbridge | Collins, p. 150 |
| 18Dec64 | Christian | Hopkinsville | Collins, p. 150 |
| 23Dec64 | Hardin | Nolin's Station | Collins, p. 150 |
| 23Dec64 | Taylor | Campbellsville | Collins, p. 150 |
| 23Dec64 | Hardin | Elizabethtown | Collins, p. 150 |
| 24Dec64 | Hardin | Elizabethtown | *O.R.*, 45-2, p. 338 |
| 27Dec64 | Oldham | Floydsburg | Collins, p. 150 |
| 28Dec64 | Henry | Lockport | *O.R.*, 45-2, p. 439 |
| 28Dec64 | Owen | | *O.R.*, 45-2, p. 440 |
| 28Dec64 | Breckinridge | Hardinsburg | Collins, p. 150 |
| 31Dec64 | Bath | Sharpsburg | *O.R.*, 45-1, p. 876 |
| 4Jan65 | Cumberland | Burkesville | Collins, p. 151 |
| 8Jan65 | Daviess | Owensboro | Collins, p. 152 |
| 9Jan65 | Nelson | New Haven | *O.R.*, 45-2, p. 560 |
| 12Jan65 | Lawrence | | Collins, p. 152 |
| 14Jan65 | Madison | Richmond | *O.R.*, 45-2, p. 593 |
| 18Jan65 | Nelson | New Haven | Collins, p. 153 |
| 21Jan65 | Hopkins | Bruce's Mills | Collins, p. 153 |
| 25Jan65 | Spencer | Mt. Eden | Collins, p. 153 |
| 25Jan65 | Nelson | Bardstown | Collins, p. 153 |

| *Date* | *County* | *Location* | *Source* |
|---|---|---|---|
| 28Jan65 | Nelson | Bloomfield | Collins, p. 153 |
| 29Jan65 | Nelson | Bardstown | Collins, p. 154 |
| 29Jan65 | Boyle | Danville | Collins, p. 154 |
| 29Jan65 | Mercer | Harrodsburg | Collins, p. 154 |
| 2Feb65 | Woodford | Midway | Collins, p. 154 |
| 8Feb65 | Franklin | Frankfort | *O.R.*, 49-1, p. 673 |
| 8Feb65 | unknown | unknown | *O.R.*, 49-1, p. 673 |
| 8Feb65 | Marion | New Market | *O.R.*, 49-1, pp. 35, 673 |
| 8Feb65 | Marion | Bradfordville | *O.R.*, 49-1, pp. 36, 673 |
| 11Feb65 | | Kentucky/Indiana border | *O.R.*, 45-2, p. 573 |
| 13Feb65 | Grayson, Breckinridge, Wade | | *O.R.*, 49-1, p. 707 |
| 14Feb65 | Jessamine | Keene | *O.R.*, 49-1, p. 715 |
| 14Feb65 | Bourbon | Paris | *O.R.*, 49-1, p. 715 |
| 20Feb65 | Ohio | Hartford | Collins, p. 155 |
| 21Feb65 | Marion | Lebanon | Collins, p. 155 |
| 21Feb65 | LaRue | Hodgenville | Collins, p. 155 |

# Notes

## Introduction

1. Thomas E. Bramlette to Secretary of War Edwin Stanton, February 7, 1865, in US War Department, *The War of the Rebellion: A Compilation of the Official Records of the Union and Confederate Armies* [hereafter cited as *O.R.*] (Washington, D.C.: Government Printing Office, 1880–1901), ser. 1, vol. 49, pt. 1, 667; James Klotter and Lowell Harrison, *A New History of Kentucky* (Lexington: Univ. Press of Kentucky, 1997), 206.

2. *Louisville Daily Courier,* January 11, 1866; August 29, 1866; October 19, 1866; September 20, 1866.

3. Reprinted in *Louisville Daily Journal,* October 26, 1867.

4. *Louisville Daily Courier,* February 20, 1866.

5. Reprinted in *Louisville Daily Courier,* December 2, 1867.

6. *Louisville Courier-Journal,* January 5, 1882.

7. On uses, abuses, and propagandistic purposes of black legends, see Phillip Wayne Powell, *Tree of Hate: Propaganda and Prejudice Affecting United States Relations with the Hispanic World* (1971; reprint, Albuquerque: Univ. of New Mexico Press, 2008), 5; William S. Maltby, *The Black Legend in England: The Development of Anti-Spanish Sentiment, 1558–1860* (Durham, N.C.: Duke Univ. Press, 1971), 10–11.

8. "Monument to Kentucky Heroes," *Confederate Veteran* 23 (January 1915), 27–28. On the Lost Cause in Kentucky, see Anne Marshall, *Creating a Confederate Kentucky: The Lost Cause and Civil War Memory in a Border State* (Chapel Hill: Univ. of North Carolina Press, 2010); on the Lost Cause more generally, see David Blight, *Race and Reunion: The Civil War in American Memory* (Cambridge, Mass.: Harvard Univ. Press, 2001); Gary Gallagher and Alan Nolan, eds., *The Myth of the Lost Cause and Civil War History* (Bloomington: Indiana Univ. Press, 2000).

9. The standard history of the war and its aftermath in Kentucky is still E. Merton Coulter, *The Civil War and Readjustment in Kentucky* (Chapel Hill: Univ. of North Carolina Press, 1926), despite its historiographical sympathies for the Dunning School and its tinges of Lost Cause ideology. On Coulter,

see John David Smith, "E. Merton Coulter, the 'Dunning School,' and the Civil War and Readjustment in Kentucky," *Register of the Kentucky Historical Society* 86 (1988): 52–69. Other standard histories of the war include Lowell Harrison, *The Civil War in Kentucky* (Lexington: Univ. Press of Kentucky, 1975); Kent Masterson Brown, ed., *The Civil War in Kentucky: Battle for the Bluegrass State* (Mason City, Iowa, Savas Publishing, 2000); James Lee McDonogh, *War in Kentucky: From Shiloh to Perryville* (Knoxville: Univ. of Tennessee Press, 1996); Harrison and Klotter, *A New History of Kentucky*, 195–212. Harrison and Klotter's work also includes a well-done bibliography that provides citations to the large number of volumes that focus on specific battles, locations, or Kentuckians.

10. In addition to the sources already cited, which generally include some information on the irregular side of the conflict in Kentucky, see James Ramage, *Rebel Raider: The Life of General John Hunt Morgan* (Lexington: Univ. Press of Kentucky, 1986); James B. Martin, "Black Flag over the Bluegrass: Guerrilla Warfare in Kentucky, 1863–1865," *Register of the Kentucky Historical Society* 86 (1988): 352–375; Daniel Sutherland, *A Savage Conflict: The Decisive Role of Guerrillas in the American Civil War* (Chapel Hill: Univ. of North Carolina Press, 2009); Brian McKnight, *Contested Borderland: The Civil War in Appalachian Kentucky and Virginia* (Lexington: Univ. Press of Kentucky, 2006); T.R.C. Hutton, *Bloody Breathitt: Politics and Violence in the Appalachian South* (Lexington: Univ. Press of Kentucky, 2013), 37–72; Robert Mackey, *The UnCivil War: Irregular Warfare in the Upper South, 1861–1865* (Norman: Univ. of Oklahoma Press, 2004), 123–194. For a focus on the reprisals meted out by Union troops against civilians in the wake of guerrilla activities, see Michael Bradley, "'I Shoot the Men and Burn Their Houses': Home Fires in the Line of Fire," in *Sister States, Enemy States: The Civil War in Kentucky and Tennessee*, ed. Kent Dollar, Larry Whiteaker, and W. Calvin Dickinson (Lexington: Univ. Press of Kentucky, 2009), 168–187.

11. Many of the works already cited cover this political aspect of Kentucky's war in some degree, but more recent scholarship has highlighted the critical importance of emancipation and racial issues in driving this conflict. See Aaron Astor, *Rebels on the Border: Civil War, Emancipation, and the Reconstruction of Kentucky and Missouri* (Baton Rouge: Louisiana State Univ. Press, 2012); Patrick Lewis, *For Slavery and Union: Benjamin Buckner and Kentucky Loyalties in the Civil War* (Lexington: Univ. Press of Kentucky, 2015); Christopher Philips, *The Rivers Ran Backward: The Civil War and the Remaking of the American Middle Border* (New York: Oxford Univ. Press, 2016), 121–122; Aaron Astor, "The Crouching Lion's Fate: Slave Politics and Conservative Unionism in Kentucky," *Register of the Kentucky Historical Society* 110 (2012): 293–326.

12. Marion Lucas, *A History of Blacks in Kentucky*, vol. 1, *From Slavery to Segregation, 1760–1891* (Frankfort: Kentucky Historical Society, 1992),

146–177; Ira Berlin et al., *Freedom: A Documentary History of Emancipation, 1861–1867,* ser. 2, *The Black Military Experience* (Cambridge, UK: Cambridge Univ. Press, 1982), 191–196, 251–278; Victor Howard, "The Civil War in Kentucky: The Slave Claims His Freedom," *Journal of Negro History* 67 (1982): 245–256.

13. Kentucky's embrace of the Lost Cause has long been a topic of interest for historians, but the treatment of Civil War memory as a discrete subject has been relatively lacking. The major work in the area of Kentucky's Civil War memory is Marshall, *Creating a Confederate Kentucky.*

14. Burbridge to "Uncle Harry," October 29, 1862, Stephen Gano Burbridge [SGB] Correspondence, 1862–1865, Filson Historical Society, Louisville, Kentucky.

15. Basil Duke, *A History of Morgan's Cavalry* (New York: Neale Publishing, 1906), 530; Nathaniel Shaler, *Kentucky: A Pioneer Commonwealth* (New York: Houghton, Mifflin, 1884), 346, 351; Thomas Speed et al., *The Union Regiments of Kentucky* (Louisville, Ky.: Courier-Journal Printing, 1897), 67; Thomas Speed, *The Union Cause in Kentucky, 1860–1865* (New York: G. Putnam and Sons, 1907), 243.

16. Coulter, *The Civil War and Readjustment in Kentucky,* 207; Edward Conrad Smith, *The Borderland in the Civil War* (New York: Macmillan, 1927), 379; Thomas Clark, *A History of Kentucky* (New York: Prentice-Hall, 1937), 346; Thomas Clark, *Kentucky: Land of Contrast* (New York: Harper and Row, 1968), 141.

17. Harrison, *The Civil War in Kentucky,* 77; Louis de Falaise, "General Stephen Gano Burbridge's Command in Kentucky," *Register of the Kentucky Historical Society* 69 (1971): 124; James M. Prichard, "Burbridge, Stephen Gano," in *Encyclopedia of the American Civil War: A Political, Social, and Military History,* vol. 1, ed. David Heidler and Jeanne Heidler (Santa Barbara, Calif.: ABC-Clio, 2000), 324.

18. Bryan Bush, *Butcher Burbridge: Union General Stephen Gano Burbridge and His Reign of Terror over Kentucky* (Morley, Mo.: Acclaim Press, 2008); James Darwin Stephens, *Reflections: A Portrait-Biography of the Kentucky Military Institute (1845–1971),* vol. 1 (Georgetown, Ky.: Kentucky Military Institute, 1991), 41; Richard Taylor, *Rail Splitter: Sonnets on the Life of Abraham Lincoln* (Monterey, Ky.: Larkspur Press, 2009), 44–45.

19. For broad summaries of this recent scholarship, see James Brewer Stewart, "Civil War: Changing Interpretations," in *The Oxford Companion to United States History,* ed. Paul Boyer (New York: Oxford Univ. Press, 2001), 133; James McPherson, *This Mighty Scourge: Perspectives on the Civil War* (New York: Oxford Univ. Press, 2007); Michael E. Woods, "What Twenty-First Century Historians Have Said about the Causes of Disunion: A Civil War Sesquicentennial Review of Recent Literature," *Journal of American History* 99

(2012): 415–439; Tony Horwitz, "150 Years of Misunderstanding the Civil War," *The Atlantic,* June 19, 2013, https://www.theatlantic.com/national/archive/2013/06/150-years-of-misunderstanding-the-civil-war/277022/.

20. Astor, *Rebels on the Border,* 3; Luke Harlow, *Religion, Race, and the Making of Confederate Kentucky, 1830–1880* (Cambridge, UK: Cambridge Univ. Press, 2014), 156; Marshall, *Creating a Confederate Kentucky,* 23. See also Philips, *The Rivers Ran Backward,* 211–234. For a review of recent Civil War scholarship on Kentucky, see John David Smith, "Whither Kentucky Civil War and Reconstruction Scholarship?," *Register of the Kentucky Historical Society* 112 (2014): 223–247.

21. de Falaise, "General Stephen Gano Burbridge's Command in Kentucky," 124.

22. Prichard, "Burbridge, Stephen Gano," 324.

## 1. Gentleman

1. On the culture of the Kentucky landed gentry, see Stephen Aron, *How the West Was Lost: The Transformation of Kentucky from Daniel Boone to Henry Clay* (Baltimore: Johns Hopkins Univ. Press, 1996), 125–129; on the figure of the Kentucky colonel in literature, see Lawrence Thompson, "Bluegrass and Bourbon: The Colonel of Kentucky Fiction," *Georgia Review* 7 (1953): 107–115.

2. Burbridge surname file, Kentucky Historical Society, Frankfort, Kentucky.

3. John Frederick Dorman, comp., *Virginia Revolutionary Pension Applications,* vol. 12 (Washington, D.C.: J. F. Dorman, 1966), 86; Thomas L. Purvis, "The Ethnic Descent of Kentucky's Early Population: A Statistical Investigation of European and American Sources of Emigration, 1790–1820," *Register of the Kentucky Historical Society* 80 (1982): 264.

4. Purvis, "The Ethnic Descent of Kentucky's Early Population," 262–264. According to Purvis, North Carolina offered its veterans land warrants for Tennessee real estate, which siphoned off potential Kentucky settlers from North Carolina into Tennessee. On George Burbridge's slave ownership, see Netti Schreiner-Yantis and Florence Speakman Love, *The 1787 Census of Virginia,* vol. 2 (Springfield, Va.: Genealogical Books in Print, 1987), 870, which shows him owning four slaves. On the emigration of Virginians generally, see Harrison and Klotter, *A New History of Kentucky,* 48; Rhys Isaac, *The Transformation of Virginia, 1740–1790* (New York: Norton, 1988), 311–312.

5. Burbridge surname file; George Armstrong Crozier, ed., *Virginia County Records,* vol. 1, *Spotsylvania County Records, 1721–1800* (Baltimore: Southern Book Co., 1955), 47, 450, 454.

6. Minnie Wilder, comp., *Kentucky Soldiers of the War of 1812* (Baltimore: Genealogical Publishing Co., 1969), 264; Virgil White, comp., *Index to War*

*of 1812 Pension Files,* vol. 1, *A-F* (Waynesboro, Tenn.: National Historical Publishing Co., 1989), 287.

7. Tax Books, Scott County, 1794–1821, Kentucky Historical Society, Frankfort, Kentucky.

8. Burbridge surname file.

9. Lindsey Apple et al., eds., *Scott County, Kentucky: A History* (Georgetown, Ky.: Scott County Historical Society, 1993), 125; Kentucky Tax Books, Scott County, Filson Historical Society, Louisville, Kentucky.

10. For the early political battles over slavery and the role of the gentry in enshrining constitutional protections for it, see Aron, *How the West Was Lost,* 89–95.

11. On the hiring-out system, see Aron, *How the West Was Lost,* 144–145; Brad Asher, *Cecelia and Fanny: The Remarkable Friendship Between an Escaped Slave and Her Former Mistress* (Lexington: Univ. Press of Kentucky, 2011), 45–47; Lucas, *A History of Blacks in Kentucky,* vol. 1, *From Slavery to Segregation,* 101–7.

12. *Administrators of the estate of George Burbridge v. John C. McGuffin* (1839), Scott County Circuit Court Civil Case Files, Kentucky Department for Libraries and Archives, Frankfort, Kentucky. George's sons Thomas and Robert were also involved in similar litigation over slave hiring contracts on their own behalf. See *Robert Burbridge (as Guardian) v. Johnson, Suggite* (1839), and *Executors of Thomas Burbridge estate v. Johnson, Suggite* (1839), Scott County Circuit Court Civil Case Files, Kentucky Department for Libraries and Archives, Frankfort, Kentucky.

13. Robert's brother Sidney had married Susan Barnes, the sister of Eliza, the previous year. Jordan Dodd et al., *Early American Marriages: Mississippi to 1825* (Bountiful, Utah: Precision Indexing Publishers, 1997), accessed via Ancestry.com, *Mississippi Compiled Marriages, 1800–1825* (Provo, Utah: Ancestry.com Operations, 1997), https://www.ancestry.com/search/collections/2093/. For Robert's slaveholdings, see Tax Books, Scott County, 1794–1821; 1823–1836; 1837–1851; 1852–1866. On the interstate slave trade, see Harrison and Klotter, *A New History of Kentucky,* 167–168; Asher, *Cecelia and Fanny,* 41–42; Walter Johnson, *Soul by Soul: Life Inside the Antebellum Slave Market* (Cambridge, Mass.: Harvard Univ. Press, 1999).

14. Aron, *How the West Was Lost,* 129; Apple et al., eds., *Scott County, Kentucky: A History,* 124; Harrison and Klotter, *A New History of Kentucky,* 135. Hemp was only one of the crops grown on the diversified farms of the Bluegrass. Corn, wheat, and other grains, as well as cattle, hogs, and horses, were all raised in varying quantities. See Apple et al., *Scott County, Kentucky: A History,* 125.

15. Marshall, *Creating a Confederate Kentucky,* 4; Phillips, *The Rivers Ran Backward,* 338. See also Maryjean Wall, *How Kentucky Became Southern: A*

*Tale of Outlaws, Horse Thieves, Gamblers, and Breeders* (Lexington: Univ. Press of Kentucky, 2010). On the influence of Virginia on the self-conception of Bluegrass planters, see Aron, *How the West Was Lost,* 90, 124–129.

16. Aron, *How the West Was Lost,* 126–127.

17. T. H. Breen, "Horses and Gentlemen: The Cultural Significance of Gambling among the Gentry of Virginia," *William and Mary Quarterly* 34 (1977): 249. See also Aron, *How the West Was Lost,* 127.

18. Apple et al., eds., *Scott County, Kentucky: A History,* 128, 143; "Famous Race Track Once at Silver Lake," in Burbridge surname file; Anne Peters, "Pedigree Analysis: Grey Eagle," Bloodhorse.com, January 9, 2015, www.bloodhorse.com/horse-racing/articles/109985/pedigree-analysis-grey-eagle.

19. The slave census of 1860 showed Burbridge owning seven slaves. US Bureau of the Census, *Eighth Census of the United States, 1860, Slave Schedules,* Kentucky, Logan County, District 2, page 39, National Archives Microfilm Publication M653, accessed via Ancestry.com (Provo, Utah: Ancestry.com Operations, 2010), https://www.ancestry.com/search/collections/7668/. On Burbridge's early military actions in support of Kentucky's slaveholders, see Ira Berlin et al., *Freedom: A Documentary History of Emancipation, 1861–1867,* ser. 1, vol. 1, *The Destruction of Slavery* (Cambridge, UK: Cambridge Univ. Press, 1985), 500–502, 506; *Janesville (Wisc.) Daily Gazette,* November 11, 1862; Burbridge to "Uncle Harry," October 29, 1862, SGB Correspondence, 1862–1865. On Burbridge's claim that being a slaveholder was a benefit in dealing with Kentucky's slaveholders, see Victor Howard, *Black Liberation in Kentucky: Emancipation and Freedom, 1862–1884* (Lexington: Univ. Press of Kentucky, 1983), 65.

20. US Bureau of the Census, *Eighth Census of the United States, 1860, Slave Schedules,* Kentucky, Logan County, District 2. The early history of the Green River Country—including Logan County—is traced in Aron, *How the West Was Lost,* 150–169.

21. US Bureau of the Census, *Eighth Census of the United States, 1860,* Kentucky, Bourbon County, Eastern Division, page 8, National Archives Microfilm Publication M653, accessed via Ancestry.com (Provo, Utah: Ancestry.com Operations, 2009), https://www.ancestry.com/search/collections/7667/; US Bureau of the Census, *Eighth Census of the United States, 1860, Slave Schedules,* Kentucky, Bourbon County, Eastern Division; *Louisville Daily Courier,* November 18, 1853; *Louisville Daily Courier* (reprinting *Paris Citizen*), July 31, 1854. On the livestock breeding interests of Bluegrass planters, see Aron, *How the West Was Lost,* 128; Harrison and Klotter, *A New History of Kentucky,* 135–136.

22. *Louisville Courier-Journal,* December 7, 1894. On Stephen F. Gano, see J. M. Armstrong, *The Biographical Encyclopedia of Kentucky of the Dead and Living Men of the Nineteenth Century,* vol. 1 (Cincinnati: J. M. Armstrong and Co., 1878), 632; Burbridge surname file. On Burbridge's academic career, see

*Catalogue of the Officers and Students of Georgetown College, Kentucky, 1845–46* (Georgetown, Ky.: Georgetown College, 1846), 9, 16; *Catalogue of the Students of Georgetown College with a List of Academical Honors Conferred by the College* (Georgetown, Ky.: Georgetown College, 1837–38). I am indebted to Georgetown College Director of Archives Sandra Baird for this information.

23. The official history of the institute gives an 1858 graduation date for Burbridge, but this seems late since he would have been twenty-seven years of age, married, and with two small children by that time. It is more likely that he was one of the earliest enrollees, graduating not later than 1856. See Stephens, *Reflections,* 1:41.

24. *Catalogue of the Officers and Cadets of the Kentucky Military Institute . . . from September 11, 1854 to June 29, 1855* (Frankfort, Ky.: A. G. Hodges and Co., 1855).

25. *Regulations of the Kentucky Military Institute* (Frankfort, Ky.: A. G. Hodges and Co., 1855).

26. "Burbridge, Stephen G.," in *The Union Army,* vol. 8, *Biographical* (Madison, Wisc.: Federal Publishing Co., 1908), 42; "Burbridge, Stephen Gano," in *The National Cyclopaedia of American Biography,* vol. 11 (New York: J. T. White Co., 1901), 317, https://archive.org/details/nationalcyclopa05whitgoog/.

27. US Bureau of the Census, *Eighth Census of the United States, 1860,* Kentucky, Logan County, District 2, page 152; US Bureau of the Census, *Seventh Census of the United States, 1850,* Kentucky, Scott County, District 1 (East part), page 26, National Archives Microfilm Publication M432, accessed via Ancestry.com (Provo, Utah: Ancestry.com Operations, 2009), https://www.ancestry.com/search/collections/8054/; *Kentucky, County Marriage Records, 1783–1965,* Scott County, 1803–1883, page 230, accessed via Ancestry.com (Lehi, Utah: Ancestry.com Operations, 2016), https://www.ancestry.com/search/collections/61372/; *Catalogue of the Teachers and Pupils of the Georgetown Female Seminary . . . for the Year 1850* (Georgetown, Ky.: Georgetown Female Seminary, 1850), 5; *Catalogue of the Georgetown Female Seminary . . . for the Year 1851* (Georgetown, Ky.: Georgetown Female Seminary, 1851), 6; *Catalogue of the Georgetown Female Seminary . . . for the Year 1852* (Georgetown, Ky.: Georgetown Female Seminary, 1852), 6; *Catalogue of the Georgetown Female Seminary . . . for the Year 1853* (Georgetown, Ky.: Georgetown Female Seminary, 1853), 4; Burbridge Surname File.

28. Kentucky Tax Books, Scott County, 1837–1851; 1852–1866.

29. *Lexington National Unionist,* November 8, 1864.

## 2. Soldier

1. Klotter and Harrison, *A New History of Kentucky,* 187–192; Coulter, *The Civil War and Readjustment in Kentucky,* 41, 145; William Ranney to

"Dear Sister," July 15, 1861, William W. Ranney Papers, 1858–1927, Special Collections Research Center, Margaret I. King Library, University of Kentucky, Lexington, Kentucky; William Freehling, *The South vs. The South: How Anti-Confederate Southerners Shaped the Course of the Civil War* (New York: Oxford Univ. Press, 2001), 69; Stephen Rockenbach, "'The Weeds and the Flowers Are Closely Mixed': Allegiance, Law, and White Supremacy in Kentucky's Bluegrass Region, 1861–1865," *Register of the Kentucky Historical Society* 111 (2013): 569.

2. Davis to Lincoln, November 29, 1861, Records of the Adjutant General's Office (RG 94), Letters Received by Commission Branch, 1874–1894, National Archives Microfilm Publication M1395.

3. Sandram to Lincoln, November 30, 1863, Records of the Adjutant General's Office (RG 94), Compiled Service Record (CSR), Stephen G. Burbridge, National Archives. One can find similar letters scattered throughout Burbridge's CSR.

4. *Cincinnati Daily Enquirer,* November 25, 1862.

5. Sherman to Burbridge, December 19, 1867, Records of the Department of the Interior (RG 48), Field Office Appointment Papers, 1849–1907, Box 288, National Archives.

6. Klotter and Harrison, *A New History of Kentucky,* 192, 196.

7. Klotter and Harrison, *A New History of Kentucky,* 193; Lewis Collins and Richard H. Collins, *Collins' Historical Sketches of Kentucky: History of Kentucky,* vol. 1 (Covington, Ky.: Collins and Company, 1874), 97, https://archive.org/details/collinshistorica01coll/page/n8/mode/2up.

8. Burbridge to Sherman, October 31, 1861, *O.R.*, ser. 1, vol. 4, 219–220; Sherman to Burbridge, November 2, 1861, Records of U. S. Army Continental Commands (RG 393), Department of the Cumberland, September–November, 1861, National Archives.

9. Klotter and Harrison, *A New History of Kentucky,* 196. For a list of the numerous small skirmishes in Kentucky, see the "Summary of Principal Events" for the period November 1861–January 1862 in *O.R.*, ser. 1, vol. 7, 1.

10. Collins and Collins, *Collins' Historical Sketches of Kentucky,* 1:97; National Park Service, "Battle Unit Details: 26th Regiment, Kentucky Infantry," www.nps.gov/civilwar/search-battle-units-detail.htm?battleUnitCode=UKY0026RI.

11. Richard Jacob to Lincoln, December 5, 1861; see also Davis to Lincoln, November 29, 1861; J. R. Underwood to Lincoln, November 29, 1861, Nathaniel Wolfe to Lincoln, November 30, 1861, Records of the Adjutant General's Office (RG 94), Letters Received by Commission Branch, 1874–1894.

12. Buell to McClellan, December 8, 1861, *O.R.*, ser. 1, vol. 7, 432.

13. Klotter and Harrison, *A New History of Kentucky,* 197.

14. Cicero Maxwell to Adjutant General John Finnell, March 8, 1862, 26th Kentucky Infantry Records, Old War Records, "History" folder, Kentucky Military History Museum, Frankfort, Kentucky; National Park Service, "Battle Unit Details: 26th Regiment, Kentucky Infantry."

15. Affidavit of James C. Lemon, September 24, 1895, US Bureau of Pensions, Sarah R. Burbridge (Widow) Pension File, Claim No. 610825, Certificate No. 418.623, National Archives; Bush, *Butcher Burbridge,* 25, 33.

16. James McPherson, *Battle Cry of Freedom: The Civil War Era* (New York: Oxford Univ. Press, 1988), 406–410.

17. Burbridge to Adjutant General John Finnell, April 10, 1862, 26th Kentucky Infantry Records, "History"; Report of Lieutenant Colonel Cicero Maxwell, April 9, 1862, *O.R.,* ser. 1, vol. 10, pt. 1, 368–369; "Organization of the Union Forces and Return of Casualties," *O.R.,* ser. 1, vol. 10, pt. 1, 107.

18. Bush, *Butcher Burbridge,* 32–33; Jack Welsh, M.D., *Medical Histories of Union Generals* (Kent, Ohio: Kent State Univ. Press, 1995), 44–45; National Park Service, "Battle Unit Details: 26th Regiment, Kentucky Infantry."

19. One of the generals, General Jeff C. Davis of Indiana, felt his honor so impugned by the insult that he soon thereafter returned and killed Nelson in the lobby of the Galt House Hotel, in one of the most controversial early episodes of the war in Kentucky. Davis was neither tried nor court-martialed for the killing. Brisbin's account was originally published by the *Philadelphia Times* and was reprinted in the *Louisville Courier-Journal,* January 29, 1880; see also George Yater, *Two Hundred Years at the Falls of the Ohio: A History of Louisville and Jefferson County* (Louisville, Ky.: Filson Club, 1987), 86; David R. Deatrick, "Nelson, William," in *The Encyclopedia of Louisville,* ed. John Kleber (Lexington: Univ. Press of Kentucky, 2001), 651.

20. Burbridge to Smith, October 13, 1862, *O.R.,* ser. 1, vol. 16, pt. 2, 615; Burbridge to Smith, October 8, 1862, *O.R.,* ser. 1, vol. 16, pt. 2, 590; Klotter and Harrison, *A New History of Kentucky,* 199–201; McPherson, *Battle Cry of Freedom,* 515–520; Bush, *Butcher Burbridge,* 34–37.

21. Burbridge to Smith, October 13, 1862, *O.R.,* ser. 1, vol. 16, pt. 2, 615; Burbridge to Smith, October 8, 1862, *O.R.,* ser. 1, vol. 16, pt. 2, 590. On "contrabands" more generally and Lincoln's attempt to persuade border state Unionists to accept compensated emancipation, see McPherson, *Battle Cry of Freedom,* 496–499.

22. Burbridge to "Uncle Harry," October 29, 1862, SGB Correspondence, 1862–1865; Klotter and Harrison, *A New History of Kentucky,* 179; Coulter, *The Civil War and Readjustment in Kentucky,* 156–157; Lucas, *A History of Blacks in Kentucky,* vol. 1, *From Slavery to Segregation,* 148–149.

23. Burbridge to "Uncle Harry," October 29, 1862, SGB Correspondence, 1862–1865; *Janesville (Wisc.) Daily Gazette,* November 11, 1862; Berlin

et al., *Freedom,* ser. 1, vol. 1, *The Destruction of Slavery,* 500–502; Lucas, *A History of Blacks in Kentucky,* vol. 1, *From Slavery to Segregation,* 148–149.

24. Official record of service, April 24, 1895, Sarah R. Burbridge (Widow) Pension File; Report of Brigadier General A. J. Smith, January 1, 1863, *O.R.*, ser. 1, vol. 17, pt. 1, 627; Bush, *Butcher Burbridge,* 40.

25. Report of Brigadier General A. J. Smith, January 1, 1863, *O.R.*, ser. 1, vol. 17, pt. 1, 627; Report of Brigadier General Stephen G. Burbridge, December 27, 1862, *O.R.*, ser. 1, vol. 17, pt. 1, 629–631.

26. Report of Brigadier General A. J. Smith, January 1, 1863, *O.R.*, ser. 1, vol. 17, pt. 1, 627.

27. See the reports on the Battle of Chickasaw Bayou from various commanders, *O.R.*, ser. 1, vol. 17, pt. 1, 625–697; McPherson, *Battle Cry of Freedom,* 577–579; Bush, *Butcher Burbridge,* 42.

28. Rear Admiral David Porter to Secretary of the Navy Gideon Welles, January 3, 1863, Naval War Records Office, *Official Records of the Union and Confederate Navies in the War of the Rebellion* (Washington, D.C.: Government Printing Office, 1894–1922), ser. 1, vol. 24, 93; Report of General John McClernand, January 11, 1863, *O.R.*, ser. 1, vol. 17, pt. 1, 701; Richard Kiper, "John Alexander McClernand and the Arkansas Post Campaign," *Arkansas History Quarterly* 56 (1997): 56–63; Mark Christ, "Battle of Arkansas Post," *The Encyclopedia of Arkansas History and Culture,* http://www.encyclopediaofarkansas.net/encyclopedia/entry-detail.aspx?entryID=525.

29. Report of General Stephen G. Burbridge, January 14, 1863, *O.R.*, ser. 1, vol. 17, pt. 1, 729–731; Kiper, "John Alexander McClernand and the Arkansas Post Campaign," 72–73; Christ, "Battle of Arkansas Post."

30. Report of General George Morgan, January 17, 1863, *O.R.*, ser. 1, vol. 17, pt. 1, 723.

31. Report of General Stephen G. Burbridge, January 14, 1863, *O.R.*, ser. 1, vol. 17, pt. 1, 731; Christ, "Battle of Arkansas Post"; Bush, *Butcher Burbridge,* 49.

32. Report of General George Morgan, January 17, 1863, *O.R.*, ser. 1, vol. 17, pt. 1, 723; Report of General Andrew J. Smith, January 16, 1863, *O.R.*, ser. 1, vol. 17, pt. 1, 727; Report of General Stephen G. Burbridge, January 14, 1863, *O.R.*, ser. 1, vol. 17, pt. 1, 731; T. J. Lucas et al. to Lincoln, January 13, 1863, CSR, Stephen G. Burbridge. On the various justifications for the assault on Arkansas Post, including redemption for the failure at Chickasaw Bluff, see Kiper, "John Alexander McClernand and the Arkansas Post Campaign," 63–66.

33. Report of General Ulysses S. Grant, January 20, 1863; General Order No. 13, January 30, 1863; McClernand to Grant, January 30, 1863; Grant to McClernand, January 31, 1863, *O.R.*, ser. 1, vol, 24, pt. 1, 8, 11–13; McPherson, *Battle Cry of Freedom,* 586–588.

34. Report of General Stephen Burbridge, February 27, 1863, *O.R.*, ser. 1, vol. 24, pt. 1, 349–352. Ironically, the reports of the Confederate commander in these skirmishes with Burbridge speak disparagingly of the wholesale and disorderly flight of his cavalry detachment, attributing the repulse of Burbridge's attack solely to the gallantry of his small group of artillerymen. See Report of Lieutenant Colonel S. W. Ferguson (CSA), February 26, 1863; February 28, 1863, *O.R.*, ser. 1, vol. 24, pt. 1, 353–355.

35. Report of General John McClernand, June 17, 1863, *O.R.*, ser. 1, vol. 24, pt. 1, 139; McPherson, *Battle Cry of Freedom*, 626–627.

36. Report of General Stephen Burbridge, May 24, 1863, *O.R.*, ser. 1, vol. 24, pt. 2, 30–31; McPherson, *Battle Cry of Freedom*, 629.

37. Report of General Stephen Burbridge, May 24, 1863, *O.R.*, ser. 1, vol. 24, pt. 2, 31–32.

38. Report of General Stephen Burbridge, May 24, 1863, *O.R.*, ser. 1, vol. 24, pt. 2, 32–33.

39. Report of General Stephen Burbridge, May 24, 1863, *O.R.*, ser. 1, vol. 24, pt. 2, 33; McPherson, *Battle Cry of Freedom*, 631–633.

40. Report of General Stephen Burbridge, May 24, 1863, *O.R.*, ser. 1, vol. 24, pt. 2, 34–35.

41. Grant to Halleck, June 18, 1863, *O.R.*, ser. 1, vol. 24, pt. 1, 43; McPherson, *Battle Cry of Freedom*, 634–636.

42. J. H. Redfield et al. to Lincoln, November 8, 1863, CSR, Stephen G. Burbridge.

43. Report of General Halleck, November 15, 1863, *O.R.*, ser. 1, vol. 24, pt. 1, 7; Klotter and Harrison, *A New History of Kentucky*, 202–3.

44. Ramage, *Rebel Raider*, 47, 93–106, 137–145. For additional accounts of Morgan and his forays into Kentucky, see Harrison and Klotter, *A New History of Kentucky*, 199, 202–3; McPherson, *Battle Cry of Freedom*, 513–516.

45. Report of Colonel John Scott (CSA), August 7, 1863, *O.R.*, ser. 1, vol. 23, pt. 1, 839–840; Klotter and Harrison, *A New History of Kentucky*, 203.

46. Lieutenant Colonel Thomas Young to Lieutenant Colonel G. B. Drake, July 30, 1863; Young to Major General George Hartsuff, July 29, 1863, *O.R.*, ser. 1, vol. 23, pt. 1, 837–838.

47. Report of General Simon B. Buckner (CSA), August 30, 1863; Report of Colonel John Scott (CSA), August 7, 1863, *O.R.*, ser. 1, vol. 23, pt. 1, 840–842.

48. Report of General Stephen Burbridge, September 30, 1863, *O.R.*, ser. 1, vol. 26, pt. 1, 317; Samuel C. Hyde, "Guerrilla Warfare in Civil War Louisiana," in *Encyclopedia of Louisiana*, ed. David Johnson, https://64parishes.org/entry/guerrilla-warfare-in-civil-war-louisiana.

49. John D. Winters, *The Civil War in Louisiana* (Baton Rouge: Louisiana State Univ. Press, 1991), 298–299; Report of General C. C. Washburn, November 7, 1863, *O.R.*, ser. 1, vol. 26, pt. 1, 357.

50. Report of General C. C. Washburn, November 7, 1863; "Return of Casualties . . . ," *O.R.*, ser. 1, vol. 26, pt. 1, 358–359; Bush, *Butcher Burbridge,* 66–68.

51. Reports of Stephen Burbridge, November 12, 1863; November 14, 1863; Franklin to Burbridge, November 14, 1863, *O.R.*, ser. 1, vol. 26, pt. 1, 362–363; Winters, *The Civil War in Louisiana,* 299.

## 3. Commander

1. Ross A. Webb, "Boyle, Jeremiah T.," and Ron Bryant, "Boyle County," in *The Kentucky Encyclopedia,* ed. John Kleber (Lexington: Univ. Press of Kentucky, 1992), 109–10.

2. Coulter, *The Civil War and Readjustment in Kentucky,* 151–153; Collins and Collins, *Collins' Historical Sketches of Kentucky,* 1:102–5; Webb, "Boyle, Jeremiah T.," 109; Ramage, *Rebel Raider,* 100.

3. Collins and Collins, *Collins' Historical Sketches of Kentucky,* 1:104–5; Coulter, *The Civil War and Readjustment in Kentucky,* 155; Harrison and Klotter, *A New History of Kentucky,* 206.

4. Collins and Collins, *Collins' Historical Sketches of Kentucky,* 1:115; Coulter, *The Civil War and Readjustment in Kentucky,* 152, 217–218.

5. Collins and Collins, *Collins' Historical Sketches of Kentucky,* 1:128; Coulter, *The Civil War and Readjustment in Kentucky,* 157–158.

6. George Blakey to Burbridge, January 5, 1864, CSR, Stephen G. Burbridge.

7. Boyle to Lincoln, January 10, 1864, *O.R.*, ser. 1, vol. 32, pt. 2, 62; see also Webb, "Boyle, Jeremiah T.," 109; Sanders, "General Jeremiah T. Boyle," https://explorekyhistory.ky.gov/items/show/17.

8. Coulter, *The Civil War and Readjustment in Kentucky,* 151; Webb, "Boyle, Jeremiah T.," 109.

9. Jonathan R. Bailey to Burbridge, January 21, 1864, SGB Correspondence, 1862–1865; Grant to Schofield, February 14, 1864, *O.R.*, ser. 1, vol. 32, pt. 2, 394; Special Order No. 41, February 15, 1864, *O.R.*, ser. 1, vol. 32, pt. 2, 401; David L. Mowery, "Brigadier General Jacob Ammen," Cincinnati Civil War Round Table, http://www.cincinnaticwrt.org/wp-content/uploads/2017/08/jacob_ammen.pdf.

10. Bramlette to Grant, March 8, 1864, *O.R.*, ser. 1, vol. 32, pt. 3, 39; Grant to Schofield, March 14, 1864, *O.R.*, ser. 1, vol. 32, pt. 3, 68; Special Order No. 85, Department of the Ohio, March 25, 1864, *O.R.*, ser. 1, vol. 52, pt. 1, 537.

11. General Edward Potter to Burbridge, March 15, 1864, *O.R.*, ser. 1, vol. 32, pt. 3, 75.

12. Burbridge to Hobson, March 29, 1864, *O.R.*, ser. 1, vol. 32, pt. 3, 186; Burbridge to Sherman, April 2, 1864, *O.R.*, ser. 1, vol. 32, pt. 3, 237; Sherman to Burbridge, April 2, 1864, *O.R.*, ser. 1, vol. 32, pt. 3, 236.

13. Sherman to Halleck, May 19, 1864, *O.R.*, ser. 1, vol. 39, pt. 2, 38; Theodore Allen, Diary, May 26, 1864, Filson Historical Society, Louisville, Kentucky; James Prichard, "Banner in the Dust: John Hunt Morgan's Last Kentucky Raid," in *Essays on America's Civil War,* vol. 4, *Confederate Generals in the Western Theater,* ed. Lawrence Lee Hewitt and Thomas E. Schott (Knoxville: Univ. of Tennessee Press, 2017), 163.

14. Schofield to Burbridge, May 22, 1864, *O.R.*, ser. 1, vol. 39, pt. 3, 43; Burbridge to Schofield, May 20, 1864, *O.R.*, ser. 1, vol. 39, pt. 3, 40; Burbridge to Bramlette, May 19, 1864; Burbridge to Sherman, May 19, 1864, *O.R.*, ser. 1, vol. 39, pt. 3, 39.

15. McKnight, *Contested Borderland,* 202; Halleck to Sherman, May 18, 1864, *O.R.*, ser. 1, vol. 39, pt. 2, 36; Ramage, *Rebel Raider,* 213. James Prichard argues that the plan to strike western Virginia was not Burbridge's independent initiative, but rather stemmed from Grant's strategy to "hammer the Confederacy on all fronts," but Sherman's reaction to Halleck's intelligence contradicts this conclusion, and Ramage suggests that Grant's offensive was not aimed at the mountains of southwestern Virginia but at the Shenandoah Valley and the Virginia & Tennessee Railroad. See Prichard, "Banner in the Dust," 165; Sherman to Halleck, May 19, 1864, *O.R.*, ser. 1, vol. 39, pt. 2, 39; Ramage, *Rebel Raider,* 211.

16. *Louisville Daily Journal,* June 11, 1864; McKnight, *Contested Borderland,* 202; Bush, *Butcher Burbridge,* 86–87; J. Bates Dickson to Bramlette, June 14, 1864, *O.R.*, ser. 1, vol. 39, pt. 1, 28, Prichard, "Banner in the Dust," 166; Ramage, *Rebel Raider,* 213.

17. *Louisville Daily Journal,* June 11, 1864; McKnight, *Contested Borderland,* 203; Bush, *Butcher Burbridge,* 91; Prichard, "Banner in the Dust," 170–175; Ramage, *Rebel Raider,* 219–221; R. A. Alston to Governor [Richard] Hawes, August 14, 1864, *O.R.*, ser. 1, vol. 39, pt. 1, 79. Burbridge's initial estimate wildly exaggerated the number of Confederate casualties after the Mount Sterling assault, reporting to Governor Bramlette that he buried two hundred enemy soldiers. Dickson to Bramlette, June 14, 1864, *O.R.*, ser. 1, vol. 39, pt. 1, 28.

18. Prichard, "Banner in the Dust," 177.

19. Hobson to J. Bates Dickson, June 24, 1864, *O.R.*, ser. 1, vol. 39, pt. 1, 33–36; Dickson to Bramlette, June 14, 1864, *O.R.*, ser. 1, vol. 39, pt. 1, 28; Hobson to Burbridge, June 22, 1864, *O.R.*, ser. 1., vol. 39, pt. 2, 138; Prichard, "Banner in the Dust," 176–179; Bush, *Butcher Burbridge,* 92–93.

20. Hobson to J. Bates Dickson, June 24, 1864, *O.R.*, ser. 1, vol. 39, pt. 1, 35–36; Hobson to Burbridge, June 22, 1864, *O.R.*, ser. 1. vol. 39, pt. 2, 138; Prichard, "Banner in the Dust," 179.

21. Dickson to Bramlette, June 14, 1864, *O.R.*, ser. 1, vol. 39, pt. 1, 28; Colonel Charles S. Hanson to General Nathaniel McLean, July 8, 1864, *O.R.*, ser. 1, vol. 39, pt. 1, 40; Bush, *Butcher Burbridge,* 94–95; McKnight, *Contested Borderland,* 203; Prichard, "Banner in the Dust," 180–184; Ramage, *Rebel Raider,* 221–223.

22. Ramage, *Rebel Raider,* 208, 216; Prichard, "Banner in the Dust," 163–165.

23. Stanton to Burbridge, July 4, 1864, *O.R.*, ser. 1, vol. 39, pt. 2, 162; Lincoln to Burbridge, June 14, 1864; Stanton to Burbridge, June 14, 1864, *O.R.*, ser. 1, vol. 39, pt. 1, 27; *Lexington National Unionist,* August 12, 1864. Burbridge's friends had been angling for his promotion for some time prior to this, however. See George Womack et al. to Lincoln and Stanton, May 30, 1864; John Latham et al. to Lincoln, February [?], 1863, CSR, Stephen G. Burbridge.

24. Burbridge to Halleck, June 23, 1864, *O.R.*, ser. 1, vol. 39, pt. 1, 21–22; Halleck to Burbridge, June 21, 1864, *O.R.*, ser. 1, vol. 39, pt. 2, 133–134; Halleck to Burbridge, June 23, 1864, *O.R.*, ser. 1, vol. 39, pt. 2, 141; Special Order No. 155, June 30, 1864, *O.R.*, ser. 1, vol. 39, pt. 2, 154.

25. W. Y. Dillard to Burbridge, July 16, 1864; Daniel W. Lindsey to Burbridge, August 20, 1864; Burbridge to Halleck, August 21, 1864, *O.R.*, ser. 1, vol. 39, pt. 2, 175, 273, 279.

26. Grant to Halleck, August 22, 1864, *O.R.*, ser. 1, vol. 39, pt. 2, 283.

27. Ramage, *Rebel Raider,* 226–244; Harrison and Klotter, *A New History of Kentucky,* 203.

28. Halleck to Burbridge, Sherman to Burbridge, August 19, 1864, *O.R.*, ser. 1, vol. 39, pt. 2, 268. For Wheeler's ineffective raiding expedition into Tennessee, see J. P. Dyer, "The Civil War Career of General Joseph Wheeler," *Georgia Historical Quarterly* 19 (1935): 40–42.

29. Adam Johnson, *Partisan Rangers of the Confederate States Army* (Louisville, Ky.: George G. Fetter Co., 1904), 164–172; Scott Tarnowieckyi, "'Branded by the Lincolnites as Guerrillas': Adam Rankin Johnson, Guerrilla Identity, and Irregular Warfare in the Lower Green River Valley in 1862," *Register of the Kentucky Historical Society* 113 (2015): 648–661, 670.

30. Johnson, *Partisan Rangers,* 164–172; Henry B. Carrington to C. H. Potter, August 9, 1864, *O.R.*, ser. 1, vol. 39, pt. 2, 236–238.

31. S. M. Starling et al. to Burbridge, August 27, 1864; Dickson to Ewing, August 12, 1864; Burbridge to Carrington, August 12, 1864, Burbridge to Hobson, August 14, 1864, *O.R.*, ser. 1, vol. 39, pt. 2, 243, 250, 309; Johnson, *Partisan Rangers,* 173–174.

32. Burbridge to Schofield, Burbridge to Halleck, September 11, 1864, *O.R.*, ser. 1, vol. 39, pt. 2, 360; Burbridge to Schofield, September 16, 1864, *O.R.*, ser. 1, vol. 39, pt. 2, 393.

33. Schofield to Burbridge, September 14, 1864, *O.R.*, ser. 1, vol. 39, pt. 2, 380; Sherman to Schofield, September 22, 1864, *O.R.*, ser. 1, vol. 39, pt. 2, 447; Schofield to Sherman, September 19, 1864, *O.R.*, ser. 1, vol. 39, pt. 2, 408; Halleck to Burbridge, September 12, 1864, *O.R.*, ser. 1, vol. 39, pt. 2, 367; Schofield to Sherman, October 1, 1864, *O.R.*, ser. 1, vol. 39, pt. 3, 10.

34. Lucas, *A History of Blacks in Kentucky*, vol. 1, *From Slavery to Segregation*, 175; McKnight, *Contested Borderland*, 207.

35. McKnight, *Contested Borderland*, 208–9; Bush, *Butcher Burbridge*, 143–145; Burbridge to Stanton, October 7, 1864, *O.R.*, ser. 1, vol. 39, pt. 1, 552.

36. McKnight, *Contested Borderland*, 209–10; Itinerary of the 1st Division, District of Kentucky, *O.R.*, ser. 1, vol. 39, pt. 1, 555–556; Bush, *Butcher Burbridge*, 145–147.

37. McKnight, *Contested Borderland*, 210–213, discusses the controversy.

38. See Gregory J. W. Urwin, *Black Flag over Dixie: Racial Atrocities and Reprisals in the Civil War* (Carbondale: Southern Illinois Univ. Press, 2004), as well as the review of Urwin's book by Michael DeGruccio, "Exposing the 'Lurid Interiors' of War," H-CivWar (August 2006), https://networks.h-net.org/node/4113/reviews/4743/degruccio-urwin-black-flag-over-dixie-racial-atrocities-and-reprisals.

39. McKnight, *Contested Borderland*, 213–215; Bush, *Butcher Burbridge*, 147; Report of Surgeon William H. Gardner, October 26, 1864, *O.R.*, ser. 1, vol. 39, pt. 1, 554.

40. Burbridge to Schofield, October 7, 1864, *O.R.*, ser. 1, vol. 39, pt. 1, 552.

41. Sherman to General J. D. Webster, September 23, 1864, *O.R.*, ser. 1, vol. 39, pt. 2, 442; Webster to Burbridge, September 27, 1864, *O.R.*, ser. 1, vol. 39, pt. 2, 497; Sherman to Webster, September 28, 1864, *O.R.*, ser. 1, vol. 39, pt. 2, 504.

42. Webster to General A. C. Gillem, October 6, 1864, *O.R.*, ser. 1, vol. 39, pt. 3, 121.

43. Schofield to Sherman, October 11, 1864, *O.R.*, ser. 1, vol. 39, pt. 3, 219.

44. Burbridge to Indiana Governor Oliver P. Morton, Colonel W. Y. Dillard to Burbridge, Burbridge to General Samuel Heintzelman, Halleck to General John F. Miller, July 16, 1864, *O.R.*, ser. 1, vol. 39, pt. 2, 173–176.

45. Grant to Halleck, August 22, 1864, *O.R.*, ser. 1, vol. 39, pt. 2, 283.

46. L. M. Dayton (aide-de-camp) to General J. D. Webster, August 23, 1864, *O.R.*, ser. 1, vol. 39, pt. 2, 291.

47. Sherman to Burbridge, August 23, 1864, *O.R.*, ser. 1, vol. 39, pt. 2, 292.

48. Sherman to General John Rawlins, April 19, 1864, *O.R.*, ser. 1, vol. 32, pt. 3, 411. See also Schofield to Burbridge, July 18, 1864, *O.R.*, ser. 1, vol. 39, pt. 2, 178, stressing that troops could not be spared for Kentucky from the front, and Sherman's response to General Rosecrans's request for more troops in Missouri, in *O.R.*, ser. 1, vol. 39, pt. 3, 530.

49. Burbridge to Schofield, October 14, 1864, *O.R.*, ser. 1, vol. 39, pt. 3, 282.

50. Burbridge to Schofield, Schofield to Burbridge, October 15, 1864, *O.R.*, ser. 1, vol. 39, pt. 3, 301–302.

51. Colonel A. A. Smith to Major B. H. Polk, October 8, 1864, *O.R.*, ser. 1, vol. 39, pt. 3, 156; General Hugh Ewing to Burbridge, Burbridge to Ewing, October 14, 1864, *O.R.*, ser. 1, vol. 39, pt. 3, 284; Burbridge to Halleck, October 17, 1864, *O.R.*, ser. 1, vol. 39, pt. 3, 343; Edward F. Williams III, "The Johnsonville Raid and Nathan Bedford Forrest State Park," *Tennessee Historical Quarterly* 28 (1969): 228–229.

52. *Lexington National Unionist,* February 7, 1865.

53. Report of Major General George H. Thomas, January 20, 1865, *O.R.*, ser. 1, vol. 45, pt. 1, 37; McKnight, *Contested Borderland,* 220.

54. Burbridge to McLean, November 21, 1864, *O.R.*, ser. 1, vol. 45, pt. 1, 980.

55. Burbridge to J. Bates Dickson, November 27, 1864, *O.R.*, ser. 1, vol. 45, pt. 1, 1103.

56. Burbridge to Dickson, Burbridge to McLean, December 5, 1864, *O.R.*, ser. 1, vol. 45, pt. 2, 67–68.

57. Stoneman to Schofield, January 6, 1865, *O.R.*, ser. 1, vol. 45, pt. 1, 811.

58. Stoneman to Schofield, January 6, 1865, *O.R.*, ser. 1, vol. 45, pt. 1, 812; McKnight, *Contested Borderland,* 221.

59. Stoneman to Schofield, January 6, 1865, *O.R.*, ser. 1, vol. 45, pt. 1, 812–813; McKnight, *Contested Borderland,* 221.

60. Burbridge to Stanton, December 28, 1864; Burbridge to Stanton, January 3, 1865, *O.R.*, ser. 1, vol. 45, pt. 1, 815–818.

61. General John C. Breckinridge (CSA) to Lieutenant Colonel W. H. Taylor, January 3, 1865, *O.R.*, ser. 1, vol. 45, pt. 1, 827.

62. McKnight, *Contested Borderland,* 221.

63. Burbridge to Halleck, October 27, 1864, *O.R.*, ser. 1, vol. 39, pt. 3, 473.

64. Burbridge to Lieutenant Colonel Bascom, November 16, 1864, included in Stoneman to Thomas, November 17, 1864, *O.R.*, ser. 1, vol. 45, pt. 1, 929.

65. *Lexington National Unionist,* February 7, 1865.

66. D. S. Towles to Hobson, December 29, 1864, Edward Henry Hobson Papers, 1767–1899, Microfilm M-284, Special Collections Research Center, Margaret I. King Library, University of Kentucky, Lexington, Kentucky.

## 4. Liberator

1. *Cincinnati Enquirer,* April 26, 1865.

2. Howard, "The Civil War in Kentucky," 253; Howard, *Black Liberation in Kentucky,* 16; Berlin et al., *Freedom,* ser. 1, vol. 1, *The Destruction of Slavery,* 502–503, 508–510; Lucas, *A History of Blacks in Kentucky,* vol. 1, *From Slavery to Segregation,* 148–152.

3. Berlin et al., *Freedom,* ser. 1, vol. 1, *The Destruction of Slavery,* 503–507.

4. Lucas, *A History of Blacks in Kentucky,* vol. 1, *From Slavery to Segregation,* 163.

5. Howard, *Black Liberation in Kentucky,* 65.

6. Berlin et al., *Freedom,* ser. 1, vol. 1, *The Destruction of Slavery,* 506, accused "the Kentucky generals and colonels" in command in the state of "scrupulously accommodat[ing] the slaveholders' claims."

7. *Lexington National Unionist,* February 7, 1865.

8. Berlin et al., *Freedom,* ser. 1, vol. 1, *The Destruction of Slavery,* 500–502; *Janesville (Wisc.) Daily Gazette,* November 11, 1862.

9. Burbridge to Stanton, June 23, 1864; Stanton to Burbridge, June 23, 1864, *O.R.,* ser. 1, vol. 39, pt. 2, 140.

10. William T. Chapman, Journals [Transcripts], January 14, 1863, January 24, 1863, Center of Archival Collections, Bowling Green State University, Bowling Green, Ohio, https://lib.bgsu.edu/finding_aids/items/show/2042.

11. Berlin et al., *Freedom,* ser. 1, vol. 1, *The Destruction of Slavery,* 504; Patrick Lewis, "'All Men of Decency Ought to Quit the Army': Benjamin F. Buckner, Manhood, and Proslavery Unionism in Kentucky," *Register of the Kentucky Historical Society* 107 (2009): 513, 535, 544; Marshall, *Creating a Confederate Kentucky,* 25.

12. Lewis, "'All Men of Decency Ought to Quit the Army,'" 531; Philips, *The Rivers Ran Backward,* 232–233; Asher, *Cecelia and Fanny,* 111; Coulter, *The Civil War and Readjustment in Kentucky,* 163; Collins and Collins, *Collins' Historical Sketches of Kentucky,* 1:118.

13. John David Smith, "The Recruitment of Negro Soldiers in Kentucky, 1863–1865," *Register of the Kentucky Historical Society* 72 (1974): 372–374; Coulter, *The Civil War and Readjustment in Kentucky,* 197–198.

14. Smith, "The Recruitment of Negro Soldiers," 371–372; *Louisville Daily Journal,* May 13, 1864; August 1, 1864.

15. Berlin et al., *Freedom,* ser. 2, *The Black Military Experience,* 191–192; Howard, *Black Liberation in Kentucky,* 58; Harlow, *Religion, Race, and the Making of Confederate Kentucky,* 163; Lorenzo Thomas to Stanton, October 5, 1865, *O.R.,* ser. 3, vol. 5, 122.

16. Smith, "The Recruitment of Negro Soldiers," 374–375.

17. Bramlette to Stanton, June 20, 1864, *O.R.*, ser. 3, vol. 4, 436; Smith, "The Recruitment of Negro Soldiers," 375–376.

18. Cope to Bramlette, February 8, 1864, Kentucky, Office of the Governor, Thomas E. Bramlette, Governor's Official Correspondence File, Military Correspondence, 1863–1867, Box 5, Folder 99, Kentucky Department for Libraries and Archives, Frankfort, Kentucky.

19. This account of Bramlette's letter and Stanton's response is drawn from Smith, "The Recruitment of Negro Soldiers," 377–378.

20. Berlin et al., *Freedom,* ser. 2, *The Black Military Experience,* 192.

21. Harlow, *Religion, Race, and the Making of Confederate Kentucky,* 156–185.

22. Hambleton Tapp, "Incidents in the Life of Frank Wolford, Colonel of the First Kentucky Union Cavalry," *Filson Club Historical Quarterly* 10 (1936): 88–91; E. Tarrant, *The Wild Riders of the First Kentucky Cavalry: A History of the Regiment, in the Great War of the Rebellion* (Louisville, Ky.: The Committee of the Regiment, 1894), 85, 88.

23. *Louisville Courier-Journal,* September 29, 1884; Collins and Collins, *Collins' Historical Sketches of Kentucky,* 1:132; Howard, *Black Liberation in Kentucky,* 58; Coulter, *The Civil War and Readjustment in Kentucky,* 199; Harrison and Klotter, *A New History of Kentucky,* 179.

24. Coulter, *The Civil War and Readjustment in Kentucky,* 199; Smith, "The Recruitment of Negro Soldiers," 380; Sydney Clay to Representative Brutus J. Clay, April 18, 1864, in Mary Clay Berry, *Voices from the Century Before: The Odyssey of a Nineteenth-Century Kentucky Family* (New York: Arcade Publishing, 1996), 391.

25. Sidell to J. B. Fry, March 13, 1864, *O.R.*, ser. 3, vol. 4, 174–175.

26. Howard, *Black Liberation in Kentucky,* 58; Coulter, *The Civil War and Readjustment in Kentucky,* 200; Sidell to Fry, March 13, 1864, *O.R.*, ser. 3, vol. 4, 174.

27. Sidell to J. B. Fry, March 13, 1864, *O.R.*, ser. 3, vol. 4, 174–175.

28. Robert Winn to "Dear Sister" [Martha], March 17, 1864, Winn-Cook Family Papers, 1861–1875, Folder 6, Filson Historical Society, Louisville, Kentucky.

29. R. E. Jeter [?] to Hobson, March [?], 1864, Edward Henry Hobson Papers, 1767–1899; Smith, "The Recruitment of Negro Soldiers," 378.

30. Ira Stout [?] to James Speed, March 11, 1864, Speed Family Papers, 1813–1981, Folder 36, Filson Historical Society, Louisville, Kentucky.

31. Sidell to J. B. Fry, March 13, 1864, *O.R.,* ser. 3, vol. 4, 175.

32. Bramlette to Burbridge, March 14, 1864, SGB Correspondence, 1862–1865; Howard, *Black Liberation in Kentucky,* 59; Coulter, *The Civil War and Readjustment in Kentucky,* 200.

33. Smith, "The Recruitment of Negro Soldiers," 368.

34. The *Frankfort Commonwealth* published what it called the original text of Bramlette's initial proclamation in its edition of May 9, 1864. There are several accounts in the secondary literature of the Frankfort meeting that rely on the same small set of primary sources and reach similar conclusions, though they differ on some of the particulars. Howard, *Black Liberation in Kentucky,* 59; Coulter, *The Civil War and Readjustment in Kentucky,* 200–201; Smith, "The Recruitment of Negro Soldiers," 382. Bramlette published his own account some years after the war when Bell accused him of fomenting resistance to federal authority during the war. See *Louisville Courier-Journal,* September 29, 1873. Bell's accusation appeared in the *Bowling Green Pantagraph,* September 17, 1873.

35. Howard, *Black Liberation in Kentucky,* 59; Coulter, *The Civil War and Readjustment in Kentucky,* 200; Smith, "The Recruitment of Negro Soldiers," 382.

36. Burbridge to Lincoln, March 16, 1864, *O.R.*, ser. 3, vol. 4, 187–188.

37. Breckinridge to Burbridge, March 26, 1864, SGB Correspondence, 1862–1865.

38. Sidell to J. B. Fry, March 13, 1864, *O.R.*, ser. 3, vol. 4, 175.

39. *Lexington National Unionist,* February 7, 1865.

40. Howard, *Black Liberation in Kentucky,* 60–61; Coulter, *The Civil War and Readjustment in Kentucky,* 203; Collins and Collins, *Collins' Historical Sketches of Kentucky,* 1:132.

41. Adjutant General E. D. Townsend, Special Order No. 140, April 6, 1864, *O.R.*, ser. 3, vol. 4, 218.

42. Quoted in *Louisville Journal,* June 14, 1864; see also Howard, *Black Liberation in Kentucky,* 63.

43. Lowell Harrison, "Slavery in Kentucky: A Civil War Casualty," *Kentucky Review* 5 (1983): 38–39, https://uknowledge.uky.edu/kentucky-review/vol5/iss1/4/.

44. Thomas B. Fairleigh, Diary, April 17, 1864, Filson Historical Society, Louisville, Kentucky; District of Kentucky, General Order No. 34, April 18, 1964, *O.R.*, ser. 3, vol. 4, 233–234.

45. Berlin et al., *Freedom,* ser. 2, *The Black Military Experience,* 193. Berlin also notes that by restricting recruiting only to provost marshals, Burbridge's order forbade the type of mounted and mobile recruitment of slaves used in Maryland and Missouri and by Captain Cunningham in western Kentucky. Thus, many slaveholders in the countryside, far from a provost marshal's office, were essentially protected from the impact of General Order No. 34.

46. Howard, *Black Liberation in Kentucky,* 63; Smith, "The Recruitment of Negro Soldiers," 385; Lucas, *A History of Blacks in Kentucky,* vol. 1, *From Slavery to Segregation,* 154; Colonel A. H. Clark to J. Bates Dickson, May 27, 1864,

Stephen G. Burbridge Papers, 1863–1864, Box 1, "Telegrams Received, 1864, May 1–31," Rubinstein Library, Duke University, Durham, North Carolina.

47. Mollie Turner to James Speed, May 2, 1864, Speed Family Papers, Folder 38.

48. District of Kentucky, General Order No. 45, June 2, 1864, *O.R,* ser. 1, vol. 39, 77; Howard, *Black Liberation in Kentucky,* 64; Lucas, *A History of Blacks in Kentucky,* vol. 1, *From Slavery to Segregation,* 155.

49. Holt to Stanton, July 31, 1864, *O.R,* ser. 1, vol. 39, pt. 2, 213–214.

50. Lorenzo Thomas, General Order No. 20, June 13, 1864, *O.R.*, ser. 3, vol. 4, 429–430.

51. *Lexington National Unionist,* March 14, 1865; Bramlette to Stanton, June 20, 1864, *O.R.*, ser. 3, vol. 4, 436–437.

52. Burbridge to Bramlette, June 16, 1864, SGB Correspondence, 1862–1865.

53. Burbridge to Stanton, June 23, 1864, *O.R.*, ser. 1, vol. 39, pt. 2, 140; Thomas to Stanton, June 29, 1864, *O.R.*, ser. 3, vol. 4, 459–460, 467; Sedgwick to Dickson, July 10, 1864, Stephen G. Burbridge Papers, 1863–1864, Box 1, "Telegrams Received, 1864, July 3–14"; Holt to Stanton, July 31, 1864, *O.R.*, ser. 1, vol. 39, pt. 2, 213; Thomas to Stanton, October 11, 1864, *O.R.*, ser. 1, vol. 39, pt. 3, 219; Thomas to Stanton, October 5, 1865, *O.R.*, ser. 3, vol. 5, 123.

54. Berlin et al., *Freedom,* ser. 2, *The Black Military Experience,* 197; Klotter and Harrison, *A New History of Kentucky,* 180.

55. Thomas to Stanton, July 16, 1864, *O.R.*, ser. 3, vol. 4, 501–502; Berlin et al., *Freedom,* ser. 2, *The Black Military Experience,* 195.

56. Thomas James, *The Life of Rev. Thomas James, by Himself* (Rochester, N.Y.: Post Express Printing Co., 1886), 17–18, http://docsouth.unc.edu/neh/jamesth/jamesth.html.

57. Richard Sears, *Camp Nelson, Kentucky: A Civil War History* (Lexington: Univ. Press of Kentucky, 2002), l–li.

58. Burbridge to Stanton, November 29, 1864, *O.R.*, ser. 1, vol. 45, pt. 1, 1165.

59. Lucas, *A History of Blacks in Kentucky,* vol. 1, *From Slavery to Segregation,* 162; Richard Sears, "John G. Fee, Camp Nelson, and Kentucky Blacks, 1864–1865," *Register of the Kentucky Historical Society* 85 (1987): 39.

60. Sears, "John G. Fee, Camp Nelson, and Kentucky Blacks, 1864–1865," 40; Berlin et al., *Freedom,* ser. 2, *The Black Military Experience,* 196–197; Lucas, *A History of Blacks in Kentucky,* vol. 1, *From Slavery to Segregation,* 160–163.

61. Lorenzo Thomas, General Order No. 20, June 13, 1864, *O.R.*, ser. 3, vol. 4, 430.

62. Thomas to Stanton, October 5, 1865, *O.R.*, ser. 3, vol. 5, 122.

63. Burbridge to Thomas, July 3, 1864, *O.R.*, ser. 3, vol. 4, 468–469.

64. Lorenzo Thomas, General Order No. 24, July 6, 1864, *O.R.*, ser. 3, vol. 4, 474; Thomas to Stanton, October 5, 1865, *O.R.*, ser. 3, vol. 5, 122.

65. Thomas to Stanton, July 3, 1864, *O.R.*, ser. 3, vol. 4, 468; Thomas to Stanton, October 5, 1865, *O.R.*, ser. 3, vol. 5, 122.

66. Burbridge to Joseph Holt, October 16, 1864, *O.R.*, ser. 1, vol. 39, pt. 3, 421.

67. Howard, *Black Liberation in Kentucky,* 73; Thomas to Stanton, October 5, 1865, *O.R.*, ser. 3, vol. 5, 123; "Biographical Note," James Sanks Brisbin Papers, 1850–1891, Montana Historical Society, http://archiveswest.orbiscascade.org/ark:/80444/xv27706/op=fstyle.aspx?t=k&q=Brisbin#bioghistID.

68. Burbridge to Stanton, August 17, 1864, *O.R.*, ser. 1, vol. 39, pt. 2, 262.

69. Holt to Stanton, July 28, 1864, *O.R.*, ser. 1, vol. 39, pt. 2, 208.

70. Thomas to Stanton, October 10, 1864, *O.R.*, ser. 1, vol. 39, pt. 3, 200; Lucas, *A History of Blacks in Kentucky,* vol. 1: *From Slavery to Segregation,* 176.

71. Major J. A. Campbell to Schofield, October 9, 1864, *O.R.*, ser. 1, vol. 39, pt. 3, 173.

72. Burbridge to Schofield, October 14, 1864, *O.R.*, ser. 1, vol. 39, pt. 3, 282; Thomas to Stanton, October 11, 1864, *O.R.*, ser. 1, vol. 39, pt. 3, 219.

73. Dickson to Meredith, October 24, 1864, *O.R.*, ser. 1, vol. 39, pt. 3, 427; Burbridge to Meredith, October 26, 1864, *O.R.*, ser. 1, vol. 39, pt. 3, 458.

74. Howard, *Black Liberation in Kentucky,* 73–74; Coulter, *The Civil War and Readjustment in Kentucky,* 208–209.

75. Lincoln to Lieutenant Colonel Glenn, February 7, 1865, *O.R.*, ser. 1, vol. 49, pt. 1, 668; Berlin et al., *Freedom,* ser. 2, *The Black Military Experience,* 273–274; Lucas, *A History of Blacks in Kentucky,* vol. 1, *From Slavery to Segregation,* 158.

76. Howard, *Black Liberation in Kentucky,* 73–74

77. Lucas, *A History of Blacks in Kentucky,* vol. 1, *From Slavery to Segregation,* 160, 164–165; Department of Kentucky, General Order No. 1, February 18, 1865, *O.R.*, ser. 1, vol. 49, pt. 1, 741; Berlin et al., *Freedom,* ser. 2, *The Black Military Experience,* 196–197; Howard, *Black Liberation in Kentucky,* 78–79.

## 5. Tyrant

1. Coulter, *The Civil War and Readjustment in Kentucky,* 214; Harrison and Klotter, *A New History of Kentucky,* 206; William Gienapp, "Abraham Lincoln and the Border States," *Journal of the Abraham Lincoln Association* 13 (1992): 26.

2. Thomas Bramlette, *Speech of Gov. Thomas E. Bramlette of Kentucky . . .* (Louisville: Lost Cause Press, 1958); *Louisville Daily Journal,* May 13, 1864.

3. Harlow, *Religion, Race, and the Making of Confederate Kentucky,* 183.

4. Sherman to Burbridge, April 2, 1864, *O.R.*, ser. 1, vol. 32, pt. 3, 237.

5. General Order No. 39, May 2, 1864, *O.R.*, ser. 1, vol. 39, pt. 2, 7.

6. *Cincinnati Enquirer,* April 6, 1864. On the suppression of the *Enquirer,* see Collins and Collins, *Collins' Historical Sketches of Kentucky,* 1:135; *New York Times,* June 20, 1864; *Cincinnati Enquirer,* July 11, 1864; July 25, 1864. A resolution by Kentucky Democratic senator Lazarus Powell to ask Lincoln to lift the suppression order was defeated by a vote of 29–3 in the Senate. Collins and Collins, *Collins' Historical Sketches of Kentucky,* 1:135.

7. General Order No. 41, May 12, 1864, *O.R.*, ser. 1, vol. 39, pt. 2, 23–24.

8. General Order No. 42, May 14, 1864, *O.R.*, ser. 1, vol. 39, pt. 2, 27.

9. General Order No. 45, May 12, 1864, *O.R.*, ser. 1, vol. 39, pt. 2, 77.

10. Howard, *Black Liberation in Kentucky,* 62.

11. Stanton to Burbridge, July 5, 1864, *O.R.*, ser. 1, vol. 39, pt. 2, 163.

12. General Order No. 233, War Department, July 19, 1864, *O.R.*, ser. 1, vol. 39, pt. 2, 180–182; Collins and Collins, *Collins' Historical Sketches of Kentucky,* 1:135; Mark Neely Jr., *The Fate of Liberty: Abraham Lincoln and Civil Liberties* (New York: Oxford Univ. Press, 1992), 90–91. Neely notes that this proclamation was unnecessary and redundant, as it merely urged enforcement in Kentucky of a previous proclamation restricting the writ of habeas corpus and imposing martial law wherever it was needed. Indeed, Neely does not see the administration's nine martial law proclamations as an ordered and logical progression, but says "the administration lurched from problem to problem drafting hasty proclamations and orders to meet the objective of the moment."

13. Halleck to Burbridge, June 23, 1864, *O.R.*, ser. 1, vol. 39, pt. 2, 140–141.

14. Sherman to Stanton, June 21, 1864; Sherman to Burbridge, June 23, 1864; Stanton to Sherman, July 1, 1864, *O.R.*, ser. 1, vol. 39, pt. 2, 131, 135, 157.

15. J. Bates Dickson to Colonel John Eve, June 26, 1864, *O.R.*, ser. 1, vol. 39, pt. 2, 146; General Order No. 61, July 26, 1864, *O.R.*, ser. 1, vol. 39, pt. 2, 205.

16. Burbridge to Sherman, August 1, 1864; Sherman to Burbridge, August 1, 1864, telegrams, *O.R.*, ser. 1, vol. 39, pt. 2, 217.

17. Proclamation by the Governor, January 4, 1864, Kentucky, Office of the Governor, Thomas E. Bramlette, Communications with the General Assembly, 1863–1867, Box 1, Folder 15-C, Kentucky Department for Libraries and Archives, Frankfort, Kentucky; *Louisville Daily Journal,* January 7, 1864, February 8, 1864.

18. Boyle to Lincoln, July 2, 1864, *O.R.*, ser. 1, vol. 39, pt. 2, 159; Klotter and Harrison, *A New History of Kentucky,* 205–206.

19. Smith, "The Recruitment of Negro Soldiers," 380–381; Coulter, *The Civil War and Readjustment in Kentucky,* 200; Howard, *Black Liberation in Kentucky,* 59; Collins and Collins, *Collins' Historical Sketches of Kentucky,* 1:134.

20. *Weekly National Intelligencer* (Washington, D.C.), September 29, 1864.

21. *Weekly National Intelligencer* (Washington, D.C.), September 29, 1864; Howard, *Black Liberation in Kentucky,* 61–62; Provost Marshal J. M. Fidler to Burbridge, May 28, 1864, Stephen G. Burbridge Papers, 1863–1864, Box 1, "Telegrams Received, 1864, May 1–31."

22. Halleck to Burbridge, June 11, 1864; Burbridge to Halleck, June 14, 1864, *O.R.*, ser. 1, vol. 39, pt. 2, 98, 116.

23. Collins and Collins, *Collins' Historical Sketches of Kentucky,* 1:137; Coulter, *The Civil War and Readjustment in Kentucky,* 206.

24. *Weekly National Intelligencer* (Washington, D.C.), September 29, 1864; Howard, *Black Liberation in Kentucky,* 62.

25. *Weekly National Intelligencer* (Washington, D.C.), September 29, 1864.

26. Burbridge to Schofield, July 17, 1864, Burbridge to Schofield, July 20, 1864, *O.R.*, ser. 1, vol. 39, pt. 2, 177, 182–183; Johnson, *Partisan Rangers,* 164–172. See also Halleck to Burbridge, June 25, 1864, *O.R.*, ser. 1, vol. 39, pt. 2, 144, authorizing him under the power of martial law to arrest anyone, including officers of the state government or elected federal representatives, guilty of aiding and abetting the rebellion.

27. Holt to Stanton, July 31, 1864, *O.R.*, ser. 1, vol. 39, pt. 2, 214; US Army, Office of the Judge Advocate General, "Report . . . on the 'Order of American Knights,' alias 'The Sons of Liberty' . . . " (1864), page 8. A copy of this pamphlet is in Joshua F. Bullitt, "Misc. items—Pamphlets," Bullitt Family Papers-Oxmoor Collection, 1683–2003, Filson Historical Society, Louisville, Kentucky.

28. Holt to Stanton, July 31, 1864, *O.R.*, ser. 1, vol. 39, pt. 2, 214.

29. Burbridge to Stanton, August 6, 1864, Stanton to Burbridge, August 7, 1864, *O.R.*, ser. 1, vol. 39, pt. 2, p. 228, 231; Collins and Collins, *Collins' Historical Sketches of Kentucky,* 1:137.

30. Frank Klement built much of his career on debunking the threat of Copperheadism and stressing the hyperbole of Republicans who tried to brand dissent as treason. See Frank Klement, "Carrington and the Golden Circle Legend in Indiana during the Civil War," *Indiana Magazine of History* 61 (1965): 31–52; Frank Klement, *The Limits of Dissent: Clement L. Vallandigham and the Civil War* (New York: Fordham Univ. Press, 1970); Frank Klement, *Dark Lanterns: Secret Political Societies, Conspiracies, and Treason*

*Trials in the Civil War* (Baton Rouge: Louisiana State Univ. Press, 1984). Klement took issue with earlier "nationalist" historians who believed too deeply in Republican propaganda about Copperhead conspiracies. More recently, Jennifer Weber has challenged Klement's conclusions by looking at grassroots Copperhead opposition to administration policies. See Jennifer Weber, *Copperheads: The Rise and Fall of Lincoln's Opponents in the North* (New York: Oxford Univ. Press, 2006). For a concise historiographical review, see Robert Sandow, "Damnable Treason or Party Organs? Democratic Secret Societies in Pennsylvania," in *This Distracted and Anarchical People: New Answers for Old Questions about the Civil War North,* ed. Andrew Slap and Michael Thomas Smith (New York: Fordham Univ. Press, 2013), 44–49.

31. Sherman to Guthrie, August 14, 1864, *O.R.*, ser, 1, vol. 39, pt. 2, 247–249.

32. *Cincinnati Enquirer,* August 1, 1864; Mildred Bullitt to Thomas W. Bullitt, September 4, 1864, "Thomas W. Bullitt, Personal Correspondence, July–December 1864," Folder 303, Bullitt Family Papers-Oxmoor Collection, 1683–2003.

33. *Lexington National Unionist,* July 22, 1864; Collins and Collins, *Collins' Historical Sketches of Kentucky,* 1:137–138; Charles Nourse to Ewing, July 27, 1864; S. W. Stone to Ewing, July 25, 1864, Hugh Boyle Ewing Papers, Box 4, Folder 1, "Correspondence, June 1864–September 1868," Ohio Historical Society, Columbus, Ohio.

34. Collins and Collins, *Collins' Historical Sketches of Kentucky,* 1:137; Charles Nourse to Ewing, July 27, 1864, Hugh Boyle Ewing Papers, Box 4, Folder 1, "Correspondence, June 1864–September 1868."

35. Kentucky, *Acts of the General Assembly,* 1864, 120–121, Kentucky Department for Libraries and Archives, Frankfort, Kentucky. On the centrality and autonomy of Kentucky's county governments, see Robert Ireland, *Little Kingdoms: The Counties of Kentucky, 1850–1891* (Lexington: Univ. Press of Kentucky, 1977), 18, 24.

36. Kentucky, *Acts of the General Assembly,* 1864, 116–117.

37. *Lexington National Unionist,* May 13, 1864. On the role of county governments during the war, see Ireland, *Little Kingdoms,* 60–63.

38. Collins and Collins, *Collins' Historical Sketches of Kentucky,* 1:137–138; Bramlette to Lincoln, September 3, 1864, *O.R.*, ser. 3, vol. 4, 688; Coulter, *The Civil War and Readjustment in Kentucky,* 186.

39. Coulter, *The Civil War and Readjustment in Kentucky,* 206.

40. Klement, *Dark Lanterns,* 244.

41. Mildred Bullitt to Thomas W. Bullitt, September 4, 1864, November 9, 1864, November 26, 1864, "Thomas W. Bullitt personal correspondence, July–December, 1864," Bullitt Family Papers-Oxmoor Collection, 1683–2003.

According to Joshua Bullitt's November 26 letter, Confederate general Nathan Bedford Forrest had engineered their release by agreeing to release some political prisoners he was holding. If such is true, it could not have bolstered Bullitt's claims of loyalty among Burbridge and other Unconditional Unionists that a Confederate general went to bat for him. See also Collins and Collins, *Collins' Historical Sketches of Kentucky,* 1:148.

42. The *Frankfort Commonwealth*'s account of Burbridge's speech was reprinted in the *Cincinnati Enquirer,* January 11, 1865; and Collins and Collins, *Collins' Historical Sketches of Kentucky,* 1:147. See also *Lexington National Unionist,* November 8, 1864. For Preston's account, see "Electioneering for President Abraham Lincoln in Kentucky, and the Outrages Committed by General Stephen G. Burbridge, from a Refugee Confederate Officer's Perspective," http://www.uky.edu/~dolph/HIS316/sources/electioneering.html, citing an original document in the Wickliffe-Preston Family Papers, 1753–1897, Box 55, Special Collections Research Center, Margaret I. King Library, University of Kentucky, Lexington, Kentucky. See also Peter Sehlinger, *Kentucky's Last Cavalier: General William Preston, 1816–1887* (Lexington: Univ. Press of Kentucky, 2004), 185–186.

43. Burbridge to Holt, October 16, 1864, *O.R.*, ser. 1, vol. 39, pt. 3, 321–322.

44. Coulter, *The Civil War and Readjustment in Kentucky,* 186–187.

45. James J. Miller et al. to Burbridge, October 28, 1864, Stephen G. Burbridge Papers, 1863–1864, Box 1, "Telegrams Received, 1864 October 1–31"; Burbridge to Maxwell, October 30, 1864, Burbridge to Holt, October 16, 1864, *O.R.*, ser. 1, vol. 39, pt. 3, 321–322, 526.

46. General Order No. 7, October 26, 1864, *O.R.*, ser. 1, vol. 39, pt. 3, 456; *Lexington National Unionist,* November 1, 1864. See also Collins and Collins, *Collins' Historical Sketches of Kentucky,* 1:144.

47. Coulter, *The Civil War and Readjustment in Kentucky,* 187–188; J. W. Throckmorton to Burbridge, November 8, 1864; Lieutenant F. Gray to Burbridge, November 8, 1864, Stephen G. Burbridge Papers, 1863–1864, Box 1, "Telegrams Received, 1864 November 1–30."

48. *Lexington National Unionist,* November 15, 1864.

49. Bramlette to Lincoln, September 3, 1864, *O.R.*, ser. 3, vol. 4, 689; *Lexington National Unionist,* May 13, 1864.

50. Bramlette to Lincoln, November 9, 1864, *O.R.*, ser. 2, vol. 7, 1114; Collins and Collins, *Collins' Historical Sketches of Kentucky,* 1:146–148; Coulter, *The Civil War and Readjustment in Kentucky,* 207. Lincoln replied to the governor that he could "scarcely believe" the allegation, for if opposition to his reelection "had been deemed sufficient cause of arrest I should have heard of more than one arrest in Kentucky on election day." See also Lincoln to Burbridge, November 10, 1864, *O.R.*, ser. 1, vol. 39, pt. 3, 739.

51. Bramlette to Burbridge, August 15, 1864; Bramlette to Burbridge, September 15, 1864, SGB Correspondence, 1862–1865.

52. Bramlette to Grant, November 9, 1864; Grant to Stanton, November 14, 1864, *O.R.*, ser. 1, vol. 39, pt. 3, 724–725.

53. Mildred Bullitt to Thomas W. Bullitt, September 4, 1864, "Thomas W. Bullitt personal correspondence, July–August, 1864," Folder 303; Mildred Bullitt to Thomas W. Bullitt, January 11, 1865, "Thomas W. Bullitt personal correspondence, 1865," Folder 304, Bullitt Family Papers-Oxmoor Collection, 1683–2003.

54. *Cincinnati Daily Enquirer,* January 25, 1865.

55. Lincoln to Burbridge, November 10, 1864; J. Bates Dickson to P. T. Swaine, November 10, 1864; Burbridge to Lincoln, November 11, 1864, *O.R.*, ser. 1, vol. 39, pt. 3, 739, 749; Burbridge to Colonel N. P. Chipman, November 23, 1864, *O.R.*, ser. 1, vol. 45, pt. 1, 1010.

56. Burbridge to Bramlette, November 10, 1864, Burbridge to Bramlette, November 12, 1864, *O.R.*, ser. 1, vol. 39, pt. 3, 749, 760; Collins and Collins, *Collins' Historical Sketches of Kentucky,* 1:146–147.

57. Bramlette's letter to Burbridge was reprinted in the *Cincinnati Enquirer,* January 11, 1865.

58. *Cincinnati Enquirer,* January 11, 1865; see also Collins and Collins, *Collins' Historical Sketches of Kentucky,* 1:147.

59. Collins and Collins, *Collins' Historical Sketches of Kentucky,* 1:138; Circular, August 2, 1864, Hugh Boyle Ewing Papers, Box 4, Folder 1, "Correspondence, June 1864–September 1868"; Bramlette to Lincoln, September 3, 1864, *O.R.*, ser. 3, vol. 4, 690.

60. Coulter, *The Civil War and Readjustment in Kentucky,* 222–224; Collins and Collins, *Collins' Historical Sketches of Kentucky,* 1:144–145.

61. Palmer Boeger, "The Great Kentucky Hog Swindle of 1864," *Journal of Southern History* 28 (1962): 59–70, quote on page 60.

62. *Lexington National Unionist,* June 21, 1864.

63. Ludington to Stanton, November 29, 1864, *O.R.*, ser. 1, vol. 45, pt. 1, 1165; Bramlette to Stanton, February 7, 1865, *O.R.*, ser. 1, vol. 49, pt. 1, 667.

64. Burbridge to Stanton, January 3, 1865, *O.R.*, ser. 1, vol. 45, pt. 2, 503.

65. Grant to Halleck, November 24, 1864, *O.R.*, ser. 1, vol. 45, pt. 1, 1015; Stanton to Grant, December 3, 1864, *O.R.*, ser. 1, vol. 45, pt. 2, 28; Halleck to Grant, and response, February 6, 1865, *O.R.*, ser. 1, vol. 46, pt. 2, 415; Lincoln to Bramlette, November 22, 1864, *O.R.*, ser. 1, vol. 45, pt. 1, 994.

66. Collins and Collins, *Collins' Historical Sketches of Kentucky,* 1:155; US War Department, Adjutant General's Office, Special Order No. 17, January 11, 1865, *O.R.*, ser. 1, vol. 45, pt. 2, 569; Stanton to Palmer, February 8, 1865, *O.R.*, ser. 1, vol. 49, pt. 1, 670.

## 6. Butcher

1. General Order No. 59, July 16, 1864, *O.R.*, ser. 1, vol. 39, pt. 2, 174.

2. General Order No. 8, October 26, 1864, *O.R.*, ser. 1, vol. 39, pt. 3, 457; Collins and Collins, *Collins' Historical Sketches of Kentucky,* 1:144.

3. Cary C. Collins, "Grey Eagle: Major General Robert Huston Milroy and the Civil War," *Indiana Magazine of History* 90 (1994): 60–62. General in Chief Henry Halleck would disavow Milroy's policies after Confederate protests were lodged against them, but Milroy continued to enjoy Lincoln's tacit support for his hardline tactics. See also Sutherland, *A Savage Conflict,* 162; McPherson, *Battle Cry of Freedom,* 303.

4. John Fabian Witt, *Lincoln's Code: The Laws of War in American History* (New York: Free Press, 2012), 191; Astor, *Rebels on the Border,* 114; Sutherland, *A Savage Conflict,* 121–125, 194; Andrew W. Fialka, "Controlled Chaos: Spatiotemporal Patterns within Missouri's Irregular Civil War," in *The Civil War Guerrilla: Unfolding the Black Flag in History, Memory, and Myth,* ed. Joseph M. Beilein Jr. and Matthew C. Hulbert (Lexington: Univ. Press of Kentucky, 2015), 53. Schofield's diary is quoted in Philips, *The Rivers Ran Backward,* 247. General Order No. 11 came on the heels of the lesser-known General Order No. 10, which exiled bushwhackers and their families from western Missouri to Arkansas.

5. Military commissions, less formal than courts-martial and conducted by officers in the field, had been instituted during the Mexican War to try American soldiers for common law crimes committed while outside the United States. Their use expanded dramatically during the Civil War, owing largely to Halleck's creative legal interpretations during his efforts to quash guerrilla activity in Missouri. Under Halleck's hand, military commissions could be used to try civilians who violated the laws of war in areas under martial law. Halleck's innovation in Missouri was approved in Washington and eventually nationalized through the issuance of the Lieber Code, a concise reformulation of the laws of war promulgated in 1863. See Gideon Hart, "Military Commissions and the Lieber Code: Toward a New Understanding of the Jurisdictional Foundations of Military Commissions," *Military Law Review* 203 (2010): 24–40; Detlev F. Vagts, "Military Commissions: A Concise History," *American Journal of International Law* 101 (2007): 38–39.

6. Neely, *The Fate of Liberty,* 130–131.

7. Breckinridge to Burbridge, January 12, 1865, *O.R.*, ser. 2, vol. 8, 57–58; Leroy Fitch to Burbridge, n.d., Stephen G. Burbridge Papers, 1863–1864, Box 1, "Telegrams Received, 1864, Aug. 1–31."

8. John M. Palmer, *Personal Recollections of John M. Palmer: The Story of an Earnest Life* (Cincinnati: Robert Clarke Company, 1901), 267; Matthew

Hulbert, "The Rise and Fall of Edwin Terrell, Guerrilla Hunter, U.S.A.," *Ohio Valley History* 18 (2018): 50.

9. Witt, *Lincoln's Code,* 191–192.

10. Witt, *Lincoln's Code,* 193–194; Hart, "Military Commissions and the Lieber Code," 37–39; Sutherland, *A Savage Conflict,* 126–127.

11. Witt, *Lincoln's Code,* 2, 231–237; Sutherland, *A Savage Conflict,* 128.

12. General Order No. 59, July 16, 1864, *O.R.*, ser. 1, vol. 39, pt. 2, 174; General Order No. 8, October 26, 1864, *O.R.*, ser. 1, vol. 39, pt. 3, 457.

13. Witt, *Lincoln's Code,* 193–194, 385–386.

14. Witt, *Lincoln's Code,* 386.

15. Witt, *Lincoln's Code,* 232–234.

16. Sherman to Burbridge, June 21, 1864, Stanton to Burbridge, July 5, 1864, General Order No. 59, July 16, 1864, *O.R.*, ser. 1, vol. 39, pt. 2, 135–136, 163, 174; Sutherland, *A Savage Conflict,* 222.

17. Christopher Phillips, "The Hard-Line War: The Ideological Basis of Irregular Warfare in the Western Border States," in *The Civil War Guerrilla: Unfolding the Black Flag in History, Memory, and Myth,* ed. Joseph M. Beilein Jr. and Matthew C. Hulbert (Lexington: Univ. Press of Kentucky, 2015), 24–25, especially note 20.

18. Samuel Haycraft, March 27, 1864, Journal, 1849–1878, Filson Historical Society, Louisville, Kentucky; Amelia Winn to "Dear Sister," September 6, 1864, Winn-Cook Family Papers, 1861–1875, Folder 16.

19. Johnson, *The Partisan Rangers,* 166.

20. Phillips, "The Hard-Line War," 15; see also Philips, *The Rivers Ran Backward,* 249; Hulbert, "The Rise and Fall of Edwin Terrell," 45.

21. *Lexington National Unionist,* February 7, 1865.

22. S. N. Starling, John Potter, and James Gowen to Burbridge, August 27, 1864, *O.R.,* ser. 1, vol. 39, pt. 2, 309.

23. N. Tunis and W. Harrison to Burbridge, August 10, 1864, in John Mason Brown Papers, 1862–1864, Folder 5, "Correspondence July–August 1864," Filson Historical Society, Louisville, Kentucky; George Blakey to Burbridge, January 5, 1864, CSR, Stephen G. Burbridge.

24. J. A. Morrison to J. S. Butler, November 28, 1864, *O.R.,* ser. 1, vol. 45, pt. 1, 1131.

25. J. H. Grider to Schofield, December 4, 1864, *O.R.,* ser. 1, vol. 45, pt. 2, 46.

26. Sherman to General William Rosecrans, Oct. 31, 1864, *O.R.,* ser. 1, vol. 39, pt. 3, 530–531. Sherman was responding to Rosecrans's request to hold back troops for the fight against guerrillas in Missouri, but Sherman's mindset applied to Kentucky as well.

27. R. J. Maxey to Bramlette, June 22, 1864, "Guerrilla letters—1864," Kentucky Military History Museum, Frankfort, Kentucky; Adjutant General

D. W. Lindsey to Maxey, June 25, 1864, Kentucky, Office of the Inspector General, Letterbook "A" (October 14, 1863 to July 29, 1864), 448, Kentucky Military History Museum, Frankfort, Kentucky.

28. John Sallee to D. W. Lindsey, July 4, 1864; G. W. Caplinger to Bramlette, June 25, 1864, "Guerrilla letters—1864"; Lindsey to Caplinger, June 27, 1864, Inspector General Letterbook "A" (October 14, 1863 to July 29, 1864), 455.

29. W. P. Westerfield to Lindsey, July 7, 1864; John Stuart to Lindsey, July 6, 1864; R. R. Bush, I. W. Bush, and W. H. Shook to Lindsey, September 19, 1864, "Guerrilla Letters—1864"; *Louisville Daily Journal,* August 3, 1864.

30. Halleck to Grant, December 3, 1864, *O.R.*, ser. 1, vol. 45, pt. 2, 29.

31. Bramlette to Stanton, February 7, 1865; Burbridge to Stanton, February 8, 1865; Stanton to Palmer, February 8, 1865, *O.R.,* ser. 1, vol. 49, pt. 1, 667–672. See also *Lexington National Unionist,* March 3, 1865.

32. Robert Cochran to D. W. Lindsey, August 14, 1864, "Guerrilla letters—1864."

33. H. H. Martin to Bramlette, November 11, 1864; W. W. Morse to Bramlette, September 25, 1864, "Guerrilla letters—1864."

34. General Order No. 3, September 13, 1864, John Mason Brown Papers, 1862–1864, Folder 11, "General Orders May 1863–November 1864."

35. Jonathan Davis to Lindsey, December 1, 1864; Davis to Lindsey, December 16, 1864, Kentucky State Militia Records, Old War Records—Hall's Gap Battalion, 1864–65, "Evidence against Major Bridgewater" folder, Kentucky Military History Museum, Frankfort, Kentucky.

36. W. P. Westerfield to Lindsey, September 21, 1864; J. J. Harrison to Bramlette, October 7, 1864, "Guerrilla letters—1864."

37. James Buford to Bramlette, November 4, 1864, "Guerrilla letters—1864."

38. "A War Reminiscence," reprinted in the *Louisville Courier-Journal,* November 12, 1876; see also "The Burbridge Bugaboo," *Louisville Courier-Journal,* January 3, 1882, which makes reference to the victims being chosen by lot. Bush, *Butcher Burbridge,* 138. Bush is unclear on how such a system ensured that someone would draw the fatal bean. *Louisville Courier-Journal,* September 28, 1896.

39. *Louisville Courier-Journal,* January 12, 1882; *Louisville Courier-Journal,* January 1, 1882; reprinted in *Louisville Courier-Journal,* January 6, 1882; *Louisville Courier-Journal,* February 18, 1882. On Duke and Confederate memory in Kentucky more generally, see Marshall, *Creating a Confederate Kentucky,* 88.

40. *Philadelphia Press* article reprinted in *Louisville Courier-Journal,* January 2, 1882; Burbridge response in *Louisville Courier-Journal,* January 9, 1882.

41. *Louisville Courier-Journal,* January 3, 1882; on the execution of the men at Midway, see Bush, *Butcher Burbridge,* 158; Collins and Collins, *Collins' Historical Sketches of Kentucky,* 1:146. Even if the men were unaware of their fate, that does not necessarily mean that they had not been subject to trial. Since these were retaliatory executions, the offense for which they may have been tried likely had nothing to do with the offense for which they were killed.

42. *Louisville Courier-Journal,* January 6, 1882.

43. *Louisville Courier-Journal,* January 9, 1882.

44. *Louisville Daily Journal,* July 29, 1864. See also articles from July 16, July 18, July 21, July 28, and August 11.

45. Dickson to Ewing July 22, 1864, *O.R.,* ser. 1, vol. 39, pt. 2, 199.

46. Burbridge to Ewing, July 25, 1864, *O.R.,* ser. 1, vol. 39, pt. 2, 203.

47. George Humphreys to Lieutenant E. B. Harlan, August 24, 1864, Hugh Boyle Ewing Papers, Box 4, Folder 1, "Correspondence, June 1864–September 1868."

48. Neely, *The Fate of Liberty,* 129.

49. See, for example, 1864 entries on May 25, May 26, May 27, July 1, July 2, July 5, and July 8, Hugh Boyle Ewing Papers, Box 6, "Journals November 8, 1847–March 1871."

50. Dickson to Ewing, September 11, 1864, *O.R.,* Ser. 1, vol. 39, pt. 2, 362.

51. The confusion over McGill/McGrew's name and his association with the Ferguson case suggests that Brown and Burbridge may actually be referring to a "Captain McGee," who was executed along with Walter Ferguson in November 1864.

52. A "drum-head court" refers to a military commission convened in the field. Hart, "Military Commissions and the Lieber Code," 3–4, especially note 18; Witt, *Lincoln's Code,* 126.

53. *Louisville Courier-Journal,* February 3, 1882.

54. Reprinted in the *Paris Kentuckian,* November 26, 1867.

55. *Louisville Courier-Journal,* January 15, 1882.

56. Witt, *Lincoln's Code,* 385–386.

57. "Proceedings of a Military Commission . . . ," Case File OO-3733, United States, Records of the Office of the Judge Advocate General (RG 153), Court-Martial Case Files, 1809–1938, National Archives.

58. *Louisville Courier-Journal,* January 3, 1882.

59. *Louisville Courier-Journal,* January 15, 1882.

60. *Louisville Courier Journal,* September 23, 1896.

61. *Louisville Courier Journal,* June 25, 1910.

62. *Louisville Courier-Journal,* January 12, 1882.

63. *Louisville Courier Journal,* January 6, 1882.

64. Mackey, *The Uncivil War,* 6–7, 14. See also Martin, "Black Flag over the Bluegrass," 353–355; Tarnowieckyi, "'Branded by the Lincolnites as Guerrillas,'" 642–644.

65. Tarnowieckyi, "'Branded by the Lincolnites as Guerrillas,'" 644–645, 672–673.

66. Martin, "Black Flag over the Bluegrass," 370–371. For examples of Jessee's activities, see reports from various correspondents in *O.R.*, ser. 1, vol. 39, pt. 3, 355, 369; ser. 1, vol. 45, pt. 2, 113, 227.

67. Quoted in Tarnowieckyi, "'Branded by the Lincolnites as Guerrillas,'" 661; *Louisville Daily Journal,* August 10, 1864; *Lexington National Unionist,* August 16, 1864.

68. *Louisville Courier-Journal,* January 3, 1882.

69. *Louisville Courier-Journal,* February 18, 1882.

70. Henry Halleck, "Retaliation in War," *American Journal of International Law* 6 (1912): 110, 112; Witt, *Lincoln's Code,* 378, 383.

71. *Louisville Courier-Journal,* February 18, 1882; *Louisville Courier-Journal,* January 5, 1882; *Louisville Daily Courier,* January 2, 1868.

72. Schofield to Sherman, October 3, 1864, *O.R.*, ser. 1, vol. 39, pt. 3, 47.

73. William Gunn to Burbridge, October 27, 1865, SGB Correspondence, 1862–1865; *Maysville (Ky.) Eagle,* January 2, 1868; *Louisville Daily Courier,* January 8, 1868.

74. *Louisville Courier-Journal,* February 18, 1882.

75. For an analysis and critique of the Union's antiguerrilla policies in Kentucky, see Andrew W. Fialka, "Federal Eyes: How the Union Saw Kentucky's Civil War," *Ohio Valley History* 18 (2018): 6–25.

76. J. S. Butler to Brown, August 12, 1864, John Mason Brown Papers, 1862–1864, Folder 5, "Correspondence, July–August 1864."

77. Burbridge to Duke, February 24, 1865, *O.R.*, ser. 1, vol. 49, pt. 1, 765; McKnight, *Contested Borderland,* 215.

78. C. J. Lawton to Burbridge, February 5, 1865, *O.R.*, ser. 1, vol. 49, pt. 1, 657; Dickson to Lawton, February 16, 1865, *O.R.*, ser. 1, vol. 49, pt. 1, 733; *Lexington National Unionist,* February 7, 1865.

79. On Lyon's raid, see correspondence by E. M. McCook to and from various federal officers, December 13–22, 1864, *O.R.*, ser. 1, vol. 45, pt. 2, 174ff; on Jessee's activities, see Alvin P. Hovey to C. H. Potter, December 16, 1864, *O.R.*, ser. 1, vol. 45, pt. 2, 227.

80. Edmund L. Starling, *History of Henderson County, Kentucky* (Henderson, Ky.: N.p., 1887), 541–544, https://archive.org/details/historyofhenders00star/page/n5.

81. *Louisville Daily Courier,* September 22, 1866; *Louisville Daily Journal,* September 24, 1866.

82. David Achtenberg, "With Malice Toward Some: United States v. Kirby, Malicious Prosecution, and the Fourteenth Amendment," *Rutgers Law Journal* 26 (1995): 275–276, 338–339.

83. *Louisville Daily Courier,* October 13, 1866.

84. *Louisville Daily Courier,* October 13, 1866.

85. *Louisville Daily Courier,* October 13, 1866.

## 7. Pariah

1. Marshall, *Creating a Confederate Kentucky,* 81, 83–84; Coulter, *The Civil War and Readjustment in Kentucky,* 275.

2. Coulter, *The Civil War and Readjustment in Kentucky,* 439.

3. Coulter, *The Civil War and Readjustment in Kentucky,* 145.

4. Ross A. Webb, *Kentucky in the Reconstruction Era* (Lexington: Univ. Press of Kentucky, 1979), 92.

5. See Marshall, *Creating a Confederate Kentucky,* 2–3, for a brief overview of the historiography.

6. Marshall, *Creating a Confederate Kentucky,* 3–5.

7. Joseph E. Brent, "Civil War Monuments in Kentucky, 1865–1935." National Register of Historic Places, Multiple Property Documentation Form, January 8, 1997, npgallery.nps.gov/pdfhost/docs/NRHP/Text/64500229.pdf. Wikipedia has an easily accessible table listing Kentucky's Civil War monuments at en.wikipedia.org/wiki/List_of_American_Civil_War_monuments_in_Kentucky. On Kentucky's monuments, see Marshall, *Creating a Confederate Kentucky,* 84–85. A general overview of Lost Cause memorialization is Gaines Foster, *Ghosts of the Confederacy: Defeat, the Lost Cause, and the Emergence of the New South, 1865–1913* (New York: Oxford Univ. Press, 1988).

8. Bush, *Butcher Burbridge,* 123–126; Collins and Collins, *Collins' Historical Sketches of Kentucky,* 1:135–136.

9. *Louisville Daily Courier,* October 3, 1866. A photo and description of the monument can be found at en.wikipedia.org/wiki/Confederate_Soldiers_Martyrs_Monument_in_Eminence.

10. *Louisville Daily Courier,* October 5, 1866.

11. *Eminence Constitutionalist,* reprinted in *Louisville Courier-Journal,* July 28, 1878; *Louisville Courier-Journal,* January 5, 1882.

12. Collins and Collins, *Collins' Historical Sketches of Kentucky,* 1:189; Marshall, *Creating a Confederate Kentucky,* 83. See the *Frankfort State Journal,* October 13, 1985, which reprinted the *Yeoman*'s article on the funeral; Collins and Collins, *Collins' Historical Sketches of Kentucky,* 1:207; Works Progress Administration, *Military History of Kentucky* (Frankfort, Ky.: State Journal, 1939), 142, kynghistory.ky.gov/Media/Publications/DMA/MilitaryHistoryKY1939AnlRpt.pdf.

13. Similar pomp and ceremony accompanied an 1866 reburial of Confederate dead at Georgetown, in Scott County, that attracted the attention of the northern press. Under the headline "Honors to Rebel Dead," the *Bangor (Maine) Daily Whig and Courier* commented that the "funeral cortege was composed of nearly six thousand soldiers and citizens at the head of whom rode Col. Basil Duke, formerly of Gen. Morgan's command." *Bangor (Maine) Daily Whig and Courier,* October 10, 1866.

14. On the cultural primacy of the Lost Cause in Kentucky, see Marshall, *Creating a Confederate Kentucky,* 155–182; on the growth of segregation and attacks on blacks' civil rights, see Harrison and Klotter, *A New History of Kentucky,* 348; George C. Wright, *A History of Blacks in Kentucky,* vol. 2, *In Pursuit of Equality, 1890–1980* (Frankfort: Kentucky Historical Society, 1992), 43–66; for the history of Confederate memory in general, see Foster, *Ghosts of the Confederacy*; Blight, *Race and Reunion*; Gallagher and Nolan, eds., *The Myth of the Lost Cause.*

15. Marshall, *Creating a Confederate Kentucky,* 155–182; on the UDC and Confederate heritage, see Karen Cox, *Dixie's Daughters: The United Daughters of the Confederacy and the Preservation of Confederate Culture* (Gainesville: Univ. Press of Florida, 2003).

16. *Louisville Courier-Journal,* April 7, 1894.

17. For images of the monument, see en.wikipedia.org/wiki/Martyrs_Monument_in_Midway. For an account of the execution, see "A War Reminiscence," *Louisville Courier-Journal,* November 12, 1876.

18. *Louisville Courier-Journal,* June 11, 1904.

19. *Louisville Courier-Journal,* June 11, 1904; June 12, 1904.

20. Marshall, *Creating a Confederate Kentucky,* 37–39, 43; Harrison and Klotter, *A New History of Kentucky,* 239–240.

21. Harrison and Klotter, *A New History of Kentucky,* 242; Marshall, *Creating a Confederate Kentucky,* 44–45.

22. *Louisville Daily Courier,* May 9, 1866; May 26, 1866.

23. *Louisville Daily Courier,* May 9, 1866; May 26, 1866.

24. *Louisville Daily Courier,* May 29, 1866.

25. *Louisville Daily Courier,* June 13, 1866.

26. *Louisville Daily Courier,* July 4, 1866; August 3, 1866.

27. *Louisville Daily Journal,* July 18, 1866; *Louisville Daily Courier,* October 24, 1866; August 29, 1866.

28. For a summary of the Hobson/Duvall election, see Harrison and Klotter, *A New History of Kentucky,* 240–241; Marshall, *Creating a Confederate Kentucky,* 40–42.

29. *Louisville Daily Courier,* December 1, 1866; January 17, 1867; January 22, 1867; February 19, 1867.

30. On Helm's election and the collapse of the Conservative Unionists, see Harrison and Klotter, *A New History of Kentucky,* 241–242; Marshall, *Creating a Confederate Kentucky,* 42.

31. Collins and Collins, *Collins' Historical Sketches of Kentucky,* 1:203; *Louisville Courier-Journal,* March 19, 1870; April 1, 1870; April 23, 1870; May 2, 1870; May 15, 1870; July 11, 1870. Beck had to publish his own separate denial over the affair and withdrew his name for reelection for his House seat. *Louisville Courier-Journal,* April 5, 1870; April 6, 1870.

32. *Louisville Journal,* October 31, 1868; United States, Congress, *Biographical Directory of the United States Congress,* https://bioguideretro.congress.gov/Home/MemberDetails?memIndex=G000271.

33. *Louisville Courier-Journal,* December 31, 1881.

34. *Louisville Courier-Journal,* December 31, 1881.

35. *Louisville Courier-Journal,* January 1, 1882.

36. *Louisville Courier-Journal,* December 31, 1881.

37. *Louisville Courier-Journal,* January 9, 1882.

38. *Louisville Courier-Journal,* January 1, 1882; January 3, 1882; January 6, 1882.

39. *Louisville Daily Courier,* February 27, 1867; March 4, 1868.

40. The *Louisville Daily Courier* reprinted Brisbin's letters to the *Cincinnati Commercial,* with appropriate derogatory comments. See *Louisville Daily Courier,* November 19, 1867; December 28, 1867. See also the *New York Times,* December 27, 1867; January 1, 1868. The *Times* denounced Brisbin's proposed project, saying it would only "stir up more bad blood" and predicting that it would do nothing to "increase the loyalty of Kentucky."

41. Reprinted in *Louisville Daily Courier,* October 30, 1867.

42. *Louisville Daily Courier,* December 28, 1867.

43. For Burbridge's self-justifications, see the articles cited earlier during the flap with Blackburn and Duke; also see *Louisville Daily Courier,* January 31, 1868; February 2, 1868; November 26, 1871.

44. James Klotter, *The Breckinridges of Kentucky, 1790–1981* (Lexington: Univ. Press of Kentucky, 1986), 88.

45. For a contemporary description of the "spoils system," albeit by an aspiring reformer of that system, see William Wedgwood, *Civil Service Reform* (Portland, Maine: Stephen Berry, 1883), 12–14, https://archive.org/details/civilservicerefo00wedg. See also A. Bower Sageser, *First Two Decades of the Pendleton Act: A Study of Civil Service Reform* (Lincoln: Univ. of Nebraska Press, 1935); Ari Hoogenboom, "Civil Service Reform," in *The Oxford Companion to United States History,* ed. Paul Boyer (New York: Oxford Univ. Press, 2001), 128–129.

46. James Halchitt to President U. S. Grant, August 4, 1870; Colonel T. W. Campbell et al. to Burbridge, July 26, 1870, Records of the Department

of the Interior (RG 48), Field Office Appointment Papers, 1849–1907, Box 288.

47. *New York Daily Herald,* April 13, 1869.

48. In addition to periodic press coverage in Kentucky's major newspapers, the records of Burbridge's job-seeking efforts can be found in Records of the Department of the Interior (RG 48), Field Office Appointment Papers, 1849–1907, Boxes 288 and 689; Records of the Department of State (RG 59), Applications and Recommendations for Public Office, Boxes 11 and 18; Records of the Department of Justice (RG 60), Appointment Files for Judicial Districts, Box 319, National Archives.

49. *Louisville Courier-Journal,* April 20, 1869; April 21, 1869; March 11, 1870. See also Thomas E. Fletcher et al. to Secretary of State William Evarts, May 7, 1877, Records of the Department of State (RG 59), Applications and Recommendations for Public Office, Box 11.

50. *Louisville Daily Courier,* September 19, 1866; September 20, 1866; October 24, 1866.

51. Robert J. Breckinridge to President U. S. Grant, June 8, 1869, Records of the Department of the Interior (RG 48), Field Office Appointment Papers, 1849–1907, Box 288.

52. W. C. Goodloe et al. to President U. S. Grant, June 1, 1869, Records of the Department of the Interior (RG 48), Field Office Appointment Papers, 1849–1907, Box 288.

53. Benjamin P. Runkle to Burbridge, August 8, 1870, Records of the Department of the Interior (RG 48), Field Office Appointment Papers, 1849–1907, Box 288.

54. *Louisville Courier-Journal,* March 16, 1872; March 27, 1872.

55. *Louisville Courier-Journal,* July 1, 1883.

## 8. Exile

1. *Louisville Courier-Journal,* December 7, 1894.

2. Robert J. Breckinridge to President U. S. Grant, June 8, 1869; W. C. Goodloe et al. to President U. S. Grant, June 1, 1869, Records of the Department of the Interior (RG 48), Field Office Appointment Papers, 1849–1907, Box 288.

3. Harrison and Klotter, *A New History of Kentucky,* 237–238; Hutton, *Bloody Breathitt,* 40–98.

4. Reprinted in *Louisville Daily Courier,* November 1, 1866.

5. *Maysville (Ky.) Eagle,* March 21, 1867.

6. *Louisville Courier,* October 14, 1867; October 18, 1867; November 2, 1867; *Russellville (Ky.) Herald,* October 16, 1867; *Cincinnati Commercial,* November 1, 1867.

7. Hutton, *Bloody Breathitt,* 74.

8. *Cincinnati Enquirer,* November 24, 1867; *Covington (Ky.) News,* January 27, 1868; *Louisville Courier,* November 29, 1867.

9. *Paris Kentuckian,* November 26, 1867.

10. Oscar Burbridge to Stephen Burbridge, May 1, 1865, SGB Correspondence, 1862–1865.

11. Oscar Burbridge to Stephen Burbridge, May 23, 1865, SGB Correspondence, 1862–1865.

12. Oscar Burbridge to Stephen Burbridge, July 2, 1865, SGB Correspondence, 1862–1865.

13. Oscar Burbridge to Stephen Burbridge, July 11, 1865, SGB Correspondence, 1862–1865.

14. Oscar Burbridge to Stephen Burbridge, July 14, 1865, SGB Correspondence, 1862–1865.

15. Oscar ended up being sued for his part in a seizure of seven hundred bales of cotton, which the plaintiff alleged were taken by fraud and force. The case hung over Oscar for years, not being decided by a jury until 1875, and even then the verdict was set aside as faulty. Ultimately, Congress passed a private bill in 1890 for the relief of the plaintiff in the case. See *Louisville Daily Courier,* June 23, 1866; December 13, 1866; *Louisville Courier-Journal,* November 20, 1875; November 21, 1875; Congressional serial set, House Report No. 1523 to accompany H. R. 2871, 51st Cong., 1st sess. (Washington D.C.: Government Printing Office, 1892).

16. Reprinted in *Louisville Daily Journal,* July 18, 1867.

17. W. C. Goodloe et al. to President U. S. Grant, June 1, 1869, Records of the Department of the Interior (RG 48), Field Office Appointment Papers, 1849–1907, Box 288.

18. *Louisville Courier,* July 25, 1868; William M. Wiecek, "The Reconstruction of Federal Judicial Power, 1863–1875," *American Journal of Legal History* 13 (1969): 356; Elizabeth Lee Thompson, *The Reconstruction of Southern Debt: Bankruptcy after the Civil War* (Athens: Univ. of Georgia Press, 2004).

19. Stephen G. Burbridge Bankruptcy Case File, Case No. 157, Bankruptcy Act of 1867 Case Files, 1867–1868, District Court for the District of Kentucky—Covington, Records of United States District Courts (RG 21), National Archives, Kansas City Regional Branch.

20. Timothy R. Mahoney, "Urban History in a Regional Context: River Towns on the Upper Mississippi, 1840–1860," *Journal of American History* 72 (1985): 329, 332n13. See also Preserved Smith, "Neile Macneale: Railroad Builder of the Middle West, 1826–1897," *Mississippi Valley Historical Review* 26 (1939): 187; City of Keokuk, "History of Keokuk," www.cityofkeokuk.org/community/history-of-keokuk.

21. Stephen G. Burbridge Bankruptcy Case File.

22. Washington, D.C., *City Directory,* 1868; Covington, Kentucky, *City Directory,* 1871; Covington, Kentucky, *City Directory,* 1872, accessed via Ancestry.com, *United States City Directories, 1822–1895* (Provo, Utah: Ancestry.com Operations, 2015), https://www.ancestry.com/search/collections/2469/; US Bureau of the Census, *Ninth Census of the United States, 1870,* Kentucky, Kenton County, City of Covington, Ward 4, page 68, National Archives Microfilm Publication M573, accessed via Ancestry.com (Provo, Utah: Ancestry.com Operations, 2009), https://www.ancestry.com/search/collections/7163/.

23. *Cincinnati Enquirer,* December 4, 1871.

24. *Louisville Courier-Journal,* November 26, 1871.

25. Applicant's Affidavit, June 9, 1892, US Bureau of Pensions, Stephen G. Burbridge (Veteran) Pension file, Claim No. 1042707, National Archives; Widow's Declaration, March 18, 1895, Sarah R. Burbridge (Widow) Pension File.

26. *Louisville Courier-Journal,* March 29, 1872. On the Liberal Republican movement, see Eric Foner, *Reconstruction: America's Unfinished Revolution* (New York: Harper and Row, 1988), 488–494, 497–499; Blight, *Race and Reunion,* 123–126.

27. *Louisville Courier-Journal,* December 8, 1894.

28. Certificate of Marriage, Sarah R. Burbridge (Widow) Pension File; "John Jacob Ridgway," *Encyclopedia of Contemporary Biography of Pennsylvania,* vol. 3 (New York: Atlantic Publishing and Engraving Co., 1898), 145–146.

29. The *Herald* article was reprinted in the *Louisville Courier-Journal,* July 22, 1883. For the history of Estelville and Jewish agricultural colonies in general, see Joseph Brandes, *Immigrants to Freedom: Jewish Communities in Rural New Jersey since 1882* (Philadelphia: Univ. of Pennsylvania Press, 1971), 67–68; Ellen Eisenberg, *Jewish Agricultural Colonies in New Jersey, 1882–1920* (Syracuse, N.Y.: Syracuse Univ. Press, 1995), 102–105.

30. Quoted in *Louisville Courier-Journal,* July 22, 1883.

31. Brandes, *Immigrants to Freedom,* 68; *St. Louis Globe-Democrat,* August 8, 1883.

32. Record of Appointment of Postmasters, 1832–1971, New Jersey: Atlantic-Mercer Counties, Records of the Post Office Department (RG 28), National Archives.

33. Applicant's Statement, December 6, 1891; copy of Death Certificate, May 4, 1895, Stephen G. Burbridge (Veteran) Pension File; Saratoga Springs, New York, *City Directory, 1888–1892,* accessed via Ancestry.com, *United States City Directories, 1822–1895,* https://www.ancestry.com/search/collections/2469/.

34. US Bureau of the Census, *Tenth Census of the United States, 1880,* District of Columbia, Enumeration District 94, page 4, National Archives Microfilm Publication T9, Ancestry.com (Provo, Utah: Ancestry.com Operations,

2010), https://www.ancestry.com/search/collections/6742/; US Bureau of the Census, *Twelfth Census of the United States, 1900,* California, Los Angeles, Ward 5, District 45, page 19, National Archives Microfilm Publication T623, Ancestry.com (Provo, Utah: Ancestry.com Operations, 2004), https://www.ancestry.com/search/collections/7602/; US Bureau of the Census, *Fifteenth Census of the United States, 1930,* California, Los Angeles, District 0600, page 13B, National Archives Microfilm Publication T626, Ancestry.com (Provo, Utah: Ancestry.com Operations, 2002), https://www.ancestry.com/search/collections/6224/; Death Record of Lillie G. B. Butler, File No. 001041, *Michigan Death Records, 1867–1952,* Ancestry.com (Provo, Utah: Ancestry.com Operations, 2015), https://www.ancestry.com/search/collections/60872/; Albert G. Burbridge Death Record, File No. 66450, *California Death Index, 1905–1939,* Ancestry.com (Provo, Utah: Ancestry.com Operations, 2013), https://www.ancestry.com/search/collections/5187/; Marriage Record of Lillie Garth Burbridge, Film No. 2026214, *District of Columbia Marriage Records, 1810–1953,* Ancestry.com (Lehi, Utah: Ancestry.com Operations, 2016), https://www.ancestry.com/search/collections/61404/.

35. *Louisville Courier-Journal,* December 7, 1894.

36. Blight, *Race and Reunion,* 4; Gallagher and Nolan, eds, *The Myth of the Lost Cause,* 4; Gary Gallagher, *Causes Won, Lost, and Forgotten: How Hollywood and Popular Art Shape What We Know about the Civil War* (Chapel Hill: Univ. of North Carolina Press, 2008), 2–4; Marshall, *Creating a Confederate Kentucky,* 6.

37. Marshall, *Creating a Confederate Kentucky,* 161; Cox, *Dixie's Daughters,* 118–140.

38. Unsigned article, *The Confederate Veteran* 30 (August 1922), 312; *Louisville Courier-Journal,* February 9, 1904. On the importance attached by the UDC to "correct" history (in other words, history with a pro-southern slant), see Cox, *Dixie's Daughters,* 94–95.

39. *Louisville Courier-Journal,* December 8, 1894.

## Conclusion

1. de Falaise, "General Stephen Gano Burbridge's Command in Kentucky," 124.

2. Ira Katznelson, "What America Taught the Nazis," *The Atlantic* (November 2017), 44.

3. *Janesville (Wisc.) Daily Gazette,* July 6, 1864.

4. Gallagher, *Causes Won, Lost, and Forgotten,* 25–27.

# Bibliography

## Newspapers and Periodicals

*Bangor Daily Whig and Courier*
*Cincinnati Daily Enquirer*
*Confederate Veteran*
*Covington News*
*Janesville Daily Gazette*
*Lexington National Unionist*
*Louisville Courier-Journal*
*Louisville Daily Courier*
*Louisville Daily Journal*
*New York Daily Herald*
*New York Times*
*Maysville Eagle*
*Paris Kentuckian*
*Russellville Herald*
*St. Louis Globe-Democrat*
*Weekly National Intelligencer*

## Federal Records

Naval War Records Office. *Official Records of the Union and Confederate Navies in the War of the Rebellion* (Washington, D.C.: Government Printing Office, 1894–1922).

Records of the Adjutant General's Office (RG 94). Compiled Service Record of Stephen G. Burbridge. National Archives.

Records of the Adjutant General's Office (RG 94). Letters Received by Commission Branch, 1874–1894. National Archives Microfilm Publication M1395.

Records of the Department of Justice (RG 60). Appointment Files for Judicial Districts. National Archives.

Records of the Department of State. (RG 59). Applications and Recommendations for Public Office. National Archives.

Records of the Interior Department (RG 48). Field Office Appointment Papers, 1849–1907. National Archives.

Records of the Office of the Judge Advocate General (RG 153). Court-Martial Case Files, 1809–1938. National Archives.

Records of the Post Office Department (RG 28). Record of Appointment of Postmasters, 1832–1971. New Jersey: Atlantic-Mercer Counties. National Archives.

Records of U.S. Army Continental Commands (RG 393). Department of the Cumberland. September–November, 1861. National Archives.

Records of U.S. District Courts (RG 21). District Court for the District of Kentucky—Covington. Bankruptcy Act of 1867 Case Files, 1867–1868. Stephen G. Burbridge Bankruptcy Case File. Case No. 157. National Archives. Kansas City Regional Branch.

United States. Bureau of the Census. *Seventh Census of the United States, 1850, Kentucky.* National Archives Microfilm Publication M432. Ancestry.com. Provo, Utah: Ancestry.com Operations, 2009. https://www.ancestry.com/search/collections/8054/.

———. *Eighth Census of the United States, 1860, Kentucky.* National Archives Microfilm Publication M653. Ancestry.com. Provo, Utah: Ancestry.com Operations, 2009. https://www.ancestry.com/search/collections/7667/.

———. *Eighth Census of the United States, 1860—Slave Schedules, Kentucky.* National Archives Microfilm Publication M653. Ancestry.com. Provo, Utah: Ancestry.com Operations, 2010. https://www.ancestry.com/search/collections/7668/.

———. *Ninth Census of the United States, 1870, Kentucky.* National Archives Microfilm Publication M573. Ancestry.com. Provo, Utah: Ancestry.com Operations, 2009. https://www.ancestry.com/search/collections/7163/.

———. *Tenth Census of the United States, 1880, District of Columbia.* National Archives Microfilm Publication T9. Ancestry.com. Provo, Utah: Ancestry.com Operations, 2009. https://www.ancestry.com/search/collections/6742/.

———. *Twelfth Census of the United States, 1900, California.* National Archives Microfilm Publication T623. Ancestry.com. Provo, Utah: Ancestry.com Operations, 2004. https://www.ancestry.com/search/collections/7602/.

———. *Fifteenth Census of the United States, 1930.* National Archives Microfilm Publication T626. Ancestry.com. Provo, Utah: Ancestry.com Operations, 2002. https://www.ancestry.com/search/collections/6224/.

United States. Bureau of Pensions. Stephen G. Burbridge Veteran's Pension File. Claim No. 1042707. National Archives.

———. Sarah R. Burbridge Widow's Pension File. Claim No. 610825. Certificate No. 418.623. National Archives.

United States. Congress. *Biographical Directory of the United States Congress, 1774–Present.* https://bioguideretro.congress.gov/.

———. Congressional Serial Set. House Report No. 1523 to accompany H.R. 2871. 51st Cong., 1st sess. Washington, D.C.: Government Printing Office, 1892.

US War Department. *The War of the Rebellion: A Compilation of the Official Records of the Union and Confederate Armies.* Washington, D.C.: Government Printing Office, 1880–1901.

## Manuscript Sources

Allen, Theodore. Diary, 1864–1865. Filson Historical Society. Louisville, Kentucky.

Brown, John Mason. Papers, 1862–1864. Filson Historical Society. Louisville, Kentucky.

Bullitt Family Papers-Oxmoor Collection, 1683–2003. Filson Historical Society. Louisville, Kentucky.

Burbridge, Stephen Gano. Correspondence, 1862–1865. Filson Historical Society. Louisville, Kentucky.

Burbridge, Stephen G. Papers, 1863–1864. Rubenstein Library. Duke University. Durham, North Carolina.

Burbridge surname file. Kentucky Historical Society. Frankfort, Kentucky.

Chapman, William T. Journals [Transcripts]. Center of Archival Collections. Bowling Green State University. Bowling Green, Ohio. https://lib.bgsu.edu/finding_aids/items/show/2042.

Ewing, Hugh Boyle. Papers, 1841–1893. Ohio Historical Society. Columbus, Ohio.

Fairleigh, Thomas B. Diary, January 1–June 7, 1864. Filson Historical Society. Louisville, Kentucky.

Haycraft, Samuel. Journal, 1849–1878. Filson Historical Society. Louisville, Kentucky.

Hobson, Edward Henry. Papers, 1767–1899. Microfilm M-284. Special Collections Research Center. Margaret I. King Library. University of Kentucky. Lexington, Kentucky.

Preston, William. "Electioneering for President Abraham Lincoln in Kentucky, and the Outrages Committed by General Stephen G. Burbridge, from a Refugee Confederate Officer's Perspective." http://www.uky.edu/~dolph/HIS316/sources/electioneering.html. [Original document in Wickliffe-Preston Family. Papers, 1753–1897. Special Collections Research Center. Margaret I. King Library. University of Kentucky. Lexington, Kentucky.]

Ranney, William W. Papers, 1858–1927. Special Collections Research Center. Margaret I. King Library. University of Kentucky. Lexington, Kentucky.

Speed Family. Papers, 1813–1981. Filson Historical Society, Louisville, Kentucky.

Winn-Cook Family. Papers, 1861–1875. Filson Historical Society. Louisville, Kentucky.

## State and Local Records

26th Kentucky Infantry Records. Old War Records. "History" folder. Kentucky Military History Museum. Frankfort, Kentucky.

*California Death Index, 1905–1939.* Ancestry.com. Provo, Utah: Ancestry.com Operations, 2015. https://www.ancestry.com/search/collections/5187/.

Crozier, George Armstrong, ed. *Virginia County Records.* Vol. 1, *Spotsylvania County Records, 1721–1800.* Baltimore: Southern Book Co.: 1955.

*District of Columbia Marriage Records, 1810–1953.* Ancestry.com. Lehi, Utah: Ancestry.com Operations, 2016. https://www.ancestry.com/search/collections/61404/.

Dodd, Jordan, et al. *Early American Marriages: Mississippi to 1825.* Bountiful, Utah: Precision Indexing Publishers, 1997. Ancestry.com. *Mississippi Compiled Marriages, 1800–1825.* Provo, Utah: Ancestry.com Operations, 1997. https://www.ancestry.com/search/collections/2093/.

Dorman, John Frederick, comp. *Virginia Revolutionary Pension Applications,* vol. 12. Washington, D.C.: J. F. Dorman, 1966.

"Guerrilla letters—1864." Kentucky Military History Museum. Frankfort, Kentucky.

*Kentucky, County Marriage Records, 1783–1965.* Ancestry.com. Lehi, Utah: Ancestry.com Operations, 2016. https://www.ancestry.com/search/collections/61372/.

Kentucky. General Assembly. Acts, 1864. Kentucky Department for Libraries and Archives. Frankfort, Kentucky.

Kentucky. Office of the Governor. Thomas E. Bramlette: Governor's Official Correspondence File. Military Correspondence, 1863–1867. Kentucky Department for Libraries and Archives. Frankfort, Kentucky.

Kentucky. Office of the Governor. Thomas E. Bramlette: Communications with the General Assembly, 1863–1867. Kentucky Department for Libraries and Archives. Frankfort, Kentucky.

Kentucky. Office of the Inspector General. Letterbook "A" (October 14, 1863 to July 29, 1864). Kentucky Military History Museum. Frankfort, Kentucky.

Kentucky. State Militia Records. Old War Records—Hall's Gap Battalion, 1864–65. Kentucky Military History Museum. Frankfort, Kentucky.

Kentucky. Tax Books. Scott County. Filson Historical Society. Louisville, Kentucky.

*Michigan Death Records, 1867–1952.* Ancestry.com. Provo, Utah: Ancestry.com Operations, 2015. https://www.ancestry.com/search/collections/60872/.

Scott County [Kentucky]. Tax Books, 1794–1821. Kentucky Historical Society. Frankfort, Kentucky.

Scott County [Kentucky]. Circuit Court. Civil Case Files. Kentucky Department for Libraries and Archives. Frankfort, Kentucky.

Schreiner-Yantis, Netti, and Florence Speakman Love. *The 1787 Census of Virginia,* vol. 2. Springfield, Va.: Genealogical Books in Print, 1987.

White, Virgil, comp. *Index to War of 1812 Pension Files.* Vol. 1, *A-F.* Waynesboro, Tenn.: National Historical Publishing Co., 1989.

Wilder, Minnie S., comp. *Kentucky Soldiers of the War of 1812.* Baltimore: Genealogical Publishing Co., 1969.

## Secondary Sources and Other Published Sources

Achtenberg, David. "With Malice Toward Some: United States v. Kirby, Malicious Prosecution, and the Fourteenth Amendment." *Rutgers Law Journal* 26 (1995): 272–342.

Apple, Lindsey, et al., eds. *Scott County, Kentucky: A History.* Georgetown, Ky.: Scott County Historical Society, 1993.

Armstrong, J. M. *The Biographical Encyclopedia of Kentucky of the Dead and Living Men of the Nineteenth Century,* vol. 1. Cincinnati: J. M. Armstrong and Co., 1878.

Aron, Stephen. *How the West Was Lost: The Transformation of Kentucky from Daniel Boone to Henry Clay.* Baltimore: Johns Hopkins Univ. Press, 1996.

Asher, Brad. *Cecelia and Fanny: The Remarkable Friendship Between an Escaped Slave and Her Former Mistress.* Lexington: Univ. Press of Kentucky, 2011.

Astor, Aaron. "The Crouching Lion's Fate: Slave Politics and Conservative Unionism in Kentucky." *Register of the Kentucky Historical Society* 110 (2012): 293–326.

———. *Rebels on the Border: Civil War, Emancipation, and the Reconstruction of Kentucky and Missouri.* Baton Rouge: Louisiana State Univ. Press, 2012.

Berlin, Ira, et al. *Freedom: A Documentary History of Emancipation, 1861–1867.* Ser. 1. Vol. 1, *The Destruction of Slavery.* Cambridge, UK: Cambridge Univ. Press, 1985.

Berlin, Ira, et al. *Freedom: A Documentary History of Emancipation, 1861–1867.* Ser. 2. *The Black Military Experience.* Cambridge, UK: Cambridge Univ. Press, 1982.

Berry, Mary Clay. *Voices from the Century Before: The Odyssey of a Nineteenth-Century Kentucky Family.* New York: Arcade Publishing, 1996.

"Biographical Note." James Sanks Brisbin Papers, 1850–1891. Montana Historical Society. http://archiveswest.orbiscascade.org/ark:/80444/xv27706/op=fstyle.aspx?t=k&q=Brisbin#bioghistID.

Blight, David. *Race and Reunion: The Civil War in American Memory.* Cambridge, Mass.: Harvard Univ. Press, 2001.

Boeger, Palmer. "The Great Kentucky Hog Swindle of 1864." *Journal of Southern History* 28 (1962): 59–70.

Bradley, Michael. "'I Shoot the Men and Burn Their Houses': Home Fires in the Line of Fire." In *Sister States, Enemy States: The Civil War in Kentucky and Tennessee,* edited by Kent Dollar, Larry Whiteaker, and W. Calvin Dickinson, 168–187. Lexington: Univ. Press of Kentucky, 2009.

Bramlette, Thomas. *Speech of Gov. Thomas E. Bramlette of Kentucky. . . .* Louisville: Lost Cause Press, 1958.

Brandes, Joseph. *Immigrants to Freedom: Jewish Communities in Rural New Jersey since 1882.* Philadelphia: Univ. of Pennsylvania Press, 1971.

Breen, T. H. "Horses and Gentlemen: The Cultural Significance of Gambling among the Gentry of Virginia." *William and Mary Quarterly* 34 (1977): 239–257.

Brent, Joseph E. "Civil War Monuments in Kentucky, 1865–1935." National Register of Historic Places. Multiple Property Documentation Form, January 8, 1997. npgallery.nps.gov/pdfhost/docs/NRHP/Text/64500229.pdf.

Brown, Kent Masterson, ed. *The Civil War in Kentucky: Battle for the Bluegrass State.* Mason City, Iowa: Savas Publishing, 2000.

Bryant, Ron. "Boyle County." In *The Kentucky Encyclopedia,* edited by John Kleber, 110. Lexington: Univ. Press of Kentucky, 1992.

"Burbridge, Stephen G." *The Union Army.* Vol. 8, *Biographical.* Madison, Wisc.: Federal Publishing Co., 1908.

"Burbridge, Stephen Gano." *The National Cyclopaedia of American Biography,* vol. 11. New York: J. T. White Co., 1901. https://archive.org/details/nationalcyclopa05whitgoog.

Bush, Bryan. *Butcher Burbridge: Union General Stephen Gano Burbridge and His Reign of Terror over Kentucky.* Morley, Mo.: Acclaim Press, 2008.

*Catalogue of the Georgetown Female Seminary . . . for the Year 1851*. Georgetown, Ky.: Georgetown Female Seminary, 1851.

*Catalogue of the Georgetown Female Seminary . . . for the Year 1852*. Georgetown, Ky.: Georgetown Female Seminary, 1852.

*Catalogue of the Georgetown Female Seminary . . . for the Year 1853*. Georgetown, Ky.: Georgetown Female Seminary, 1853.

*Catalogue of the Officers and Students of Georgetown College, Kentucky, 1845–46*. Georgetown, Ky.: Georgetown College, 1846.

*Catalogue of the Officers and Cadets of the Kentucky Military Institute . . . from September 11, 1854 to June 29, 1855*. Frankfort, Ky.: A. G. Hodges and Co, 1855.

*Catalogue of the Students of Georgetown College with a List of Academical Honors Conferred by the College*. Georgetown, Ky.: Georgetown College, 1837–38.

*Catalogue of the Teachers and Pupils of the Georgetown Female Seminary . . . for the Year 1850*. Georgetown, Ky.: Georgetown Female Seminary, 1850.

Christ, Mark. "Battle of Arkansas Post." *The Encyclopedia of Arkansas History and Culture*. http://www.encyclopediaofarkansas.net/encyclopedia/entry-detail.aspx?entryID=525.

City of Keokuk. "History of Keokuk." www.cityofkeokuk.org/community/history-of-keokuk.

Clark, Thomas. *A History of Kentucky*. New York: Prentice-Hall, 1937.

———. *Kentucky: Land of Contrast*. New York: Harper and Row, 1968.

Coleman, J. Winston. *Lexington in the Civil War*. Lexington, Ky.: Commercial Printing Co, 1938.

Collins, Cary C. "Grey Eagle: Major General Robert Huston Milroy and the Civil War." *Indiana Magazine of History* 90 (1994): 48–72.

Collins, Lewis, and Richard H. Collins. *Collins' Historical Sketches of Kentucky: History of Kentucky*, vol. 1. Covington, Ky.: Collins and Company, 1874. https://archive.org/details/collinshistorica01coll/page/n8/mode/2up.

Coulter, E. Merton. *The Civil War and Readjustment in Kentucky*. Chapel Hill: Univ. of North Carolina Press, 1926.

Cox, Karen. *Dixie's Daughters: The United Daughters of the Confederacy and the Preservation of Confederate Culture*. Gainesville: Univ. Press of Florida, 2003.

Crawford, Byron. "Two Executions in Kentucky Aided Neither Union nor Unity." *Louisville Courier-Journal*. May 2, 1980.

Deatrick, David R. "Nelson, William." In *The Encyclopedia of Louisville*, edited by John Kleber, 650–651. Lexington: Univ. Press of Kentucky, 2001.

de Falaise, Louis. "General Stephen Gano Burbridge's Command in Kentucky." *Register of the Kentucky Historical Society* 69 (1971): 101–127.

DeGruccio, Michael. "Exposing the 'Lurid Interiors' of War." H-CivWar (August 2006). https://networks.h-net.org/node/4113/reviews/4743/degruccio-urwin-black-flag-over-dixie-racial-atrocities-and-reprisals.

Duke, Basil. *A History of Morgan's Cavalry.* New York: Neale Publishing, 1906.

Dyer, J. P. "The Civil War Career of General Joseph Wheeler." *Georgia Historical Quarterly* 19 (1935): 17–46.

Eisenberg, Ellen. *Jewish Agricultural Colonies in New Jersey, 1882–1920.* Syracuse, N.Y.: Syracuse Univ. Press, 1995.

Fialka, Andrew W. "Controlled Chaos: Spatiotemporal Patterns within Missouri's Irregular Civil War." In *The Civil War Guerrilla: Unfolding the Black Flag in History, Memory, and Myth,* edited by Joseph M. Beilein Jr. and Matthew C. Hulbert, 43–70. Lexington: Univ. Press of Kentucky, 2015.

———. "Federal Eyes: How the Union Saw Kentucky's Civil War." *Ohio Valley History* 18 (2018): 6–25.

Foner, Eric. *Reconstruction: America's Unfinished Revolution.* New York: Harper and Row, 1988.

Foster, Gaines. *Ghosts of the Confederacy: Defeat, the Lost Cause, and the Emergence of the New South, 1865–1913.* New York: Oxford Univ. Press, 1988.

Freehling, William. *The South vs. The South: How Anti-Confederate Southerners Shaped the Course of the Civil War.* New York: Oxford Univ. Press, 2001.

Gallagher, Gary. *Causes Won, Lost, and Forgotten: How Hollywood and Popular Art Shape What We Know about the Civil War.* Chapel Hill: Univ. of North Carolina Press, 2008.

Gallagher, Gary, and Alan Nolan, eds. *The Myth of the Lost Cause and Civil War History.* Bloomington: Indiana Univ. Press, 2000.

Gienapp, William. "Abraham Lincoln and the Border States." *Journal of the Abraham Lincoln Association* 13 (1992): 13–46.

Halleck, Henry. "Retaliation in War." *American Journal of International Law* 6 (1912): 107–118.

Harlow, Luke. *Religion, Race, and the Making of Confederate Kentucky, 1830–1880.* Cambridge, UK: Cambridge Univ. Press, 2014.

Harrison, Lowell. *The Civil War in Kentucky.* Lexington: Univ. Press of Kentucky, 1975.

———. "Slavery in Kentucky: A Civil War Casualty." *Kentucky Review* 5 (1983): 32–41. https://uknowledge.uky.edu/kentucky-review/vol5/iss1/4/.

Hart, Gideon. "Military Commissions and the Lieber Code: Toward a New Understanding of the Jurisdictional Foundations of Military Commissions." *Military Law Review* 203 (2010): 1–77.

Head, James. *The Atonement of John Brooks: The Story of the True Johnny Reb Who Did Not Come Marching Home.* Geneva, Fla.: Heritage Press, 2001.

Hoogenboom, Ari. "Civil Service Reform." In *The Oxford Companion to United States History,* edited by Paul Boyer, 128–129. New York: Oxford Univ. Press, 2001.

Horwitz, Tony. "150 Years of Misunderstanding the Civil War." *The Atlantic,* June 19, 2013. https://www.theatlantic.com/national/archive/2013/06/150-years-of-misunderstanding-the-civil-war/277022/.

Howard, Victor. *Black Liberation in Kentucky: Emancipation and Freedom, 1862–1884.* Lexington: Univ. Press of Kentucky, 1983.

———. "The Civil War in Kentucky: The Slave Claims His Freedom." *Journal of Negro History* 67 (1982): 245–256.

Hulbert, Matthew. "The Rise and Fall of Edwin Terrell, Guerrilla Hunter, U.S.A." *Ohio Valley History* 18 (2018): 42–61.

Hutton, T.R.C. *Bloody Breathitt: Politics and Violence in the Appalachian South.* Lexington: Univ. Press of Kentucky, 2013.

Hyde, Samuel C. "Guerrilla Warfare in Civil War Louisiana." In *Encyclopedia of Louisiana,* edited by David Johnson. https://64parishes.org/entry/guerrilla-warfare-in-civil-war-louisiana.

Ireland, Robert. *Little Kingdoms: The Counties of Kentucky, 1850–1891.* Lexington: Univ. Press of Kentucky, 1977.

Isaac, Rhys. *The Transformation of Virginia, 1740–1790.* New York: Norton, 1988.

James, Thomas. *Life of Rev. Thomas James, by Himself.* Rochester, N.Y.: Post Express Printing Co, 1886. http://docsouth.unc.edu/neh/jamesth/jamesth.html.

"John Jacob Ridgway." *Encyclopedia of Contemporary Biography of Pennsylvania,* vol. 3. New York: Atlantic Publishing and Engraving Co., 1898.

Johnson, Adam. *Partisan Rangers of the Confederate States Army.* Louisville, Ky.: George G. Fetter Co, 1904.

Johnson, Walter. *Soul by Soul: Life Inside the Antebellum Slave Market.* Cambridge, Mass.: Harvard Univ. Press, 1999.

Katznelson, Ira. "What America Taught the Nazis." *The Atlantic,* November 2017: 42–44.

Kiper, Richard. "John Alexander McClernand and the Arkansas Post Campaign." *Arkansas History Quarterly* 56 (1997): 56–79.

Kleber, John E., ed. *The Kentucky Encyclopedia.* Lexington: Univ. Press of Kentucky, 1992.

Klement, Frank. "Carrington and the Golden Circle Legend in Indiana during the Civil War." *Indiana Magazine of History* 61 (1965): 31–52.

———. *Dark Lanterns: Secret Political Societies, Conspiracies, and Treason Trials in the Civil War.* Baton Rouge: Louisiana State Univ. Press, 1984.

———. *The Limits of Dissent: Clement L. Vallandigham and the Civil War.* New York: Fordham Univ. Press, 1970.

Klotter, James. *The Breckinridges of Kentucky, 1790–1981.* Lexington: Univ. Press of Kentucky, 1986.

Klotter, James, and Lowell Harrison. *A New History of Kentucky.* Lexington: Univ. Press of Kentucky, 1997.

Lewis, Patrick. "'All Men of Decency Ought to Quit the Army': Benjamin F. Buckner, Manhood, and Proslavery Unionism in Kentucky." *Register of the Kentucky Historical Society* 107 (2009): 513–549.

———. *For Slavery and Union: Benjamin Buckner and Kentucky Loyalties in the Civil War.* Lexington: Univ. Press of Kentucky, 2015.

"List of American Civil War Monuments in Kentucky." en.wikipedia.org /wiki/List_of_American_Civil_War_monuments_in_Kentucky.

Lucas, Marion. *A History of Blacks in Kentucky.* Vol. 1, *From Slavery to Segregation, 1760–1891.* Frankfort: Kentucky Historical Society, 1992.

Mackey, Robert. *The UnCivil War: Irregular Warfare in the Upper South, 1861–1865.* Norman: Univ. of Oklahoma Press, 2004.

Mahoney, Timothy R. "Urban History in a Regional Context: River Towns on the Upper Mississippi, 1840–1860." *Journal of American History* 72 (1985): 318–339.

Maltby, William S. *The Black Legend in England: The Development of Anti-Spanish Sentiment, 1558–1860.* Durham, N.C.: Duke Univ. Press, 1971.

Marshall, Anne. *Creating a Confederate Kentucky: The Lost Cause and Civil War Memory in a Border State.* Chapel Hill: Univ. of North Carolina Press, 2010.

Martin, James B. "Black Flag over the Bluegrass: Guerrilla Warfare in Kentucky, 1863–1865." *Register of the Kentucky Historical Society* 86 (1988): 352–375.

McDonogh, James Lee. *War in Kentucky: From Shiloh to Perryville.* Knoxville: Univ. of Tennessee Press, 1996.

McKnight, Brian. *Contested Borderland: The Civil War in Appalachian Kentucky and Virginia.* Lexington: Univ. Press of Kentucky, 2006.

McPherson, James. *Battle Cry of Freedom: The Civil War Era.* New York: Oxford Univ. Press, 1988.

———. *This Mighty Scourge: Perspectives on the Civil War.* New York: Oxford Univ. Press, 2007.

Mowery, David L. "Brigadier General Jacob Ammen." Cincinnati Civil War Round Table. http://www.cincinnaticwrt.org/wp-content/uploads/2017 /08/jacob_ammen.pdf.

National Park Service. "Battle Unit Details: 26th Regiment, Kentucky Infantry." www.nps.gov/civilwar/search-battle-units-detail.htm?battleUnitCode =UKY0026RI.

Neely, Mark, Jr. *The Fate of Liberty: Abraham Lincoln and Civil Liberties.* New York: Oxford Univ. Press, 1992.

Palmer, John M. *Personal Recollections of John M. Palmer: The Story of an Earnest Life.* Cincinnati: Robert Clarke Company, 1901.

Peters, Anne. "Pedigree Analysis: Grey Eagle." Bloodhorse.com. January 9, 2015. http://www.bloodhorse.com/horse-racing/articles/109985/pedigree-analysis-grey-eagle.

Philips, Christopher. "The Hard-Line War: The Ideological Basis of Irregular Warfare in the Western Border States." In *The Civil War Guerrilla: Unfolding the Black Flag in History, Memory, and Myth,* edited by Joseph M. Beilein Jr. and Matthew C. Hulbert, 13–42. Lexington: Univ. Press of Kentucky, 2015.

Philips, Christopher. *The Rivers Ran Backward: The Civil War and the Remaking of the American Middle Border.* New York: Oxford Univ. Press, 2016.

Powell, Phillip Wayne. *Tree of Hate: Propaganda and Prejudice Affecting United States Relations with the Hispanic World.* 1971. Reprint, Albuquerque: Univ. of New Mexico Press, 2008.

Prichard, James M. "Banner in the Dust: John Hunt Morgan's Last Kentucky Raid." In *Essays on America's Civil War.* Vol. 4, *Confederate Generals in the Western Theater,* edited by Lawrence Lee Hewitt and Thomas E. Schott, 163–193. Knoxville: Univ. of Tennessee Press, 2017.

———. "Burbridge, Stephen Gano." In *Encyclopedia of the American Civil War: A Political, Social, and Military History,* vol. 1, edited by David Heidler and Jeanne Heidler, 323–324. Santa Barbara, Calif.: ABC-Clio, 2000.

Purvis, Thomas L. "The Ethnic Descent of Kentucky's Early Population: A Statistical Investigation of European and American Sources of Emigration, 1790–1820." *Register of the Kentucky Historical Society* 80 (1982): 253–266.

Ramage, James. *Rebel Raider: The Life of General John Hunt Morgan.* Lexington: Univ. Press of Kentucky, 1986.

*Regulations of the Kentucky Military Institute.* Frankfort, Ky.: A. G. Hodges and Co, 1855.

Rockenbach, Stephen. "'The Weeds and the Flowers Are Closely Mixed': Allegiance, Law, and White Supremacy in Kentucky's Bluegrass Region, 1861–1865." *Register of the Kentucky Historical Society* 111 (2013): 563–589.

Sageser, A. Bower. *First Two Decades of the Pendleton Act: A Study of Civil Service Reform.* Lincoln: Univ. of Nebraska Press, 1935.

Sanders. "General Jeremiah T. Boyle." https://explorekyhistory.ky.gov/items/show/17.

Sandow, Robert. "Damnable Treason or Party Organs? Democratic Secret Societies in Pennsylvania." In *This Distracted and Anarchical People: New Answers for Old Questions about the Civil War North,* edited by Andrew

Slap and Michael Thomas Smith, 42–59. New York: Fordham Univ. Press, 2013.

Sears, Richard. *Camp Nelson, Kentucky: A Civil War History.* Lexington: Univ. Press of Kentucky, 2002.

———. "John G. Fee, Camp Nelson, and Kentucky Blacks, 1864–1865." *Register of the Kentucky Historical Society* 85 (1987): 29–45.

Sehlinger, Peter. *Kentucky's Last Cavalier: General William Preston, 1816–1887.* Lexington: Univ. Press of Kentucky, 2004.

Shaler, Nathaniel. *Kentucky: A Pioneer Commonwealth.* New York: Houghton, Mifflin, 1884.

Smith, Edward Conrad. *The Borderland in the Civil War.* New York: Macmillan, 1927.

Smith, John David. "E. Merton Coulter, the 'Dunning School,' and the Civil War and Readjustment in Kentucky." *Register of the Kentucky Historical Society* 86 (1988): 52–69.

———. "The Recruitment of Negro Soldiers in Kentucky, 1863–1865." *Register of the Kentucky Historical Society* 72 (1974): 364–390.

———. "Whither Kentucky Civil War and Reconstruction Scholarship?" *Register of the Kentucky Historical Society* 112 (2014): 223–247.

Smith, Preserved. "Neile Macneale: Railroad Builder of the Middle West, 1826–1897." *Mississippi Valley Historical Review* 26 (1939): 181–192.

Speed, Thomas. *The Union Cause in Kentucky, 1860–1865.* New York: G. Putnam and Sons, 1907.

Speed, Thomas, et al. *The Union Regiments of Kentucky.* Louisville, Ky.: Courier-Journal Printing, 1897.

Starling, Edmund L. *History of Henderson County, Kentucky.* Henderson, Ky.: N.p., 1887. https://archive.org/details/historyofhenders00star/page/n5.

Stephens, James Darwin. *Reflections: A Portrait-Biography of the Kentucky Military Institute (1845–1971),* vol. 1. Georgetown, Ky.: Kentucky Military Institute, 1991.

Stewart, James Brewer. "Civil War: Changing Interpretations." In *The Oxford Companion to United States History,* edited by Paul S. Boyer, 133. New York: Oxford Univ. Press, 2001.

Sutherland, Daniel. *A Savage Conflict: The Decisive Role of Guerrillas in the American Civil War.* Chapel Hill: Univ. of North Carolina Press, 2009.

Tapp, Hambleton. "Incidents in the Life of Frank Wolford, Colonel of the First Kentucky Union Cavalry." *Filson Club Historical Quarterly* 10 (1936): 82–99.

Tarnowieckyi, Scott. "'Branded by the Lincolnites as Guerrillas': Adam Rankin Johnson, Guerrilla Identity, and Irregular Warfare in the Lower

Green River Valley in 1862." *Register of the Kentucky Historical Society* 113 (2015): 641–673.

Tarrant, E. *The Wild Riders of the First Kentucky Cavalry: A History of the Regiment, in the Great War of the Rebellion.* Louisville, Ky.: The Committee of the Regiment, 1894.

Taylor, Richard. *Rail Splitter: Sonnets on the Life of Abraham Lincoln.* Monterey, Ky.: Larkspur Press, 2009.

Thompson, Elizabeth Lee. *The Reconstruction of Southern Debt: Bankruptcy after the Civil War.* Athens: Univ. of Georgia Press, 2004.

Thompson, Lawrence. "Bluegrass and Bourbon: The Colonel of Kentucky Fiction." *Georgia Review* 7 (1953): 107–115.

Urwin, Gregory J. W. *Black Flag over Dixie: Racial Atrocities and Reprisals in the Civil War.* Carbondale: Southern Illinois Univ. Press, 2004.

*U.S. City Directories 1822–1995.* Ancestry.com. Provo, Utah: Ancestry.com Operations, 2015.

Vagts, Detlev F. "Military Commissions: A Concise History." *American Journal of International Law* 101 (2007): 35–48.

Wall, Maryjean. *How Kentucky Became Southern: A Tale of Outlaws, Horse Thieves, Gamblers, and Breeders.* Lexington: Univ. Press of Kentucky, 2010.

Webb, Ross A. "Boyle, Jeremiah T." In *The Kentucky Encyclopedia,* edited by John Kleber, 109. Lexington: Univ. Press of Kentucky, 1992.

———. *Kentucky in the Reconstruction Era.* Lexington: Univ. Press of Kentucky, 1979.

Weber, Jennifer. *Copperheads: The Rise and Fall of Lincoln's Opponents in the North.* New York: Oxford Univ. Press, 2006.

Wedgwood, William. *Civil Service Reform.* Portland, Maine: Stephen Berry, 1883. https://archive.org/details/civilservicerefo00wedg.

Welsh, Jack D., M.D. *Medical Histories of Union Generals.* Kent, Ohio: Kent State Univ. Press, 1995.

Wiecek, William M. "The Reconstruction of Federal Judicial Power, 1863–1875." *American Journal of Legal History* 13 (1969): 333–359.

Williams, Edward F., III. "The Johnsonville Raid and Nathan Bedford Forrest State Park." *Tennessee Historical Quarterly* 28 (1969): 225–251.

Winters, John D. *The Civil War in Louisiana.* Baton Rouge: Louisiana State Univ. Press, 1991.

Witt, John Fabian. *Lincoln's Code: The Laws of War in American History.* New York: Free Press, 2012.

Woods, Michael E. "What Twenty-First Century Historians Have Said about the Causes of Disunion: A Civil War Sesquicentennial Review of Recent Literature." *Journal of American History* 99 (2012): 415–439.

Works Progress Administration. *Military History of Kentucky*. Frankfort, Ky.: State Journal, 1939. kynghistory.ky.gov/Media/Publications/DMA/MilitaryHistoryKY1939AnlRpt.pdf.

Wright, George C. *A History of Blacks in Kentucky*. Vol. 2, *In Pursuit of Equality, 1890–1980*. Frankfort: Kentucky Historical Society, 1992.

Yater, George. *Two Hundred Years at the Falls of the Ohio: A History of Louisville and Jefferson County*. Louisville, Ky.: Filson Club, 1987.

# Index